STATE THEORIES

STATE THEORIES

CLASSICAL, GLOBAL, AND FEMINIST PERSPECTIVES

THIRD EDITION

MURRAY KNUTTILA
AND WENDEE KUBIK

FERNWOOD PUBLISHING
ZED BOOKS

Editing: Robert Clarke
Design and production: Beverley Rach
Printed and bound in Canada by: Hignell Printing Limited

Some of the material in chapter nine has been adapted from Murray Knuttila, *Introducing Sociology: A Critical Perspective* (Toronto: Oxford University Press, 1996).

Fernwood Publishing Company Limited gratefully acknowledges the financial support of the Department of Canadian Heritage and the Canada Council for the Arts for our publishing program.

Published in Canada by Fernwood Publishing Ltd.
Box 9409, Station A
Halifax, Nova Scotia
B3K 5S3

Published in the rest of the world by Zed Books Ltd.
7 Cynthia Street, London NI 9JF, UK
and Room 400, 175 Fifth Avenue,
New York, 10010, USA
Distributed in the USA exclusively by Palgrave,
a division of St. Martins Press, LLC, 175 Fifth Ave., New York, 10010, USA.

Zed Books
ISBN 1 85649 032 7 Paper
ISBN 1 85649 027 0 Cloth

British CIP available from the British Library
American CIP has been applied for

Canadian Cataloguing in Publication Data

Knuttila, Kenneth Murray

State theories

3rd ed.

Previous editions have subtitle: From liberalism to the challenge of feminism.
First ed.: Toronto: Garamond Press, 1987.
Includes bibliographical references.
ISBN 1-55266-025-7

1. State, The. I. Title.

JC11.K56 2000   320.1   C00-950043-X

CONTENTS

ACKNOWLEDGEMENTS

The author remains grateful to those who assisted with the First and Second editions of this book. We would like to thank all those who took the time to read and comment on the Third Edition—in particular, Phil Hansen, Joanne Boucher, Trevor Harrison, and Gregg Olsen. Special mention must be made of the continuing work of Wayne Antony and Fernwood Publishing for their assistance, work, and encouragement. Canadian publishing remains alive due to their efforts. Once again, thanks to Robert Clarke who made countless improvements. As well, credit is due to the production group at Fernwood Publishing—Beverley Rach, Debbie Mathers and Tim Dunn. All errors and omissions are, of course, the responsibility of the author.

For Erin and Lee

ABOUT THE AUTHORS

Wendee Kubik is currently an Interdisciplinary Doctoral Candidate in the Canadian Plains Studies Program in the Canadian Plains Research Center at the University of Regina. Her dissertation is focusing on the "Changing Roles of Farm Women and the Consequences for their Health, Well-being, and Quality of Life." She holds a BA (Honours) in Psychology and an MA in Canadian Plains Studies. The author and co-author of numerous papers on issues relating to farm women, stress, social change and rural issues, she is currently the Book Review Editor of *Prairie Forum*.

Murray Knuttila teaches in the Department of Sociology and Social Studies at the University of Regina where he is also Dean of Arts. His biography, *That Man Partridge: E.A. Partridge, His Thoughts and Times* tells the story of an important figure in Canadian history. He is also the author of *Introducing Sociology: A Critical Perspective* and numerous articles on the state in capitalist society and on the historical role of the state in structuring Western Canadian society.

INTRODUCTION

> The state—or apparatus of "government"—appears to be everywhere, regulating the conditions of our lives from birth registration to death certification. Yet, the nature of the state is hard to grasp. This may seem peculiar for something so pervasive in public and private life, but it is precisely this pervasiveness which makes it difficult to understand. There is nothing more central to political and social theory than the nature of the state, and nothing more contested. (Held 1983: 1)

This observation by David Held served to introduce the earlier editions of this book. Despite recent suggestions that the state in capitalist society has become less relevant, we maintain that the state remains both important and pervasive. We also remain convinced that, despite centuries of analysis, thought, and debate, social scientists have not yet reached anything close to agreement on the essential nature, role, and character of the state in capitalist society. The debates continue. Those interested in understanding their society are still faced with the challenge of exploring the various approaches to the state and deciding which of them, if any, provides the best explanation of how the state works and how is has developed.

The Third Edition of *State Theories* brings a number of important changes, with the most important being the formal introduction of a co-author, Wendee Kubik. Wendee played an important role in the development of many of the ideas presented in the earlier editions, and has since become more directly involved in this project, thus, making the formal recognition both timely and appropriate.

As with the first and second editions, this book aims to assist our understanding by introducing a variety of different theoretical perspectives on the study of the state. While we do not claim to be comprehensive, we have attempted to present a broad selection of positions, approaches, and theories that represent the major historical and contemporary streams of thought in social theory, from "classical" or "founding" figures to current theorists.

In selecting the classical figures, we selected thinkers and perspectives whose influence is manifest in contemporary theories and approaches. We have also made a deliberate effort to be interdisciplinary because too often the treatment of political theory is conditioned by disciplinary boundaries and, as a result, omits a wealth of material. Ordinarily, certain theorists are "covered" by those studying politics or political philosophy while others are left to the sociologist. We contend that an adequate grasp of the manner in which the state has been understood in western social science requires familiarity, for example, not only with Hobbes, Locke, Michels, or the idea of

11

pluralism, but also with Durkheim, Weber, Parsons, and functionalist thought.

An undertaking such as ours faces a number of challenges, not the least of which are fundamental disagreements relating to the concept of the state, to the basic world views adopted, the meanings ascribed to various concepts, and the very definition of politics. In recent years some scholars have gone on to challenge even the possibility of the sort of systematic knowledge that many of the theorists discussed here attempted to develop.

As one begins to explore theories of the state some inherent problems become evident immediately. For example, the theories and approaches discussed here are typically informed by radically different conceptions of the state that are predicated on equally differing conceptions and understandings of human beings and their behaviour in society. Theorists differ in their view of "human nature," and have radically different understandings of what has made human beings develop and organize themselves in certain ways. As we will see, some theorists argue that there is a fixed and static human nature, that human beings are, by nature, self-centred, egotistical, aggressive, and possessive individuals. Others argue that there is no such thing as a fixed "human nature" and maintain that human beings are largely the products of the social environments into which they are born and in which they develop.

The conceptions held about the fundamental character of the species obviously have significant implications for any view of society and, ultimately, for a view of the state. If in fact we are aggressive, self-centred, greedy, and possessive individualists, certain types of society and certain related forms of the state would appear to be most appropriate. If, however, we are to a significant degree products of our social environment, we would take on different views about how society is organized and how the state has come to play its particular role. In discussing various theories of the state, then, this book attempts to link, especially, the differing conceptions held by theorists on humans, society, and the state—in other words, we emphasize the starting points.

When we recognize the difficulty of arriving at an acceptable or all encompassing definition of concepts such as democracy, politics, or even the state, the task then becomes one of attempting to reach some understanding of how these concepts are used and employed within the various approaches. For example, there are fundamental differences in the use of a concept such as "democracy" in the works of Thomas Hobbes, John Locke, Max Weber, and Karl Marx. Further, in examining basic concepts of the state employed in functionalist, pluralist, elite, and feminist theory it becomes apparent that there is a real lack of agreement regarding the meanings of these common concepts and terms.

The *Oxford Dictionary* defines democracy as a "form of government in which sovereign power resides in the people as a whole, and is exercised either directly by them or by their elected representatives; State having this form of government." The definition, rather than clarifying the concept, serves to raise further questions: How do we define people? What is the basis for participation in the affairs of government? Who is eligible to determine the choice of sovereign? What powers should the sovereign assume?

There are, indeed, radically different conceptions of democracy, and most theorists would agree that a dictionary definition is far too narrow, and the reality far more complex. Democracy, some argue, must include control over one's total existence including economic activities and practices. In the context especially of feminist theory, it must also include control over one's own body, of its reproductive functions, for instance. That is, a broader definition of democracy takes the question of what politics involves beyond the mere selection of government representatives and into the realm of the problems and issues of everyday life.

What we hope to do here is elaborate on the historical questions and contested concepts through an examination of a variety of perspectives. One of our central objectives is to introduce these various positions at a basic level to the student of society. To achieve this objective we have integrated a large number of quotations into the text, partly to provide a sense or flavour of the original writer. We also hope the extracts will encourage readers to form their own interpretations of these treatises on the state, and to look more closely and fully at the originals.

There is a certain historical logic in the organization of the discussion. We have tried, for instance, to provide connections between different concepts of the state as well as between those concepts and the historical context out of which they emerged. In addition we have made an effort to locate the positions examined in the social, political, and intellectual context of their times.

Chapter One provides an overview of the works of the "classical liberals"; our definition of classical liberal is wide enough to take in the work of Hobbes, Locke, James Mill, Bentham, and John Stuart Mill. Chapter Two sets up a contrasting approach to the state by introducing a number of writers located in what is broadly called "a sociological perspective." The emergence of sociology in the works of Comte and Durkheim is closely related to the context of the classical liberal concepts of society, and Chapter Two attempts to illustrate the differences between these two currents of thought. Chapter Three introduces what is commonly referred to as "elite theory"; the primary focus of attention is on how elite theory explains, or fails to explain, inequalities of power.

Chapter Four is essentially a straightforward consideration of American "pluralism" from its origins and founding tenets through to the works of Robert Dahl. Chapter Five explores the theories of "classical marxism," with an overview of the developing concept of the state in the work of Marx and, to a lesser extent, Engels and Lenin. Chapter Six introduces selected efforts by "neo-Marxist" thinkers to understand the state in capitalist society, drawing out especially the substantial differences among those who are attempting to build on and extend Marx's work. Chapter Seven introduces the basic positions of key anarchist thinkers and the general trends of the "anarchist critique" of western state structures.

The major changes to this edition are found in Chapters Eight, Nine, and the new Conclusion. Among the most striking changes in the political economy of the capitalist world has been dual recognition by many social scientists of the fact that the capitalist system is a world system, and of a systematic attack and critique of the welfare state. The new Chapter Eight attempts to introduce a historical basis for the ongoing debate of the implications of global capitalism for the nation-state, and to link elements of this debate to the disparities about the legitimacy and efficacy of the welfare state. We end the chapter by commenting on some recent developments within the pluralist and new-Marxian approaches, including brief discussions of "regulation theory" and "power resource theory."

The new Chapter Nine builds on the obvious fact that all of the major theories tend to have emerged from, to borrow Mary O'Brien's term, "malestream" thought. Although the structured subordination of women has been an essential dimension of human relations in western society over the past several centuries, few theoretical approaches have addressed this issue. Chapter Nine examines the issue of the gendered nature of the state by looking to some feminist scholars who have offered new perspectives that not only present an analytical framework, but also point to an emancipatory political agenda as well.

Chapters One through Nine are essentially expository in character: they present some of the various positions and arguments that have emerged as western social scientists and thinkers have addressed the issue of the polity over the last several hundred years. The final chapter presents a series of critical comments and asks a series of key questions that point to limitations in most of the approaches presented in the earlier chapters. It also tries to develop a more adequate approach to the study of the polity in advanced capitalist society. Although there are limitations, theoretical work is fundamentally necessary. However, most of the existing approaches to the study of the polity fail to adequately locate formal political structures and processes within the context of the larger social order, that is, within the structures of advanced capitalist, or liberal-democratic society. We suggest an approach that offers an alternate way of understanding the structures of capitalist society as well as a specific mode of connecting the state to the economic and reproductive practices upon which society stands. More than anything the last chapter seeks to stimulate a critical re-examination of our thinking in this direction.

What follows is only an introduction to some very complex ideas and arguments. Our main objective remains to whet readers' appetites; to stimulate them to go back to the original sources and to undertake more serious and systematic investigations of these and other perspectives. In the end, good social science is not just presenting theory. Rather, good social science uses theories and theoretical ideas to help explain the world we live in.

• ONE •

CLASSICAL LIBERALISM

Twentieth-century students of society understandably find it difficult to comprehend a social, economic, and political system that undergoes little apparent change for over eight hundred years. Yet this was the case in the western precapitalist or medieval era. From around 600 A.D. to about 1450, a remarkable stability in economic, social, and political structures characterized society in western Europe. It is, somewhat ironically, easier for students today to make sense of the relatively rapid upheavals that followed. By the fifteenth century major changes began to occur, and in the following two centuries virtually all vestiges of the old order were swept away.

These transformations were economic, social, and political, involving the emergence of new economic relations and practices, new family, religious, and educational institutions, and new state or political structures. The unity and coherence of life that characterized feudal society disappeared, and in no realm was this more apparent than in economic existence. In his discussion of the transition to the modern world Andrew Gamble argues that the central development was the emergence of a sphere of human activity largely concerned with materials production and distribution. Gamble notes, "In the seventeenth and eighteenth centuries this new form of economic society became known as *civil society*" (Gamble 1981: 29). Unlike the regulated, limited (in that it was centred on a local community), and traditional economic activity that tended to characterize feudalism, the new order was "mobile, restless, aggressive, competitive and individualistic." This transformation was part of a larger set of structural changes:

> The conditions for the formation and reproduction of civil society were economic (new ways of organizing production and distribution), but also political (new rules and agencies for maintaining a private sphere of free competition and exchange) and ideological (new modes of thought and evaluation). The first gave rise to capitalism, the second to the modern state and ultimately liberal democracy, and the third to science. (29-30)

The rise of new classes; the emergence of new modes of economic activity and conduct geared to expanding the private accumulation of wealth; the emergence of nation-states and the affiliated concentration and centralization of political power in the hands of monarchs; the decline of the church; European expansion; and the emergence of a new science: All of these developments stimulated a re-evaluation of existing social, economic, and political theory. Within this context also emerged the first—what we will term "modern"—political theories of the state in capitalist society.

While these transformations were ultimately to produce the liberal-democratic state, initially the essential feature of the state in emerging capitalist society was its fundamentally undemocratic nature. The terms "absolute monarchies" or "absolutism" are commonly and appropriately used to describe the new state forms that emerged in England after the War of Roses and during the Tudor period, and in France under Louis XIII, Louis XIV, and their advisors, Richelieu and Colbert. These were states predicated on a strong monarch or royal court working in conjunction with the rising merchant classes. A symbiotic relationship emerged, based on the monarch's insatiable appetite for increased revenues and the merchant's desire for a strong central state that would establish the preconditions for an expanded market economy. Broadus Mitchell describes the relationship as one in which "Two ambitions worked together to make mercantilism. They were the demand of the new national states for power, and the eagerness of the new middle class of businessmen for profits" (Mitchell 1967: 34-35). Mitchell notes, "Government and bourgeois needed each other. Neither could prosper without a partner."

The emerging merchant class was willing to contribute its part through the payment of a variety of different taxes and the provision of loans to the government. In return the merchant class expected the state to take certain actions to facilitate trade and commerce: currency standardization and regulation, standardization of weights and measures, improvements in transportation facilities. Merchants also relied on the state's enforcement of law and order, which made longer distance trade and commerce feasible. The relationship between the monarchs and the merchants ultimately produced the mercantilist state, a state that was active, interventionist, expansive, and expensive. Such a state structure served the interests of both merchants and monarch. For a certain period of time it established the preconditions for the accumulation of wealth by the merchants and, by virtue of its very existence, enhanced the power and grandeur of the monarch.

The phrase "for a period of time" is important. The stability of precapitalist society contrasts sharply with the dynamic nature of capitalism. The formative stage of capitalism—mercantilism—soon underwent a transformation as radical as the one that characterized its emergence. Once again the transformation involved fundamental structural changes in the economic, social, and political institutions. In their economic history of Europe Clough and Cole provide a concise summary:

> Changes in the scope and character of economic activity and of social classifications had their repercussions in the sphere of politics. Capitalists had supported one feudal lord, the king, in his struggle to bring

other feudal barons into subjection and in the establishment of a strong monarchial state. It was easier to do business in a country with a centralized government than in one ruled by innumerable semiautonomous princes. But after this step had been taken, capitalists frequently discovered that they could not secure the legislation they desired, nor could they escape paying heavy taxes for the support of a luxurious court. They therefore waged a campaign for obtaining political power. (Clough and Cole 1967: 347-75)

The historical developments, then, led to an emerging struggle for political power between the mercantile middle class and the monarchs. This struggle in turn provided the impetus for the first systematic efforts by social and political philosophers to understand the nature of the state in capitalist society.

HOBBES AND THE ABSOLUTE STATE

As David Held notes: "While the works of Niccolo Machiavelli (1496-1527) and Jean Bodin (1520-96) are of great importance in these developments, Thomas Hobbes (1588-1679) directly expressed the new concerns" (Held 1938: 2). Indeed, no thinker of the modern era better addresses the full range of "new concerns" than Hobbes. His interest in the emerging scientific method, the role of the state, the relationship of state to society, and the emerging problem of order places his work as an essential point of departure for studying subsequent efforts to conceptualize and understand the state in capitalist society.

As C.B. Macpherson points out, the thought of Hobbes exhibits the influences of classical deductive modes of thought and an acceptance of the newly emerging empirical scientific method. Classical deductive thought, as exemplified in geometry, moves from accepted or self-evident simple propositions to demonstrable, more complex propositions. The application of this method to politics or social affairs generally is made difficult by the absence of self-evident first principles that would provide the basis for subsequent knowledge. Hobbes found a source of such principles in the application of the scientific method of his day, a method that tended to emphasize the use of observation in knowledge production. Through observation Hobbes sought to establish the basic principles from which an understanding of the state could be deduced (Macpherson 1973: 245). As Brian Nelson points out, in actual fact the observations Hobbes made should not be confused with simple direct observations; rather, the task involved "thought experiments" and a good deal of speculation (Nelson 1982: 138-39).

In his best known work, *The Leviathan*, Hobbes uses deductive thought and a version of the new scientific method to explain the relationship between human nature, society, and the state. Beginning with an extended discussion of human nature in "The First Part," entitled "Of Man," Hobbes establishes the basis of his argument that the state is necessary for the very existence of human society.

Hobbes begins his arguments, as an adherent of the science of his day might, with an analysis of human beings as, basically, material in motion. There are in humans, Hobbes states, two kinds of motions. First there are the vital motions that have to do with a variety of involuntary bodily processes. The second type, "otherwise called voluntary motion," is made up of the human actions of speech and voluntary bodily movements. The voluntary movements involve human intelligence since they "depend always upon a precedent thought of *whither, which way,* and *what*" (Hobbes 1969: 118). Human motions are the basis of actions, which in turn are the basis of endeavours. Endeavours, which are geared to "something which causes it," yield appetites and aversions (119). Human motions thus produce endeavours or appetites and desires for food, drink, and a variety of other basic physical necessities. The human animal also endeavours to avoid certain phenomena, situations, and conditions, a practice Hobbes refers to as aversion. Appetites and aversions are basic human characteristics.

Some appetites and aversions are natural in that humans are born with them, while others are learned from experience. The object of appetite, Hobbes says, man "for his part calleth Good" (120). It follows then that because humans have appetites and desires for these things called "Good," they seek to use their endeavours to secure them. The ability to satisfy appetites and desire for "Good" is what Hobbes terms power. "The Power of a Man, (to take it Universally) is his present means to obtain some future apparent Good" (150).

Hobbes leads us from human material existence as motions, thorough appetites, desires, and aversions, to endeavours to secure "Good," and finally to power. Power thus introduced becomes the central concept in the subsequent arguments, especially as they relate to the question of the state.

Hobbes notes that there are two types of power, "either *Originall or Instrumentall*" (150). Original, also termed "Naturall Power," relates to "the eminence of the Faculties of Body, or Mind: an extraordinary Strength, Forme, Prudence, Art, Eloquence, Liberality, Nobility." Instrumental power, on the other hand, is power acquired through the use of these physical or mental abilities or by fortune. This power in turn provides the potential for acquisition of even more power. Power, residing in the very nature of human existence, is thereby a central factor in human behaviour or, perhaps more fittingly, a central aspect of the human condition. Hobbes states:

> So that in the first place, I put for a generall inclination of all mankind, a perpetuall and restlesse desire of Power after power, that ceaseth only in Death. And the cause of this, is not always that a man hopes for a more intensive delight, than he has already attained to; or that he cannot assure the power and means to live well, which he hath present, without the acquisition of more. (161)

The human condition, then, resolves itself into a constant motion, which produces desires for "Good," which in turn produces power. Power, inasmuch as it is the means to attaining the "Good," becomes what humans restlessly and perpetually pursue. Explicit in this discussion of power is the fact that power, once secured, begets more power. "For the nature of Power, is in this point, like to Fame, increasing as it proceeds; or like the motion of heavy bodies, which the further they go, make still the most hast" (150).

Despite the fact that these arguments suggest a potential, fundamental, unequal acquisition of power, Hobbes states in Chapter XIII of *Leviathan* that nature has made men fundamentally equal.

> Nature hath made men so equall, in the faculties of body, and mind; as that though there bee found one man sometimes manifestly stronger in body, or of quicker mind than another; yet when all is reckoned together, the difference between man, and man, is not so considerable, as that one man can thereupon claim to himselfe any benefit, to which another may not pretend, as well as he. (183)

He notes that individual differences are such that "the weakest has strength enough to kill the strongest, either by secret machination, or by confederacy with others, that are in some danger with himself" (183). Hobbes summarizes, "So that in the nature of man, we find three principall causes of quarrell. First, Competition; Secondly, Diffidence: Thirdly, Glory, (185). Such a condition is incompatible with human development, if not survival. In what is possibly his most oft-quoted statement Hobbes argues:

> Whatsoever therefore is consequent to a time of Warre, where every man is Enemy to every man, the same is consequent to the time, wherein men live without other security, than what their own strength, and their own invention shall furnish them withall. In such condition, there is no place for Industry; because the fruit thereof is uncertain: and consequently no Culture of the Earth; no Navigation, nor use of the commodities that may be imported by Sea; no commodious Building, no Instruments of moving, and removing such things as require much force; no Knowledge of the face of the Earth; no account of Time, no Arts; no Letters; no Society; and which is worst of all, continuall feare, and danger of violent death; And the life of man, solitary, poore, nasty, brutish, and short.

In such a world, under such conditions, when human existence is a "warre of every man against every man," there is no such thing as right, wrong, justice or injustice. There is no law or dominion in "the ill condition which man by mere Nature is actually placed in." There is, however, also because of Nature, a possibility to come out of it, consisting partly in the Passions, partly in his Reason. The "Passions" in question are the fear of death, desire for life, and a hope for industry, while "Reason" suggests a solution (188).

To explain the solution that human beings ultimately develop, Hobbes presents a series of basic laws of nature. The essential process involves the realization that under conditions of a continual and perpetual war, passions cannot be satisfied. As creatures with the capacity to reason, humans seek a solution that offers them a way out of an undesirable condition but which is still in accordance with the laws of nature.

The solution developed is the social contract by which individuals give up certain rights of "self-government," as David Held describes it, and in return are assured an improvement in their condition. The rights that all men yield are transferred to a single authority—a sovereign—that not only becomes the holder of these rights but also enjoys sole legitimate power over them, and is thereafter authorized to act on behalf of the "subject." This sovereign, in Hobbes's formulation, can be either a person—a monarch—or a body, such as an assembly. The contract between men and sovereign is carried out "on the condition that every individual does the same" (Held 1983: 6). The result is the creation of a powerful sovereign, which cannot be limited in its authority since the sovereign requires considerable power to formulate laws, enforce agreements, ensure contracts: in a word, to bring order to the previous natural condition of disorder.

In his Chapter XIX Hobbes discusses the various forms that the sovereign, or more precisely the sovereign state, can take. He identifies the form associated with a single ruler as "Monarchy," and that associated with the rule by an "Assembly of All" as "Democracy." He sees the rule of an assembly that represents only a portion of the population as an "Aristocracy." In comparing the various forms of government Hobbes concludes that monarchy is the most appropriate form:

> It follows that where the publique and private interests are most closely united, there is the publique most advanced. Now in the Monarchy, the private interest is the same with the publique. The riches, power, and honour of a Monarch arise onely from the riches, strength and reputation of his Subjects. For no King can be rich, nor glorious, nor secure; whose Subjects are either poore, or contemptible, or too weak through want, or dissention, to maintain a war against their enemies. (Hobbes 1968: 241-42)

For Hobbes the power of the sovereign state is absolute, to be accepted without question. The sovereign state is responsible only to God. Hobbes lists ways that the sovereign state, and thus peace and security, could be destroyed: for instance, making the sovereign state subject to civil law; or allowing individuals absolute proprietorship of their goods. In his introductory comments to a discussion of the office of the sovereign Hobbes summarizes his absolutist position:

> The Office of the Sovereign, (be it a Monarch, or an Assembly) consisteth in the end, for which he was trusted with the Sovereign Power, namely the procuration of *the safety of the people*; to which he is obliged by the Law of Nature, and to render an account thereof to God, the Author of that Law, and to none but him. (376)

To those who would argue that this absolute power of the sovereign state is unacceptable, Hobbes had two responses, which Martin Carnoy summarizes: "First, subjugation is better than civil war (death), and second, it would not be in the interest of the sovereign to do this to his (or its) subjects because the sovereign's strength consists in the vigor of those subjects" (Carnoy 1984: 16). Indeed, Hobbes would argue, the existence of a sovereign state represents an essential precondition for the existence of a civilized human society; any human interaction beyond that of continual war against all requires a state. The state is thus at the core of human existence. It is the constitution, the basis of all social structures. As Held concludes, "The state does not simply record or reflect socio-economic reality, it enters into its very construction by establishing its form and codifying its forces" (Held 1983: 8).

Although Hobbes developed this concept of the state on the basis of a substantial measure of deductive thought, there was ample empirical evidence in his day for the necessity of a strong sovereign or state. The establishment of a market society necessitated substantial state intervention and regulation. The essence of Hobbes's era was a unity of merchant and monarch in a mutually beneficial relationship. The relationship ultimately turned out to be perhaps too beneficial: It resulted in an increasing divergence of interests between the partners as mercantilism itself developed. The ultimate transformation of mercantilism brought with it a fundamental questioning of the political structures of absolutism, a process that would result in the emergence of a radically different understanding of the state in market society.

JOHN LOCKE: THE PRESERVATION OF CIVIL SOCIETY

The decline of the absolutist state in Britain was linked to the increasing strength of what would become the capitalist class. The expansion of Europe through outward colonization had served both the interests of the absolute monarch and the merchant element of the capitalist class. However, it was the growing middle class that ultimately benefited most from trade and commerce. In Britain James I, upon assuming the throne in 1603, was the first monarch to face a serious challenge from the middle class over the issue of taxation. James's successor, Charles I, became embroiled in serious conflicts with the parliamentary representatives of the middle class over taxation, property rights, and the question of the relationship of the sovereign to the laws of the land. The outcome of these and other conflicts was, in brief, civil war, a short-lived republic, a restoration, and finally the assumption of power by the middle class with the Glorious Revolution of 1688.

John Locke (1632-1704) has been referred to as the theorist if not the apologist of the Glorious Revolution. While care must be taken in imputing historical motives, it is clear that the concept of the state that emerges from the writing of Locke was more appropriate for the emerging industrial era than it was for the mercantile absolutist state. Like Hobbes, Locke bases his concept of the state on principles of human nature. But in fact his conception of human nature is notably different, as is the concept of the state that he develops.

Locke begins his book *The Second Treatise of Government* with an outline of his essential purpose and begins the main argument in Chapter II, entitled "Of the State of Nature." The chapter begins:

> To understand political power right and derive it from its original, we must consider what state all men are naturally in, and that is a state of perfect freedom to order their actions and dispose of their possessions and persons as they think fit, within the bounds of the laws of nature, without asking leave or depending upon the will of any other man. (Locke 1952: 4)

Several paragraphs later Locke further delineates the "laws of nature":

> The state of nature has a law of nature to govern it, which obliges every one; and reason, which is that law teaches all mankind who will but consult it that, being all equal and independent, no one ought to harm another in his life, health, liberty or possessions. (5)

In the state of nature therefore humans enjoy life, health, liberty, and possessions, elements that Locke links together in subsequent arguments. Locke states that God has given "the world to men in common" as well as "reason to make of it the best advantage of life and convenience." As a result, in their labours human beings use the property they possess to appropriate a portion of nature to meet their various basic needs. Having mixed their labour with nature, they make a portion of nature their property. "Whatsoever then he removes out of the state that nature has provided and left it in, he has mixed labour with, and joined to it something that is his own, and thereby makes it his property" (17). Human activity in the state of nature produces private property.

Locke, while appearing to disagree with Hobbes's contention that the state of nature is a state of war, nevertheless argues that certain difficulties emerge for humans in the state of nature, where there are equal rights to life, health, liberty, and possessions. If an individual invades another's rights or does harm to another—that is, breaks the laws of nature—then *"every man has a right to punish the offender and be executioner of the law of nature"* (7). If everyone has these rights a problem develops because of the possibility "that self love will make men partial to themselves and their friends, and, on the other side, that ill nature, passion, and revenge will carry them too far in punishing others, and hence nothing but confusion and disorder will follow" (9). Such confusion and disorder can, Locke argues, result in the emergence "Of the State of War," the title of Chapter III.

Locke, maintaining that the state of war is not synonymous with the state of nature, argues that war emerges when there are transgressions against the laws of nature and no common judge. A state of war exists when the rights of an individual are violated by force or the threat of force in the absence of a common superior. A state of war clearly implies a threat to the natural rights of all individuals. The solution? Clearly the establishment of a common superior power, or in Hobbes's terms a sovereign.

In Locke's work the process of establishing a common superior is not unlike that found in Hobbes. Reasonable humans realize that the preservation of property—that is, their life, liberty, and estate—against the injuries and attempts of other men without arbitrary individual judgements and punishments against transgressors demands a common superior. The result is an agreement through which individuals give up some of their natural power to a common superior in exchange for assurances of common security.

In discussing the emergence of a common superior power Locke at first used the term community. Individuals give up powers to a community, which results in individuals no longer being able to judge violations of their rights. Rather, "The community comes to be umpire by setting standard rules, indifferent and the same to all parties." The community judges all members according to established laws. Humans thus divest themselves of some of their natural rights, such as absolute self-protection, in exchange for security in a broader sense. The process involves the establishment of a political structure as individuals "unite into a community for their comfortable, safe, and peaceable living amongst another, in a secure enjoyment of their properties and a greater security against any that are not of it" (54).

Locke's common superior, his community, later referred to as the legislative power, is considerably less absolute than Hobbes's sovereign. In Chapter XI, "Of the Extent of the Legislative Power," Locke specifically limits the power of the legislature. In a famous statement he notes, the "great end of men's entering into society being the enjoyment of their properties in peace and safety," then the fundamental purpose which must govern the activities of the legislature "is the preservation of society and, as far as will consist with the public good, of every person it" (75). Elsewhere, unlike Hobbes, he argues that a legislature cannot enjoy absolutely arbitrary power over the people, it cannot "rule by extemporary, arbitrary decrees," nor can it "take from any man part of his property without his own consent." In his summary Locke specifically notes again that the government must govern according to laws designed for the good of the people and must not raise taxes on the property of the people without their consent (81).

Perhaps no point better illustrates the differences between Hobbes's sovereign and Locke's legislature than the question of consent. For Hobbes the sovereign is absolute, with its, his, or her rule not predicated on the will of the subjects. For Locke the legislature cannot rule in any arbitrary manner and it requires the consent of the population. Indeed, Locke develops this point to the extent that he recognizes the possibility of rebellion and a withdrawal of consent should the government act inappropriately. The inappropriate acts include: violation of the laws of nature, failure to provide the necessary "umpirage," or the passing of arbitrary laws. In the event that consent is withdrawn, Locke does not foresee a return to the state of nature, but the reconstitution of the state. He writes:

> In these and the like cases, when the government is dissolved, the people are at liberty to provide themselves by erecting a new legislative, differing from the other by the change of persons or form, or both as they shall find it most for their safety and good. (123)

The sole purpose of the legislative power is to act as a guardian of the people. "The end of government is the good of mankind" (128). Who is to decide as to whether or not a "prince or legislative" has broken the trust? Locke is clear: "To this I reply: The people shall judge" (38). Ultimately God is the judge but in matters of controversy between the government and the people, "I should think the proper umpire in such a case should be the body of the people" (139).

Locke, however, is not at all clear on what constitutes a breach of trust, the form that rebellion might take, the modes of activity that might go into the selections of a new legislative power, or even who constitutes the all powerful people. Although his concept of the state was to become central to liberal-democratic theory, he was not a democrat himself, in the sense of advocating a system involving periodic electoral inputs into the constitution of the legislature. He does at one point note that legislative power has its origins in "the compact and agreement and the mutual consent of those who make up the community" (Carnoy 1984: 19). Considering that the "community" was originally defined in terms of property, it is safe to assume that the "people" are defined as property holders.

In his brilliant analysis of Locke's thoughts, C.B. Macpherson demonstrates the contradictions in Locke's liberalism, which explicitly denied a growing majority the opportunity to achieve full rational human development through the acquisition of property. The assumption of Locke and his peers is that property equals full human rationality and is thus the criterion for full human participation in civil society.

At the same time Locke recognized the limitations on the continued private appropriation of nature via human labour. Given that nature possesses finite resources, individuals are increasingly faced with a situation of having to alienate their labour in order to survive, and in the process they lose their ability to own property. Macpherson writes: "For Locke, then, a commercial economy in which all the land is appropriated implied the existence of wage labour" (Macpherson 1962: 217).

The recognition of the existence of propertyless individuals leads to interesting philosophical questions. Because participation in civil society is the basis of community membership, should those not participating in civil society have no role in the "consenting process" with regard to state? Locke's government clearly had as its central role the preservation of civil society—market society—which means the preservation of the property, structures, and practices of capitalism. Locke's arguments, as Macpherson points out, whether by design or not "led logically to differential class rights and so to the justification of a class state" (251).

Locke's notion of a sovereign being responsible to the full citizenry of civil society, in the sense that the citizenry is the ultimate source of legitimation for the state, was influential in the political events that led to the 1688 Revolution. Following 1688 the British Parliament emerged supreme and the developing British bourgeoisie assumed political power. In the period that followed, as the industrial revolution began, the very character of the rising bourgeoisie underwent a radical transformation.

THE UTILITARIANS: BENTHAM AND JAMES MILL

The mid-1770s, as Clough and Cole suggest, are a key watershed in the emergence of the industrial era. By the mid-1770s most mercantile doctrines were in retreat as a new economic and political ideology, commonly termed laissez-faire, became more widespread. In 1776 Adam Smith published *The Wealth of Nations*, a systematic attack on key mercantilist and interventionist state policies. The regulated market and overwhelmingly commercial activities of the capitalist class were replaced by a freer market and expanded industrial activities. A new concept of wealth emerged, replacing the static mercantilist concept. The mercantilist class tended to conceive of wealth in limited terms, advocating as much accumulation as possible through trade and commerce. The emerging industrial capitalist class believed that wealth could be created, produced, and enhanced through the application of new technologies and machines to the productive process. The ultimate outcome of this belief was the development of industrial capitalism.

This new era ushered in a number of radical changes. The obvious transformation of economic relations, techniques, and practices was accompanied by a restructuring of family, educational, and political institutions. The new industrial middle class developed a new concept of the appropriate role of the state. With the decline of mercantilism and the associated decline in support for an interventionist state, the mercantilist state, which had ultimately created the essential preconditions for industrial capitalism, came under attack.

At the same time, the writings of Hobbes and Locke had established the foundations of the liberal concept of the state: that is, the state as the guarantor of order, safety, stability, and progress in civil society. There were substantial differences between Hobbes and Locke around the extent to which such a role required absolute power and the extent to which the true members of civil society were justified in criticizing a state that exceeded certain boundaries. Both agreed, however, that a state (sovereign or legislative power) was essential for the continued functioning of civil society. As capitalism continued to develop and the production of industrial commodities replaced trade and commerce as the essential basis of accumulation, a new conception of the relationship of the state to civil society emerged. In the process liberalism became liberal democracy, political philosophy flourished, and new modes of thinking in the "social sciences" emerged.

Although Locke was arguably not a liberal-democrat, he did demand a measure of legislative responsibility. Central to his position was a belief in the ultimate power of the people to withdraw consent from a legislature or ruler no longer fulfiling its mandate. David Held notes that while Locke "certainly never imagined that such power might be exercised directly by the citizens themselves, i.e. in some form of self government," such an idea does emerge from his thought (Held 1983: 14). The notions of consent based on the active electoral participation of the propertied citizenry was a logical extension in the development of the liberal-democratic concept of the state, especially within the context of a growing industrial middle class. The theorists commonly associated with this particular era in the development of liberal-democratic theory are Jeremy Bentham (1748-1832), James Mill (1773-1836), and Mill's son John Stuart Mill (1806-1873). Both Bentham and his contemporary James Mill argued in favour of a much more direct means of linking the government to the population than was evident in Locke. Rather than attempting to control the government and make it accountable through "Devices for legal limitation on sovereignty such as bills of rights, the separation of powers, and checks and balances," Bentham suggested eventual universal suffrage of a well-educated population (Sabine 1937: 695). He further suggested that a parliament with a shorter life span would have an increased sense of responsibility to the electorate.

Bentham was the chief advocate of utilitarianism, a philosophical system based on the principle of self-interest, and which considered the purpose of government as maximizing the sum of the happiness of the greatest number of individuals. Bentham argued that is was vital for government to understand the wishes and will of the people, since this was the only way of ensuring its proper functioning. Government was a human contrivance, with one essential function: to provide for the public good. Bentham and other utilitarians defined the notion of "the public good" as ensuring "by means of careful calculation, the achievement of the greatest happiness for the greatest number" (Held 1983: 15). Governmental knowledge as to what constitutes the public good must necessarily come from society at large. Society at large was composed of utilitarian individuals calculating individually how to maximize pleasure and minimize suffering and it was deemed essential to have some mode of linking these individuals with government. A more direct link was required between the state and civil society in order to maximize utilities.

The idea of an affinity of interest between the sovereign, the government, legislators, or state, and the people it serves predates even Hobbes. However, the utilitarians made it a more central part of political philosophy than in previous modern theory. James Mill's position on the importance of the enfranchisement of the industrial middle class flowed from a concern with establishing a congruence of interests between civil society and the state. A state controlled by the individuals who composed civil society would remove the possibility of that state working against the interests of the population. Held summarizes the importance of these arguments:

> Bentham, Mill and the Utilitarians generally provided one of the clearest justifications for the liberal-democratic state which ensures the conditions necessary for individuals to pursue their interests without risk of arbitrary political interference, to participate freely in economic transactions, to exchange labour and goods on the market and to appropriate resources privately. (16)

As Sabine (1961) argues, the utilitarians attempted to synthesize an egotistical conception of individual human beings with a concept of a government or state that seeks to work out policies in tune with a "general social harmony" (697). The essential assumption is that a commonality of interests exists among those to whom the government is responsible; that is, a commonality of interests within civil society.

The concept of a commonality of interests within civil society was, however, increasingly inappropriate for British society towards the end of Bentham's life. Bentham died the very year of the passing of the 1832 Reform Act, a measure commonly associated with the consolidation of the industrial bourgeoisie as the predominant political force in Britain. The triumph of British industrial capitalism had created fundamental divisions within civil society. After the turn of the nineteenth century these divisions threatened the very stability of that society. The necessity of the Reform Act illustrates the divisions which had emerged within the rising middle class as the industrial faction now demanded a greater share of political power. As well as the divisions within the bourgeoisie, there was the coincidental emergence of a working class. In addition there were remnants of other social groupings, such as the feudal aristocracy, the independent craft producers, and a dwindling agrarian population. In terms of material interests, ideology, and political demands, civil society did indeed lack a sense of commonality of position and interest.

Perhaps no process better exemplifies the emerging recognition of these realities than the state's reactions to the emergence of the English working class. The interventionist mercantilist state had always been willing to take actions affecting the emerging working class. In 1563 the Statute of Artificers sought to fix wages and regulate such things as the location of industry and the training of workers. The emergence of working-class associations and clubs throughout the next two centuries led to such state reactions as the 1793 Friendly Societies Act, which recognized the existence of workers' societies but not for the purposes of collective bargaining. A short time later the 1798-1800 Combination Acts declared unions to be criminal conspiracies and made "combinations" of workers illegal. In 1819 the Six Acts ushered in an even more repressive era as magistrates were given broad powers, including the power to search homes. The same Acts controlled public meetings and placed a high tax on newspapers in an effort to control reform and workers' papers. The various strikes and confrontations of the period also led to the Luddite activities between 1811 and 1816. The repeal of the Combination Acts in 1824 resulted in a massive increase in trade union growth, with much of its political energy directed at supporting the larger middle-class reform movement.

The broader reform movement was successful in the sense that the 1832 Reform Bill did increase the political power of a wider cross-section of the middle class, in particular the industrial bourgeoisie. The working class was not rewarded for its support although the subsequent emergence of major national trade union centrals and an increasing working-class interest in various forms of socialism resulted in a series of parliamentary concessions of sorts. In the era during which the British state was controlled by a class and individuals committed to a radical laissez-faire, the government did nevertheless enact some regulatory legislation, such as the 1833 Factory Act, the 1843 reforms to the Poor Laws, and the 1847 Ten Hours Act. Indeed, one could argue that continued growth of trade unions and the Chartist movement of the post-1832 period all contributed to the eventual recognition of the need for a broader franchise. The 1867 Reform Bill substantially extended the cote, although the extensions were still only to certain male citizens—and women were still totally excluded.

JOHN STUART MILL

The new realities of a class-divided civil society were systematically incorporated into the political theorizing of the most important liberal-democrat of the mid-nineteenth century, John Stuart Mill. The son of James Mill, John Stuart Mill was well versed in the works of Bentham and utilitarian theory as well as continental thought. His own works display important first efforts to create a theory of democratization of the liberal state. While the twentieth century mind may find fault with many of his limitations of democratic participation, it is clear that his concepts of participation and consent went far beyond anything that previous liberal thinkers will willing to contemplate.

Perhaps the central differentiating characteristic of Mill's thought is its underlying developmental orientation. Mill does not view human nature as static, fixed, or unchanging. Rather, he adopts a perspective that views human beings as developing, progressing, indeed both evolving and improving in some manner. Mill's emphasis on education and the potentials of education to improve the human condition is illustrative. The very criteria of good government are placed in a developmental context:

> We have now, therefore, obtained a foundation for a two-fold division of the merit which any set of political institutions can possess. It consists partly of the degree in which they promote the general mental advancement of the community, including under the phrase advancement in intellect, in virtue, and in practical activity and efficiency; and partly of the degree of perfection with which they organize the moral, intellectual, and active worth already existing so as to operate with the greatest effect on public affairs. A government is to be judged by its action upon men, and by its action upon things; by what it makes of the citizens, and what it does with them; its tendency to improve or deteriorate the people themselves, and the goodness or badness of the work it performs for them. (Mill 1958: 27-28)

This line of argument leads to the following declaration:

> And the one indispensable merit of a government, in favour of which it may be forgiven almost any amount of other demerit compatible with progress, is that its operation on the people is favourable, or not unfavourable, to the next step which is necessary for them to take in order to raise themselves to a higher level. (30)

The changes apparent here in the legitimate role of the state, as compared to Hobbes, Locke, and Bentham, are dramatic. The state now is conceived of as having a positive function, namely the "raising," "improving," even "development" of the people. What form should this, once again, much more active state assume? Mill answers: "This ideally best form of government will be found in some one or other variety of the Representative System" (36). A further question emerges: Who should control the representative government? Again, Mill's own words are illuminating: "The meaning of representative government is, that the whole people, or some numerous portion of them, exercise through deputies periodically elected by themselves the ultimate controlling power, which in every constitution must reside somewhere" (quote in Held 1983: 99).

The question of ultimate control is not satisfactorily addressed in these remarks, for they simply identify the whole people or some numerous portion of them. How is this portion to be defined? In examining this question, the limitations of Mill's democracy become apparent, for despite his views that ultimately the franchise would be extended as more and more people became educated and thus competent, he does initially limit the franchise. "Mill's theory dilutes universal suffrage by denying the right to vote to persons who cannot read, write, or do simple arithmetic, who pay no taxes, or who receive welfare (parish relief)" (D.F. Thompson 1976: 99). Two considerations appear to justify this limitation: the question of competence and the issue of vested interests.

The issue of voter competence, because it enters Mills' system elsewhere, is easier for him to address. At one point he suggests that those who are more competent should be given a greater voice than the incompetent. This could be accomplished by not denying the vote to anyone provided the competent be given more than one vote—a concept of plural voting. For Mill the essential basis for evaluating opinions is mental capacity. "The only thing which can justify reckoning one person's opinion as equivalent to more than one is individual mental superiority" (Mill 1958: 137). If one is able to establish some empirical indicator of differential mental abilities, then it follows that the basis of differential opinions is present. Under such a circumstance, the superior elements must be given their due. After discussing indicators of inequalities in mental capacity, Mill states: "Subject to some such condition, two or more votes might be allowed to very person who exercises any of these superior functions" (138).

Despite these limitations on the franchise, Mill was cognizant of the importance of class and the possibilities of class domination in a state control-led by select elements of civil society. In discussing the question, Mill's liberal conception of the importance of self-interest once again emerges. However, for Mill the basic problem is the danger that "an exclusive class" may neglect those classes not represented because "it suffices that, in the absence of its natural defenders, the interests of the excluded is always in danger of being overlooked" (Held 1983: 98). Mill makes this point in stronger language elsewhere: "One of the greatest dangers ... of democracy, as in other forms of government, lies in the sinister interest of the holders of power: it is the danger of class legislation; of government intended for (whether really effecting it or not) the immediate benefit of the dominant class, to the lasting detriment of the whole" (99-100).

As a classical democrat Mill illustrates the substantial development of liberal theory towards liberal-democratic theory. Mill is clearly more democratic in his view of the role and extent of the franchise than the other theorists discussed, yet his work is not without its problems. As C.B. Macpherson notes, Mill was unable to recognize or at least satisfactorily address the problem inherent in attempting to synchronize a concept of the state which was fully democratic within a civil society that was predicated on class divisions. In Mill's civil society humans are liberal-possessive individuals and ultimately unequal, yet a market-based civil society offers them no assured mode of achieving the standing necessary for democratic participation, In Mill, classical liberalism reached a point of theoretical development that raised questions that began to be answered in alternate theoretical frameworks or substantial revisions of the classical liberal positions.

• TWO •

SOCIOLOGICAL CONCEPTIONS
OF THE STATE

The dangers inherent in simple attempts to link intellectual and theoretical perspectives to concrete historical situations are apparent when we consider the emergence of sociology and sociological conceptions of the state. The term sociology was first systematically used by August Comte (1798-1857) to describe the new science he was attempting to found. Comte was a contemporary of Bentham, James Mill, and John Stuart Mill, yet he ultimately attempted to develop a social theory offering a much different explanation of the momentous changes that were sweeping Europe. Comte can be credited for not only popularizing the term sociology, but also for introducing to modern social science a conception of society that contrasted radically with that of his day.

Comte's overwhelming concern with the basis of social order must be viewed in the context of his times. He was born into, and raised in, the monumental social and political confusion of post-revolutionary France, and an understanding of this epoch is central to an understanding of Comte's theoretical work and conclusions. According to Ronald Fletcher, Comte's "fundamental and lifelong preoccupation was how to replace disorder by order: how to accomplish the total reconstruction of society" (Fletcher 1971, Vol. 1: 165). Fletcher provides a concise summary of the historical period that informed this preoccupation:

> The *ancien regime* was gone, fallen to pieces, shown to be totally inadequate for the new trends and conditions of scientific knowledge and industrialization. There was no adequate order of institutions of the new changes in society. The social action of men was ungoverned and ill-directed. The thought of men was disoriented. There were great cleavages between belief and knowledge. And the feelings of men lacked coherence, confidence, and worthwhile objectives. In the spheres of social loyalty, traditional allegiance, moral purpose, men were adrift. (165)

The disorder and discord that so concerned Comte seemed to have emerged, ironically, from an era in which there was an increasing emphasis on reason, science, progress, and individual rights. The term most often associated with the intellectual currents of the eighteenth century is "Enlightenment." As Gamble notes, the period of the Enlightenment was one of intellectual stimulation during which new modes of thought came to be applied to virtually all aspects of human existence.

> Central to the concerns of the intellectual Enlightenment were reflections upon the emerging shape of the new state, the new economy, and the new science.... The faith in reason, in natural science, in progress, and in the individual, were central themes running through the contributions, which covered all branches of human knowledge.... Its intellectuals were interested in everything, dabbled in everything and wrote on everything. (Gamble 1981: 14)

That this new, apparently rational and scientific world view produced disorder and chaos rather than order and progress was Comte's central concern. In addressing the problem of order Comte sought to use the intellectual perspective founded in science. He studied mathematics and physics and was impressed by the capacity of science to facilitate an understanding of the order and regularity of nature. In the "natural world" scientific knowledge had provided a basis of progress through assisting in the understanding of the orderly working of nature. In the realm of the social, however, Comte noticed a radical difference. He saw that much Enlightenment thinking and philosophy had been essentially critical, even negative, in its attitudes towards the existing social structures. The end result, Comte maintained, was an era of confusion and conflict. What Comte proposed was a more positive form of knowledge in the social sciences, a new kind of knowledge founded on the scientific method. The application of the methods of science to the realm of the social and the political would make possible the transformation of society in accordance with the laws of nature. Positive science would be the basis of a positive reconstruction of society.

COMTE'S SOCIOLOGY: EARLY FUNCTIONALISM

The conception of society underlying classical liberal theory was based on an assumption that humans and human nature could be examined separately from society. The Hobbesian notion of presocial humans deciding to form a state to ensure order within civil society illustrated the classical liberal conception of the relationship of individuals to society. The assumption was that a universal human nature existed, and it was ultimately the task of social sciences to uncover this nature in order to provide a basis upon which society would be reconstructed. The whole, society, was assumed to be merely the sum of the parts, the individuals who compose it. Social arrangements were merely conveniences to maximize individual pleasures and benefits. The individual and his or her characteristics were *a priori*, basic, and had to be accommodated if social structures were to avoid conflict, chaos, and breakdown.

Comte's conception of society must be understood in the context of his positions on human understanding and the evolution of science. Comte argues that human intelligence and human knowledge pass successively through three theoretical stages: "the theological or fictitious, the metaphysical or abstract, and the scientific or positive" (Comte 1953, Vol. 1: 2). At each of these different stages radically different assumptions and procedures guide human intelligence in its search for knowledge. The essential point is that the culmination of the process of human knowledge production is science. Comte examines the growth and evolution of positive or scientific knowledge, establishing a hierarchy of science based, in part, on the complexity of the phenomenon studied. At the top of the hierarchy is sociology, the science of human affairs, the crowning achievement of human knowledge as represented by the application of the methods of positive science to human affairs. The reconstruction of human society in accordance with knowledge provided by science represents the crowning achievement of human history. "We have only to complete the Positive Philosophy by bringing Social phenomena within its comprehension, and afterwards consolidating the whole into one body of homogeneous doctrine" (15).

In this writing Comte explicitly criticizes the basic assumptions of utilitarian and social contract theories of society. Human society for Comte is not the outcome of deliberate human action, but rather emerges because of "Man's social tendencies" (Comte 1953, Vol. 2: 127-128). Human society must be understood as an essentially spontaneous outcome of the social inclinations of humans.

Comte therefore disagreed with the classical liberal notion of a static and fixed human nature and the corresponding thesis that a certain form of society was more appropriate for that nature. Comte argues that human society changed, developed, and evolved in a manner similar to many biological entities. Indeed, the usage of a biological analogy for analysis of human society became a central aspect of Comte's work. Human society, a collective organism, must be understood in a manner analogous to the biological approach to the study of living organisms. Comte even used biology's basic concepts— elements, tissues, and organs—as the basis of social analysis. He furthermore argued that these various components must be understood as linked into a system. The key to understanding the social system is "to study social phenomena in the only right way—viewing each element in the light of the whole system" (81).

In more concrete terms this means that each aspect of the social system, from individuals to families and ultimately governments, must be understood as parts of a larger whole. The large whole, moreover, is an evolving, developing, even progressing whole, which must be understood as "a cumulative process of institutions, knowledge, skills, traditions, values, beliefs" which cannot "be simply deduced from the nature of man as a biological individual" (Fletcher 1971, Vol. 1: 177). Comte argues that the basis for an analysis of the social organism was present in "the incomparable Aristotle." Comte credits Aristotle for understanding that "the true principle of every collective organism" was the "distribution of functions and the combination of labour" (Comte 1953, Vol. 1: 129).

Comte thus established a theoretical position based on a new conception of society. He sought to establish a new science dedicated to examining social phenomena and ultimately a practical application of that knowledge to assist the reconstruction of society. The methods to be used in the scientific analysis of society were historical, comparative, and functional. Each of the elements as well as the entire collective organism was subject to historical and evolutionary development and thus had to be studied historically. Each component of the social structure was also a part of a large functioning unity and thus social analysis had to examine the components in functional terms.

Comte is thus an early representative of what would later emerge as functional analysis, which directs our attention specifically to what a phenomenon does or how it performs within a large system. To use a biological analogy, to explain the role of the heart in an organism such as the human body, a functional analysis would proceed by referring to the work of the heart as a pump operating to ensure the circulation of blood to the various other organs within the body. The role of other organs would be explained in a similar way. In social analysis, functionalist explanation looks at various social structures, institutions, and practices in terms of their functions for society as a whole.

COMTE'S CONCEPT OF THE STATE

When Comte claimed, while criticizing utilitarian theory, that humans possessed fundamental social tendencies, he was not absolutely ruling out the concept of self-interest. Indeed, he specifically noted the presence in humans of both personal and social affections. Personal affections are the basis of those behaviours geared to securing personal satisfaction and comfort, while social affections are, as the name implies, the basis of social actions. While personal and social affections are different, they are not contradictory, nor do they necessarily conflict. Indeed, it follows from Comte's statement about human social tendencies that the social affections seem to predominate. Despite acknowledging the existence of strong personal affections, Comte refers to "natural benevolence" and "universal benevolence" as part of the integration of personal and social affections in the formation of social units, including the family.

For Comte the family is the basic unit for social analysis. The family is the most elementary social unit, the "avenue that Man comes forth from his mere personality, and learns to live in another" (Comte 1953, Vol. 2: 133). The family, Comte states, "is, and will ever be, the basis of social spirit, through all the gradual modifications which it may have to undergo in the course of human evolution" (133). He goes on to include the family as the basic building block in a larger structure: society as a whole.

Within the family there is a division of functions that, Comte argues, makes it necessary to human development and evolution. In examining society further, he develops the idea that specialization in functions facilitates the development and evolution of a phenomenon. Indeed, he states that the basis of "the superiority of the social to the individual organism is ... the more marked speciality of the various functions fulfiled by organs more and more distinct but interconnected" (140). Society is thus superior because it brings together and co-ordinates the endeavours of a variety of individuals, and the result is beneficial to all. Human beings as individuals bring into society natural differences and specializations in skills and abilities, with the result being a distribution of employments, or specialization of social tasks, in the social organism. These differences, however, have a negative side in that they provide the basis of conflict in human society. There emerge, Comte says, "mischievous intellectual consequences of the spirit of speciality which at present prevails" (143). The end result is a threat to the very basis of society, a process which Comte sees as a fundamental contradiction: "Thus it is that principle by which alone general society could be developed and extended, threatens, in another view, to decompose it into a multitude of unconnected species" (144).

Comte's approach thus takes us through the postulation of an essentially social human being, who through family structures exists in a society or collective organism. Within the family and within the larger society there emerges a specialization of labour, which then becomes the basis of social conflict as it produces the basis of divisions, differences, and ultimately conflict. Society comes to the position recognized by classical liberalism: that it requires some mode of assuring order.

Like the classical liberals, Comte also introduces a concept of government. However, he places it within the social organism as opposed to above or apart from civil society. Comte's functional analysis comes to the fore:

> Thus it appears to me that the social destination of government is to guard against and restrain the fundamental dispersion of ideals, sentiments, and interests, which is the inevitable result of the very principle of human development, and which if left to itself would put a stop to social progression in all important respects. (144)

Government's function is to maintain peace, order, and stability in the society. Disorder can only be prevented by setting up government "as a new special function, which shall intervene in the performance of all the various functions of the social economy" (145). The government is an integral part of the large collective organism, an organ like others with a special function. As typical of functional analysis, Comte pays little or no attention to the history of the organ; indeed the government in Comte's analysis is simply another spontaneous organ (147).

While Comte's analysis differed from the liberals in many respects, he did acknowledge certain points of agreement. At one point Comte notes that Hobbes was correct in maintaining that government must rest on force if it is to be effective in ensuring peace, and he points out that while force is essential, it is not in and of itself sufficient to maintain order in the long run. Government and society are maintained over time by a combination of physical and intellectual force. For Comte, intellectual force means moral sanctions and mechanisms or a mode of controlling those with political power. Comte argues that social control in this last sense amounts to modes of control by which society as a whole curbs possible excesses by the holders of political power.

To summarize, Comte understood the state as an integral part of society. In turn, he saw society as an organic entity with each component structure integrated into and functioning for the larger whole. The importance of Comte's work lies in his elaboration of an organic approach, an approach that came to dominate French sociology with the later emergence of the work of Emile Durkheim.

EMILE DURKHEIM

If we view the emergence of the sociological perspective as a counterpoint to the classical liberal conception of human nature and the associated reductionist view of society, the work of Emile Durkheim (1858-1917) becomes central. Durkheim's intellectual life was devoted to legitimizing the scientific stature of sociology. In the process he addressed issues such as liberal and utilitarian individualism, the appropriate methods of sociology, and the nature and importance of moral authority in society.

Durkheim is perhaps best known for his study of the evolution of industrial society, *The Division of Labour in Society* (1893), in which he elaborated his revolutionary perspective on the development of industrial society. In this, Durkheim placed special emphasis on the role of norms, values, belief systems, or—to use his own term—moral facts in providing a basis for social solidarity, stability, and order. By comparing human society to a living organism, Durkheim argues that industrial society evolved from a primitive pre-industrial mode and that during the course of this evolution numerous changes took place. The key changes involve an increasing social division of labour or specialization of individual tasks and functions. This evolving social division of labour has two dimensions: first, individual occupational specialization; secondly, at a more general level, institutional specialization. As industrial society emerged there was a transformation of the basic individual and social structural "sameness" and similarity that characterizes pre-industrial society. Specialized occupations develop alongside of, and with, specialized institutions.

As the process of social transformation becomes established, its first fruits are not necessarily desirable. Pre-industrial society was characterized by a social order and stability predicated on "mechanical solidarity." This mechanical solidarity springs from the "strongly defined moral consensus" of these societies, "an enveloping *conscious collective*" (Giddens 1972: 5). Anthony Giddens explains:

> The unity of such a society, in other words, is to be found in the fact that there exists a strongly defined set of values and beliefs which ensures that the actions of all individuals conform to common norms.... The term [mechanical solidarity] indicates an analogy with simple organisms, which have a mechanical structure in this sense, such that each cell is wholly comparable to every other, and such that a cell or a group of cells can split away without destroying the unity of the parent organism. (Giddens 1972: 6)

In essence, the virtual sameness of employment, activity, institutional and personal experience, and structure yielded a population with a high degree of common consciousness. The emergence of occupational specialization and institutional differentiation erodes this sameness and creates the potential for a variety of differences and factions. The end result of the process is not, however, a fractured social structure, because the new industrial society produces the basis for a new order by virtue of its structural characteristics.

An industrial society, with its specialization of occupation, its division of labour, and its institutional differentiation, generates a new form of social solidarity. In a pre-industrial society people possessed a marked degree of independence, even self-sufficiency, in that they were capable of most types of labour. In industrial society this independence is replaced by an interdependence as people, specializing now in certain labours or activities, become dependent on others to perform a wider and wider range of tasks to complement their own. All specialized occupations come to require the services and labours of other occupations merely to survive. Similarly, institutions that have become specialized perform narrow, closely defined tasks or functions for society and they too become less independent. Modern industrial society increasingly functions like a complex organism with a structure composed of specialized parts all performing specialized functions for the whole. In an industrial society each institution functions in a manner similar to the separate parts of an organism: It meets a need or performs some function for the whole.

Durkheim refers to the basis of social solidarity which evolves in industrial society as organic solidarity. It is based on a shared moral code or normative belief system that emphasizes individual and institutional interde-

41

pendence. The growth of the division of labour may *appear* to result in the emergence of a society that is merely a collection of atomized individuals; however, something quite different is happening:

> Consequently, even where society relies most completely upon the division of labour, it does not become a jumble of juxtaposed atoms, between which it can establish only external transient contacts. Rather the members are united by ties which extend deeper and far beyond the short moments during which the exchange is made. Each of the functions that they exercise, in a fixed way, depend upon others, and with them forms a solitary system. Because we fill some certain domestic or social function, we are involved in a complex of obligations from which we have no right to free ourselves. (Durkheim 1933: 227)

Durkheim goes on to note that one organ is particularly important in the maintenance of the unity of the social organism: the state.

The essence of Durkheim's concept of the state is thus located in his functional analysis and his concern with the basis for and role of moral authority. The state performs an essential function for society. This function is related to the necessity of re-establishing a system or moral authority or a moral code appropriate for an advanced industrial society. Anthony Giddens has summarized this aspect of Durkheim's work, noting that for Durkheim "economic reorganization alone will exacerbate rather than resolve the crisis facing the modern world, since this is a crisis which is moral rather than economic" (Giddens 1971: 99). While Durkheim recognized the economic dimensions of the problem, he saw the dilemma as essentially the lack of a shared moral code that would provide a basis for integration and order. The state's role in solving the crisis must address the cause of the problem. Thus, "The state must play a moral as well as an economic role: and the alleviation of the *malaise* of the modern world must be sought in measures which are in general moral rather than economic" (99).

To understand the nature of this moral role we must reconsider the nature of the moral problem that an industrializing or industrial society faces. With the development of the division of labour and individual/institutional specialization there is a concomitant breakdown of the moral code which was previously the basis of stability and order. If instability, conflict, and discord are to be avoided, the moral vacuum that has developed must be filled with a new normative or moral order. In part an essential function of the state becomes that of facilitating the emergence of a new moral order, a new *conscious collective*. In addition, some mode of collective decision-making becomes necessary in the advanced organic society and thus the state must take on that additional responsibility. Decision-making for the organic collectivity and the formulation and dissemination of a new normative order become the state's essential functions. In the context of a discussion of the emergence of collective policies and ideas Durkheim states:

> There is always, or at least usually, some sort of deliberation, and an understanding of the circumstances as a whole that make the decision necessary; and it is precisely this inner organ, the state, that is called upon to conduct these debates. Thus we have the councils, assemblies, debates and rulings which control the pace at which ideas are formulated. We may say, in summary: the state is a specialised agency whose responsibility is to work out certain ideas which apply to the collectivity. These ideas are distinguished from the other collective representations by their more conscious and deliberate character. (quoted in Giddens 1972: 192)

In addition to discussing the role or function of the state, Durkheim also considered the question of the form of the state. How are individuals related to the state? How do individuals in a collective organism influence a central organ such as the state? How is the state related to other social institutions?

Durkheim, we must always bear in mind, was first and foremost interested in furthering the sociological mode of analysis and thought. It is thus not surprising that he linked individuals to the state through an intervening social unit—the occupational group or corporation—which necessarily emerges in an industrial society with its multiplicity of occupations and professions.

The occupational group becomes an integral aspect of Durkheim's analysis of industrial society for a number of reasons, including its central role in the provision and dissemination of the appropriate moral code. But we must take care not to understand the occupational or corporate group in narrow terms, related only to economic functions associated with the division of labour. In the Preface to the Second Edition of the *Division of Labour* Durkheim extends the basis of corporatist groups to include those associated with educational institutions, aesethetic life, sport and recreation, and societies of mutual aid. He concludes: "The corporative activity can thus assume the most varied form" (Durkheim 1933: 27). The picture that emerges is one of an advanced organic industrial society composed of individuals engaged in a variety of specialized occupations which are organized or structured into specialized institutions. Individuals, in addition to being located in institutional structures, participate in or are organized into occupational or corporate groups based literally on occupation or on some other social attribute or activity. The occupational or corporate group becomes the key integrating structure, co-ordinating and reorganizing the multitude of individuals into the large social organism. In the area of politics these groups play a similar role. Durkheim notes, "There is every reason to suppose that the corporation will become the foundation or one of the essential bases of our political organization" (27).

Durkheim was also concerned about the possible social consequences of the excessive individualism that tended to accompany the development of the division of labour. In an obvious reference to the classical liberal notion of the state, Durkheim notes: "A society composed of an infinite number of unorganized individuals, that a hypertrophied state is forced to oppress and contain, constitutes a veritable sociological monstrosity" (28). In such a society the state would be too complex, remote, distant, and detached for the individual. This type of society would not be democratic, a matter of some importance to Durkheim, who saw the necessity for a strong state that established a *reciprocal* relation between the "unconsciously" evolved movements taking place in the lower levels of society and "the more articulate and deliberate activities of the state." Democracy had to ensure "an active interplay between the state and the rest of society" (Giddens 1972: 19-20). If the state were unable to perform its integrative functions the society, Durkheim concludes, would disintegrate. The solution, for Durkheim, was to give the occupational groups an openly political role:

> A nation can be maintained only if, between the state and the individual, there is intercalated a whole series of secondary groups near enough the individuals to attract them strongly in their sphere of action and drag them, in this way into the general torrent of social life. We have just shown how occupational groups are suited to fill this role, and that is their destiny. (Durkheim 1964: 28)

The concept of the state that emerges in Durkheim's work is clearly functionalist in that the state performs a variety of functions for the social collectivity or the social organism. Durkheim's position is also pluralist; he argues that occupational groups, corporations, or secondary groups are required to maintain flows of communications between individuals and the state and to counterbalance the potential abuse of powers by those in state institutions (Giddens 1978: 60-61). Giddens summarizes this point: "It is this assertion of the need for pluralism which draws the connection between Durkheim's theory of the state and his conception of democracy, and from thence with his call for the resurgency of occupational associations (corporations)" (Giddens 1971: 101-102).

It is important, then, to note that Durkheim's conception of democracy is influenced by the importance he attaches to secondary groups. Democracy is not direct democracy, but a system of control and influence on the state which is predicated on the various secondary groups or associations that characterize an advanced industrial society. Democracy does not imply a weak state, because the state is an essential social organ. Rather, for Durkheim, "A democratic society is one in which the state is independent and strong enough to accomplish these tasks, but nevertheless in close communication with the ideas of the mass of the population" (Giddens 1978: 60).

TALCOTT PARSONS AND SYSTEMS ANALYSIS

Durkheim's work was to have a strong impact on subsequent western sociology. In North America it was first brought systematically to the fore through the work of the leading western sociologist of the post-World War II period, Talcott Parsons (1902-1979). As Alvin Gouldner argues, the work of Parsons, like that of Durkheim and Comte, emerged out of a historical period characterized by crisis and instability (Gouldner 1970). For Comte the immediate post-French Revolution period had provided a context; for Durkheim the context was the continued instability of French society and politics of the late nineteenth century. In turn, the Great Depression of the 1930s was the epoch during which the Parsonian system took its initial shape. As a result, like Comte and Durkheim, Parsons was greatly concerned with the problem of order.

Parsons' theoretical work in the discipline of sociology is founded in his larger perspective on the goal of the social sciences. In a short summary of Parsons' work Peter Hamilton states: "All of the social or 'human' sciences (perhaps a more apt term) are primarily concerned with human *action* in all of its spheres: Parsons works with the assumption that 'action' is the single most characteristic attribute of 'human-ness'; is a highly differentiated quality, and that each of the social sciences study action at different empirical levels" (Hamilton 1983: 86). Sociology as a discipline focuses on human action in its group context, and the most significant group is society. As his work developed Parsons more and more focused on the social system and society, seeking to present a theoretical orientation that would allow an understanding of these phenomena and thus contribute to a large general theory of human action.

Social systems face, Parsons argues, certain invariable problems which they must solve in order to survive. Parsons summarizes four basic problems or system prerequisites in his A-G-I-L schema, which refers to the fundamental problems of Adaptation, Goal Attainment, Integration, and Latency or Pattern Maintenance:

> 1) that concerned with the maintenance of the highest "governing" or controlling patterns of the system; 2) the internal integration of the system; 3) its orientation to the attainment of goals in relation to its environment; 4) its more generalized adaptation to the broad conditions of the environment—e.g., the non-action, physical environment. (Parsons 1966: 19-20)

Parsons thus argues that individual human beings are to be understood as actors oriented towards actions; these actions take place in the context of social systems which face a number of invariant problems. Perhaps *the* central problem is the co-ordination of the multiplicity of actors and actions within a unified and stable system. Because human actors and systems of social relationships possess, to use Parsons' own phrase, an "inherent potential for conflict and disorganization," the central social problem is the problem of order (Parsons 1969: 8). The problem of order is at least partially solved by securing solutions to the problems associated with the broader A-G-I-L schema.

Parsons links system problems or prerequisites with action and the larger social system through the concept of institution. Social institutions are to be understood in the context of human action and system problems. Thus, for example, economic actions are oriented by and to economic institutions, addressing the problem referred to as adaptation. In assigning institutional spheres to the different prerequisites, Parsons assumes that the problems related to goal attainment are the purview of the polity, which refers to "a set of structures and processes, a subsystem parallel to the economy" (206).

The central function of the polity in the overall social system is goal attainment, or more specifically the mobilization of society's resources in the interest of specific goals. The mobilization of resources is essentially how Parsons defines power; thus, the polity has to do with the "generation and distribution of power." Parsons does not focus on the competitive or conflictual dimensions of power but rather on power and politics in the context of collective goal attainment (Bourricaud 1981: 143).

The structures and processes related to the polity include the government, which Parsons argues performs specific functions as defined in the constitution. Parsons summarizes these constitutionally defined functions as "the conduct of foreign relations, the regulation of commerce between the states, the enforcement of rights (personal freedom, opportunity, property), the ensuring of justice and internal order and the promotion of the 'general welfare'" (Parsons 1969: 207). The functions of the larger polity, however, are broader, including the legitimization of the powers of government, overall co-ordination of society's operations, and the mobilization of support for the actions and operation of legitimate governmental actions.

The essential nature of the functions of the polity in Parsons' scheme can best be grasped by considering his ideas about systems analysis. As a subsystem of the larger social system the polity is involved in sets of exchanges with that larger system as well as with other subsystems, with each subsystem contributing to the larger whole. Parsons identified four subsystems, each with a specialized primary function. In addition to the polity there is the economy specializing in the adaptive functions; the societal community (such as kinship-household units, religious and educational institutions) ensuring integration; and the pattern maintenance subsystem, which is responsible for the dissemination of shared values throughout the social system (Parsons 1971: 10-14).

The polity provides the collectivity with leadership, goals, and policy directions in exchange for political support, legitimized authority, commitments to implement the polity's goals, and regular input. The exchange relations between the polity and the larger social system can be understood in terms of inputs from the larger system into the subsystem and subsequently certain outputs from the subsystem. In Parsons' own schematic representation, the public inputs into the polity are "generalized support" and "advocacy of policies" while the polity's outputs are "effective leadership" and "binding decisions" (Parsons 1969: 209).

STRUCTURAL FUNCTIONALISM

Because Parsons never undertook a detailed study of the polity, and because of the difficult nature of his abstract analysis, his specific work on the polity or state has had less lasting influence than the different modes of functional analysis his work influenced. Indeed, a conception of the state based on Parsons' work—the general sociological approach commonly referred to as structural functionalism—has become widely accepted in the social sciences.

While there are numerous variations among those viewing themselves as functionalists, there are also several basic points of agreement. First, human society or human social systems face a number of basic problems that must be solved if the system is to survive. Functionalists usually examine the state or the polity as an institution within the context of a set of system prerequisites. Although the precise number of system prerequisites varies among different functionalist theorists, several are commonly assumed, including the establishment and articulation of collective goals, and various forms of social regulation are viewed as the basis of system survival. Functionalists assume that failure to establish some forms of institutional arrangements to address these problems would have pathological implications for the social system.

Rossides, for example, declares: "The major function of the polity, in short, is to make adjustments between the other institutions of society so as to integrate them and at the same time to facilitate the successful performance of their specialized functions" (Rossides 1968: 195). Others have examined government in a similar manner, noting explicitly its essential functions. For example, Hunt and Colander have elaborated on the primary functions of government as: maintaining internal order and external security, ensuring justice, safeguarding individual freedoms, and promoting general welfare and certain regulatory functions (Hunt and Colander 1984: 303-306). Seymour Martin Lipset, perhaps the best known U.S. political sociologist, uses a similar definition of the polity: The polity may be viewed as that part of the social system which is responsible for allocating the resources and facilities of the society" (Lipset 1968: 157).

Whatever the term—state, government, or polity—all are thus examined through their functioning within the context of a larger social system. In the social system each institution performs a series of specialized functions for the whole, meeting certain system prerequisites, solving certain problems for the whole. The basis of institutional analysis is an understanding of an institution's functions. The state is understood to be performing certain central functions for the social system as a whole.

In general, structural functionalist analysis would not suggest any specific state form as necessarily appropriate or desirable. The precise nature of the institutional arrangements and structures which make up the polity will vary from society to society depending on the nature of the society's normative and value systems. The state system or, perhaps more appropriately, the state subsystem, operates in the context of a normative value system that provides the basis of the functioning of that subsystem and a basis for inter-institutional functioning (Rossides 1968: 183-185).

When they address the operation and structures of the state in capitalist society—in particular western liberal democracies—functionalists tend to adopt a specific position: a pluralist approach. In an article in a book edited by Talcott Parsons, S.M. Lipset notes: "Perhaps the largest single field of inquiry in political sociology has been the study of voting behavior" (Lipset 1969: 165). This analysis of voting and electoral behaviour locates the centre of political analysis in processes of the selection of government personnel. Other functionalists have focused their attention on the processes of pressure group lobbying and the role of various associations in the ongoing political processes (Rossides 1968: 198-99).

Max Weber and the Modern State

Perhaps no other sociologist of the "classical" era developed an approach to the discipline as complex—and misunderstood—as that of Max Weber (1864-1920). Despite criticisms to the contrary by theorists such as Ritzer (1983), Weber produced a consistent and pertinent body of work within which political sociology, or the study of the state, plays an important role.

Weber defines sociology as "a science concerning itself with the interpretative understanding of social action and thereby with a causal explanation of its course and consequences" (Weber 1978: 4). He states that action as implied in this definition relates to individual human beings; thus the project of sociology becomes interpreting, understanding, and explaining the social actions or behaviours of individual human beings. This is, needless to say, an enormously complex project, a fact that Weber incorporated into the very core of his method and approach. In his consideration of the methodological issues facing the social sciences Weber notes the difficulty of the task:

> The type of social science in which we are interested is an *empirical science* of concrete *reality (Wirklichkeitswissenschaft)*. Our aim is the understanding of the characteristic uniqueness of the reality in which we move. We wish to understand on the one hand the relationships and the cultural significance of individual events in their contemporary manifestations and on the other the causes of their being histori-

cally *so* and not *otherwise*. Now, as soon as we attempt to reflect about the way in which life confronts us in immediate concrete situations, it presents an infinite multiplicity of successively and coexistently emerging and disappearing events, both "within" and "outside" ourselves. The absolute infinitude of this multiplicity is seen to remain undiminished even when our attention is focused on a single "object," for instance, a concrete act of exchange, as soon as we seriously attempt an exhaustive description of *all* the individual components of this "individual phenomenon," to say nothing of explaining it causally. All the analysis of infinite reality which the finite human mind can conduct rests on the tacit assumption that only a finite portion of this reality constitutes the object of scientific investigation, and that only it is "important" in the sense of being "worthy of being known." But what are the criteria by which this segment is selected? (Weber 1949: 72-73)

Social scientists, with their finite minds, face, Weber notes, an infinitely complex reality. What is the social scientist to do? Rather than suggesting that social scientists throw up their collective hands in despair, Weber outlines a point of departure. He presents some of the factors that must be considered to start grasping this infinite complexity of reality. In his most important work, *Economy and Society,* first published in 1921, Weber presents a preliminary indication of the sorts of issues, considerations, or factors that must be examined in order to begin interpreting and explaining social actions. A survey of the table of contents illustrates Weber's tact: He introduces us to the study of economic action, forms of domination and legitimation, social norms, kin groups, religion, ethnic groups, law, and historical analysis.

The complexity of the structure of *Economy and Society* mirrors the complexity of the reality that social scientists face in their efforts to explain and interpret social action. In short, sociologists must be prepared to consider these and more factors if they are to understand and interpret social action.

Among the more important factors that must be considered, Weber declares, are forms of domination. In one of his most forceful passages he declares: "Domination in the most general sense is one of the most important elements of social action."

Of course, not every form of social action reveals a structure of dominancy. But in most of the varieties of social action domination plays a considerable role, even where it is not obvious at first sight.... Without exception every sphere of social action is profoundly influenced by structures of dominancy. (Weber 1978: 941)

The message is clear: Social scientists and especially sociologists must consider, understand, and take account of domination.

Understanding domination is, however, also a complex process. Weber maintains that domination is a special case of power and, further: "Domination in the quite general sense of power, i.e. of the possibility of imposing one's own will upon the behaviour of other persons, can emerge in the most diverse forms" (942). Among the various forms of structures of domination and power is the phenomenon of political power.

Political power is, for Weber, related to the "striving to share power or striving to influence the distribution of power either among states or among groups within the state" (Weber 1946: 78). Weber defines power as the "probability that one actor within a social relationship will be in a position to carry out his own will despite resistance, regardless of the basis on which this probability rests" (Weber 1978: 53). When power is exercised within a given territorial area, and when those holding power have a monopoly over the use of legitimate force within that area, we are dealing with a form of political organization that we might refer to as a state. Weber's famous definition of the state notes, "A state is a human community that (successfully) claims the *monopoly of legitimate use of physical force* within a given territory" (Mills and Gerth 1958: 78). The basis of the legitimacy may vary among tradition, charisma, and rational/logical systems, but the essence of a state and political action relates to some actors using the state to their advantage because the state, like all political institutions, "is a relation of men dominating men" (78).

For Weber, then, power relations and domination are essential aspects of human social action. Among the many kinds of power are: economic power, which relates to the market and class; power related to the distribution of honour, which relates to status and status groups; and a more general dimension of power that Weber refers to as social power. Social power relates to "influencing social action no matter what its content may be" (Weber 1978: 938). One type of social power is political power, which has to do with the activities of parties and efforts to share or influence the state.

Weber's political analyses were ultimately heavily influenced by his overall concern with the direction of western civilization and his lifelong concern with understanding the origins and direction of modern capitalism. In this context it is possible to understand his ultimate support for a parliamentary system of political organization. Parliamentary representative government provided some possibility for countering the growing rationalization and bureaucratization of the political processes. Like all other aspects of life in the west, political organizations tend to become routinized and rationalized. The logical extension of this process is the large-scale bureaucratic state. Parliamentary democracy, for Weber, offers the possibility of greater input into the process and therefore a degree of resistance to the general trends (Weber 1978: 1381-84; Giddens 1972: 19).

Weber's work, then, takes a distinctive approach to politics and the state. He essentially argues that political power is but one dimension of the larger phenomenon of power and domination in human relations. Human social action inevitably involves some form of power relations, which in turn raises the probability of domination. Power and domination can relate to a variety of action situations, including economic activity, the distribution of honour or prestige, and finally the distribution of social power. Political or state power, the capacity to influence social action in the context of a territory and the legitimate use of force, may be based on a number of considerations, including class interest, family traditions, and ideological inclination.

Political power is thus an enormously complex matter. Like all other issues facing the social scientist it must be approached with an eye to making some sense out of the potentially infinite data. For Weber the point of departure for such analysis is an understanding of the essential nature of power and domination in human social action, some mode of classifying the basis of legitimacy of political power, an understanding of the relationship of political power to the larger social tendencies towards rationalization, and an appreciation of the various forms of state or political structures that humans are capable of establishing. Human conduct is infinitely complex, and power and domination in the political sphere are a part of that pattern. Weber's final conclusion is that although definitive knowledge of these phenomena will continue to elude us, we can nevertheless make some inroads towards understanding them.

STABILITY OR CONFLICT?

Both classical liberal and sociological theorists, then, are concerned with the question of social order and the state's role in providing a basis for order. However, the modes of theorizing the state and its role are quite different. For the classical liberal, the state stands outside and even above civil society, serving the role of an umpire in the contests and conflicts that permeate market society. The state's role is not to eliminate conflict, but rather to provide for a minimal basis of order and to adjudicate conflicts when they arise.

The sociological thinkers, especially Comte, Durkheim, and Parsons, understand the state as an institution much more organically integrated into the larger social system. Indeed, they conceptualize the state as an institution. Like other institutions it performs some specialized functions, meeting a particular need or solving a particular problem for the collective social organism. Its function is linked to providing a basis of social solidarity and social integration. Its integrative functions provide the possibility of eliminating or at least dramatically reducing social conflict, tension, and discord. A properly functioning state would ensure a degree of social harmony and consensus far beyond the hopes of the classical liberal thinkers.

Although the precise manner by which the state would perform this function varies from theorist to theorist, Weber's work presents a different view in that he articulates an alternate project for sociology, different from that found in Comte and Durkheim. He maintains that relations of power and domination are inherent in market society and, as a result, the elimination of conflict by the state was at the very least an unrealistic dream.

51

• THREE •

ELITE THEORY

At first glance a workable definition of the term "elite" seems simple enough. The *Oxford Dictionary*, for example, defines it as "Choice part, best (of); select group or class." A standard dictionary of social science concepts defines elite as either: "The most influential and prestigious stratum in a society" or as "The highest stratum within a field of competition" (Theodorson and Theodorson 1969: 129). This definition assumes, incidentally, that those in the highest stratum are the most influential members of social organizations, groups, and even societies.

The term "elite" has, as might be expected, experienced a somewhat more complicated history of development and definition in the hands of political philosophers and social scientists. The theorists who have used it as a tool for studying the role and organization of the state and society have taken differential approaches in its meaning and use. The term as used here refers to certain conceptions of power, inequality, and politics as found in the works of Vilfredo Pareto, Gaetano Mosca, Robert Michels, and more recently C.W. Mills and John Porter. Each of these theorists argues that various human societies have in fact produced elites. While they have differing explanations for why this happens, they do agree that these elites come to be the key actors in shaping and structuring the central characteristics of their societies.

CLASSICAL ELITE THEORY: VILFREDO PARETO
The social and political environment that influenced the classical elite thinkers—Pareto, Mosca, and Michels—was the environment of Durkheim and Weber: one of rapid political change and an intense shift to industrialization. More specifically, the thinking of these founders of elite theory was influenced by the Italian intellectual movement. What was unique was the focus on a search for constants in human nature. Lewis Coser summarizes the impact of this intellectual tradition on Italian social theorizing:

> The point of departure of the Italian tradition in social thought ever since Machiavelli was not socialized man involved in a web of relations and shaped by institutions, but rather human nature. Men, the Italian thinkers felt, have certain unchanging characteristics and the social thinker should mainly be concerned with highlighting and scrutinizing human nature so as to determine conduct under different circumstances.... In the Machiavellian tradition, the social analyst is enjoined to cultivate a cool, sceptical ability to penetrate the

mainsprings of human nature. (Coser 1977: 408)

Into this tradition came Vilfredo Pareto (1848-1923), a thinker whose training was initially in engineering and mathematics, but who studied and wrote in the areas of political economy, politics, and finally sociology. Indeed, as he sought to apply the methods of the scientific sociology advocated by Comte, Pareto's work also took a shifting political stance, moving away from his earlier liberalism to an anti-liberal position since linked with fascism (Zeitlin 1981: 206-207).

Society, Pareto maintained, is a mechanical system with interrelated elements or parts. In order to understand the system it is necessary to study and understand its elements or parts. He argued that three categories of elements must be studied: 1) the geographical and physical environment; 2) spatial and historical considerations that have an impact on the society's relations with other societies; and 3) internal elements (Pareto 1976: 251). Pareto focuses his attention on the third group, the so-called "internal elements."

In essence, what Pareto means by internal elements are human characteristics, human behaviour, and human actions. Social theorizing, then, begins with a consideration of human beings themselves. Human behaviour must be understood in the context of a distinction between logical and nonlogical actions. Logical actions are those undertaken with clear and deliberately chosen objectives in mind. According to Pareto, not much human action falls into this category. Most human action falls into the nonlogical category. Nonlogical behaviour is not the same as illogical; it is just that it is not directed or motivated with clearly articulated and understood objectives in mind.

Nonlogical behaviour is understandable if we examine the basic structures and operation of the human mind and personality. Pareto bases his understanding of the human mind and personality on a biologically based explanation of human action. In a complex argument, Pareto explains human action as being rooted in motivating forces or dispositions, which he calls *residues*. Residues in turn stem from what he terms *sentiments*, which in turn are understandable in the context of basic biophysical states termed *instincts*.

The entire gamut of behaviour which comprises human actions is determined by the presence or absence of various residues in any given individual, and the determination of whether residues are present or absent in an individual is essentially a biological event. The essential point is the fact that no two individuals possess exactly similar distributions of these residues. As a result all humans are different, not only in their behaviour and personalities but also in their interests, abilities, aptitudes, and capacities. The unequal distribution of residues, the basic substance of human actions, is the essence of the human condition.

Pareto summarizes: "Whatever certain theorists may like to think, human society in fact is not a homogeneous thing, and individuals are physically, morally and intellectually different" (247).

The differences among people, Pareto argues, are so fundamental as to make it possible for us to develop an index or grading system to evaluate their efforts in whatever area of human action we might choose to examine. If we were to undertake this task, Pareto says, we would conclude that it is possible to divide the population into two broad categories. The first category would be those who excel at whatever tasks they have undertaken. The second category, the majority, would be those whose performance we would consider "average." The implications of this fundamental division for society as a whole are very significant. The fundamental inequalities characteristic of humans, the basic elements of society, result in a society that by necessity exhibits inequality.

Pareto eventually characterizes those individuals whose performance is superior as the elite. He develops the central point of his social and political theory in this passage:

> Let us therefore make a class for those people who have the highest indices in their branch of activity, and give to this class the name of *elite*.... We have therefore two strata in the population: 1. the lower stratum, the non elite ... and 2. the upper stratum, the elite class. (248-49)

Pareto's social theory thus builds from his propositions concerning human individuals existing with biologically based inequalities, to the emergence of elites within society. Those individuals favourably endowed with certain residues will emerge as superior performers in their endeavours and will eventually become part of the elite. Pareto also points out divisions within and among elites, including a division between the governing elite and the nongoverning elite: "The first elite class includes those who directly or indirectly play a significant part in government and in political life; the second comprises the rest of the elite personnel, those who have no significant role in government and politics" (248).

To understand government and politics in a specific society it is necessary, then, to understand the role of the governing elite. The manner by which elites govern is, for Pareto, the basis of a typology of governments. History reveals two basic types of government: "Type I. Governments which rely mainly on physical force and on religious or other similar situations.... Type II. Governments which rely mainly on intelligence and cunning" (274-75). The former type of government is controlled by the "lions" while the "foxes" use cunning and intelligence to maintain their rule. There are of course mixes of these types of government. The essential lesson that every elite must learn in its efforts to retain power is how to avoid the fate of past elites. In a famous declaration Pareto warns, "History is the graveyard of elites" (249).

The most serious error that an elite may make is to fail to provide for circulation, for people to move up into its ranks and for people to move out. Elites, once in power, are not self-perpetuating:

> Aristocracies decay not only in number but also in quality, in the sense that their energy diminishes and there is a debilitating alteration in the proportion of the residues which originally favoured their capture and retention of power.... The governing class is renovated not only in number but also—and this is more important—in quality, by recruiting to it families rising from the lower classes, bringing with them the energy and proportions of the residues necessary for maintaining them in power. It is renovated also by the loss of its more degenerate elements. (249)

The necessity of a circulation of elites is thus obvious. Pareto takes some care to elaborate on the implications for an elite that fails to consider the lesson of history:

> By the circulation of elites, the governing elite is in a state of continuous and slow transformation. It flows like a river, and what it is today is different from what it was yesterday. Every so often, there are sudden and violent disturbances. The river floods and breaks its banks. Then, afterwards, the new governing elite resumes again the slow process of self-transformation. The river returns to its bed and once more flows freely on.... Revolutions occur because—either through a slowing down in the circulation of elites or from other causes—the upper strata accumulate decadent elements which no longer retain the residues appropriate to the maintenance of power and which shrink from the use of force; while among the lower strata, elements of superior quality are increasing which do possess the residues suitable for governing and are prepared to use force.... In revolutions individuals of the lower strata are generally led by individuals from the upper strata because these latter possess the intellectual qualities needful for devising strategy and tactics; the combative residues they lack are provided by individuals from the lower strata. (250)

In Pareto we thus find a biologically based, psychologically oriented elite theory. The biologically based and psychological (intellectual, aptitudinal, and moral) differences explain the individual inequalities he observed among the population. Individual inequalities become manifest at the social and political level with the emergence of elites. The implications of these processes for politics and government are obvious. Societies will tend to be governed by a political elite. The existence of elites, including political governing elites, is an inescapable condition, given the realities of human biological and psychological existence. Democracy in any sense of the word is manifestly impossible and the best political system would be one that provides for a measure of mobility for the superior elements of the population into the elite through a circulatory process.

GAETANO MOSCA

Perhaps the weakness in Pareto most easily identified by social scientists is his biological determinism. The work of Pareto's contemporary Gaetano Mosca (1858-1941) can be viewed in part as an effort to establish a more sociological basis for the existence of elites. Mosca's most important work, *The Ruling Class*, begins with a consideration of the possible explanations of why "an individual, or a class of individuals, might succeed in achieving supreme power in a given society and in thwarting the efforts of other individuals or groups to supplant them" (Mosca 1939: 1).

Mosca considers two possible explanations for the persistent existence of elites. First he examines what he refers to as the "constant trends in human society"—meaning biological factors such as race. After an examination of this line of argument, Mosca concludes that "Social contacts and historical circumstances" are central to understanding human behaviour. In the terms of the debate, still ongoing, Mosca argues that we focus our attention on environment/nature as opposed to biology/nurture. Innate human predispositions are not, however, eliminated from the argument as Mosca also contends that human existence is characterized by the constant struggle for what he terms pre-eminence. "To put the situation in a few words, the struggle for *existence* has been confused with the struggle for *preeminence*, which is really a constant phenomenon that arises in all human societies" (29).

Human beings engage in ongoing competition, which "is focused upon higher position, wealth, authority, control of the means and instruments that enable a person to direct many human activities, many human wills, as he sees fit" (30). This competition produces, as competition is wont to do, winners and losers. The ultimate outcome of the process is the emergence of the ruling class. Since competition is inherent to human existence, so is the existence of ruling classes:

> Among the constant facts and tendencies that are to be found in all political organisms, one is so obvious that it is apparent to the most casual eye. In all societies—from societies that are very meagerly developed and have barely attained the dawnings of civilization, down to the most advanced and powerful societies—two classes of people appear—a class that rules and a class that is ruled. The first class, always the less numerous, performs all political functions,

monopolizes power and enjoys the advantages that power brings, whereas the second, the more numerous class, is directed and controlled by the first, in a manner than is now more or less legal, now more or less arbitrary and violent, and supplies the first, in appearance at least, with material means of subsistence and with the instrumentalities that are essential to the vitality of the political organism. (50)

As in Pareto's work, inequalities, now manifest in the form of ruling classes, are an inevitable feature of human society. Mosca's explanation for their existence is, however, quite different, rejecting as he does the biologically based accounts of human behaviour, even if he holds to the position that human competition is inevitable. Ruling classes emerge because some humans prove to be more capable in competitive struggles. The superior ability of some to compete is not primarily a function of biology, but rather of acquired skills, aptitudes, talents, and capacities. Those with special abilities belonging to aristocracies "owe their special qualities not so much to the blood that flows in their veins as to their very particular upbringing, which has brought out certain intellectual and moral tendencies in them in preference to others" (62).

Having established the inevitability and basis of the existence of ruling classes in human society, Mosca turns his attention to how ruling classes maintain their positions and thus maintain order. In an argument similar to Pareto's, he suggests that ruling classes tend to use force or a political formula that includes value systems and ideologies to bind society together in the interests of the ruling class. Long-term stability resides in achieving a balance between these strategies as well as achieving a balance among the various forces in society. With the dangers inherent in the absolute control of any single social force, Mosca sees parliamentary systems as offering certain advantages, including the allowance of inputs from various sections and interests, at least in appearance. In reality, however, he recognizes that elements in the population, those most capable of winning the competition involved, will rule. "In elections, as in all other manifestations of social life, those who have the will and, especially the moral, intellectual and material *means* to force their will upon others take the lead over the others and command them" (154).

ROBERT MICHELS

The best known of the "classical elite theorists" is surely Robert Michels (1876-1936), a German-born academic who spent most of his adult life in Italy. The full title of Michel's most influential book, published in 1911, indicates its essential contents: *Political Parties: A Sociological Study of the Oligarchical Tendencies of Modern Democracy*. In his preface Michels states his objectives, the most central one being to examine the problems democracy encounters in attempting to avoid oligarchy—problems that both Pareto and

Mosca would consider insurmountable. Michels will reach a similar conclusion, but through a different route.

In his preface Michels notes three tendencies leading democracy in the direction of oligarchy: 1) the nature of human individuals; 2) the nature of political struggle; and 3) the nature of organization. The third consideration is the central focus of the analysis.

Like Pareto and Mosca, Michels incorporates the concept of instinct in his analysis, maintaining that humans possess a "peculiar and inherent instinct" which leads them to view political power as something to be acquired and then passed on to successive generations. The fact that humans seek to acquire political power and, once successful, maintain their position in order to pass it on to the next generation is a central factor in the historical tendency of human societies to generate aristocracies. The so-called instinctual factor is, however, in the final analysis not central to the overall argument Michels develops as he goes on to examine the nature of organizations and how they contribute to the transformation of democracy.

Michels leads us into a consideration of organizations by first considering their necessity if democracy is to operate successfully. Any class, group, or association wishing to have an impact on the political process in a democracy must be organized. In modern industrial societies these organizations will, by necessity, be large and complex, representing large numbers of members. Large organizations representing members dispersed over large geographic areas become increasingly complex. As a result the everyday operation of these organizations generates a demand for specialization and an internal division of labour. These processes in turn generate a hierarchy:

> The principle of division of labor coming more and more into operation, executive authority undergoes division and subdivision. There is thus constituted a rigorously defined and hierarchical bureaucracy. In the catechism of party duties, the strict observance of hierarchical rules becomes the first article. The hierarchy comes into existence as the outcome of technical conditions, and its constitution is an essential postulate of the regular functioning of the party machine. (Michels 1962: 72)

The emergence of a hierarchy within complex organizations becomes the central stimulus for the emergence of leadership positions within the organization. Individuals occupying these positions, which are necessary for the organization, gain experience and expertise, and a cycle begins. The individuals become the most qualified to continue to hold leadership positions, and thus their competence assists the organization. The masses of members themselves encourage the process in that, as Michels argues, they actually desire to be led. Apathy, incompetence, and the desire to be led dovetail with the desire of the leadership of the organization to maintain its power, with devastating results for democracy.

The movement from democracy to oligarchy is thus understandable in human and organizational terms. Michels summarizes his analysis in an oft-quoted remark:

> It follows that the explanation of the oligarchical phenomenon which thus results is partly PSYCHOLOGICAL; oligarchy derives, that is to say, from the psychical transformations which the leading personalities in the parties undergo in the course of their lives. But also, and still more, oligarchy depends upon what we may term the PSYCHOLOGY OF ORGANIZATION ITSELF, that is to say, upon the tactical and technical necessities which result from the consolidation of every disciplined political aggregate. Reduced to its most concise expression, the fundamental sociological law of political parties (the term "political" being here used in its most comprehensive significance) may be formulated in the following terms: "It is organization which gives birth to the dominion of the elected over the electors, of the mandataries over the mandators, of the delegates over the delegators. Who says organization, say oligarchy." (365)

CONTEMPORARY ELITE THEORY: MILLS, PORTER, FIELD, AND HIGLEY

An examination of what I have referred to as the "classical elite theorists" reveals a trend towards the emergence of a more sociologically based analysis. While Michels retains a role for innate human behavioural predispositions, his overall analysis is primarily predicated on a sociological analysis of organizations, their inherent structure and logic, and how they produce elites. Contemporary elite theory has attempted to build on the organizational focus initiated by Michels.

Perhaps one of the most significant efforts to adopt elements of elite theory and apply it to North American society was C. Wright Mills' 1956 volume *The Power Elite*. Mills, one of the most controversial figures in American social science during the 1950s and even after his death in 1962, examined power, society, and politics within the context of social sciences dominated by pluralism and functionalism. Mills also operated during the era of the Cold War, McCarthyism, and the post-war "celebration" of a mass consumption society.

While Mills rejected much of what passed for social science in the functionalist and pluralist approaches, he was never able to fully embrace conventional Marxian analysis (Eldridge 1983: 31-36). Mills was also not steeped in classical elite theory. Rather, his thinking was influenced by a combination of influences: Marx, Weber, Thorstein Veblen, social behaviouralism, and American pragmatism (Martindale 1975: 83-85). What is perhaps most significant is how the trajectory of Mills' own work led him to conclude that the United States was governed by a small elite.

The Power Elite followed the publication of two previous books in which Mills examined labour leaders *(The New Men of Power)* and the middle class *(White Collar)* and uncovered the existence of a high degree of domination and manipulation of the working and middle classes. It was a logical third step from there to his examination of the upper or ruling class and his discovery of a small ruling elite in *The Power Elite*.

In *The Power Elite* Mills argues that an elite composed of three different elements had assumed control in the United States, that U.S. social and economic development had resulted in the emergence of three predominant institutional orders: the economic, political, and military. In the words of Mills:

> At the pinnacle of each of the three enlarged and centralized domains, there have arisen those higher circles which make up the economic, the political, and the military elites. At the top of the economy, among the corporate rich, there are the chief executives; at the top of the political order, the members of the political directorate; at the top of the military establishment, the elite of soldier-statesmen clustered in and around the Joint Chiefs of Staff and the upper echelon. As each of these domains has coincided with the others, as decisions tend to become total in their consequence, the leading men in each of the three domains of power—the warlords, the corporate chieftains, the political directorate—tend to come together, to form the power elite of America. (Mills 1956: 8-9)

Unlike some elite thinkers who focus on the personal or individual characteristics of the members of the elite, Mills explicitly locates social position as the central consideration.

> For power is not of a man. Wealth does not center in the person of the wealthy. Celebrity is not inherent in any personality. To be celebrated, to be wealthy, to have power requires access to major institutions, for the institutional positions men occupy determine in large part their chances to have and to hold these valued experiences. (10-11)

The majority of people in institutionally defined elite positions ultimately owe their position to the possession of wealth. The United States, Mills argues, has produced a bourgeoisie which "has monopolized not only wealth but prestige and power as well" (12). The elite that emerged is thus "a set of higher circles whose members are selected, trained and certified and permitted intimate access to those who command the impersonal institutional hierarchies of modern society" (15).

For Mills the usage of the term elite as opposed to class was important because the concept of class, he argues, is an economic term. To speak of a ruling class would, for Mills, oversimplify the nature of power relations because the power elite is not just an economic class which rules politically. The liberal notion of political representatives in control of the state also misses the mark because it fails to recognize the interplay between the corporate power holders, the military, and the state. Mills states:

> We hold that such a simple view of "economic determinism" must be elaborated by "political determinism" and "military determinism"; that the higher agents of each of these three domains now often have a noticeable degree of autonomy and that only in the often intricate ways of coalition do they make up and carry through the most important decisions. Those are the major reasons we prefer "power elite" to "ruling class" as a characterizing phrase for the higher circles when we consider them in terms of power. (277)

In the hands of C. Wright Mills analysis of elites becomes a critical tool. Far from accepting and/or justifying the rule of elites, Mills forcefully criticizes the society which the U.S. power elite has been instrumental in producing. In his final chapter, entitled "The Higher Immorality," he concludes:

> The men of the higher circles are not representative men; their high position is not a result of moral virtue; their fabulous success is not firmly connected with meritorious ability. Those who sit in the seats of the high and the mighty are selected and formed by the means of power, the sources of wealth, the mechanics of celebrity, which prevail in their society. They are not men selected and formed by a civil service that is linked with the world of knowledge and sensibility. They are not men shaped by nationally responsible parties that debate openly and clearly the issues this nation now so unintelligently confronts. They are not men held in responsible check by a plurality of voluntary associations which connect debating publics with the pinnacles of decision. Commanders of power unequaled in human history, they have succeeded within the American system of organized irresponsibility. (361)

The ascension to positions of power of members of the power elite is accompanied by the drift of American society as a whole into what Mills terms mass society. He contrasts the unified power elite to the fragmented, passive, and powerless bottom part of mass society (1965: 324). Under such circumstances the ideal of U.S. democracy, open politics, and intelligent citizens debating political alternatives become impossible to realize. Despite the fact that for

Mills elite rule is neither natural nor necessary, the picture of society he creates is one of manipulation and domination by the elites and of mass acceptance by the majority.

Shortly after the publication of *The Power Elite* a major study of class and power in Canada was published. John Porter's *The Vertical Mosaic*, which adopts an explicitly elite-oriented approach, stands out as one of the most important social science volumes published in Canada.

Like Mills, Porter focuses his analysis on the major institutions he sees as central in Canadian society, and on their leadership. He argues that this approach is best suited to understanding complex modern society:

> Institutional systems are ... hierarchically organized, and individuals or groups at the top of our institutions can be designated as elites. Elites both compete and co-operate with one another: they compete to share in the making of decisions of major importance for the society, and they co-operate because together they keep the society working as a going concern. Elites govern institutions which have, in the complex world, functional tasks. The economy must produce, governmental bureaucracies must administer, governments must govern, the military must maintain the defences, and the churches, or some counterpart in the epoch of mass media, must continue to provide a view of the world in which the whole process is legitimate and good and in conformity with dominant social values. It is elites who have the capacity to introduce change, but changes bring about shifts in the relations between elites. Because they all have power as their institutional right they can check each other's power, and, therefore, co-operation and accommodation, as well as conflict, characterize their relations. (Porter 1965: 27)

A major portion of the over 600-page volume is devoted to examining the background, education, social status, ethnic background, religion, and political affiliation of the leading elites: economic, labour, political, bureaucratic, and ideological. Each elite is examined in detail, and though Porter located many interconnections and interrelations he avoids any definite declaration of anything approaching Mills' power elite. Indeed, Porter maintains that the existence of various elites can results in conflict and competition among elites, providing less chance for any particular elite to become dominant. In his concluding remarks Porter acknowledges the necessity of elite rule but holds out the possibility of open recruitment—Pareto's notion of circulation—as providing some measure of equality in society:

> Although it has a class structure peculiar to its own history and geography, Canada is probably not unlike other western industrial

nations in relying heavily on its elite groups to make major decisions and to determine the shape and direction of its development. The nineteenth-century notion of a liberal citizen-participating democracy is obviously not a satisfactory model by which to examine the processes of decision-making in either the economic or the political contexts. Given the complexities of modern societies it is unlikely that widespread participation can develop without very great changes and institutional experimentation. If power and decision-making must always rest with elite groups, there can at least be open recruitment from all classes into the elites. (558)

With the exception of Mills, the theorists discussed in this chapter have tended to accept if not embrace and justify the necessity of elites in society. The tendency for elite theory to not be critical of structured inequality and non-democratic social and political processes is most apparent in the book *Elitism* by G. Lowell Field and John Higley.

Elitism is an explicit restatement of the value of elite theory and the political necessity of elites in society. The authors identify their position as explicitly elitist, arguing that there is "almost certainly some necessary amount of power concentration in all societies" (Field and Higley 1980: ix). They suggest that there is a necessity for people in power to recognize the realities of social life:

> At the same time we are equally concerned to show that a much more explicitly *elitist* viewpoint or orientation among persons in influential positions generally is necessary to meet the current problems of developed and developing societies realistically and practically. (x)

For the rest of the text the authors remain true to this objective, evaluating the relationship of elite theory and liberalism and restating elite theory in terms of recognizing its merits as imposing "an obligation." The analysis presented attempts to link different elite structures to different periods of phases of world history. While the basis of elites is understood in a manner similar to that found in the work of Michels, the discussion of international power relations raises some controversial points (20, 80).

The problems of international development/underdevelopment are cast in the terms of elite theory:

> A major category of current international problems falls under the rubric of the North-South conflict. The "North" consists of the developed countries. The "South" consists of the less developed countries in the so-called Third World. As we shall show, the dynamics of this

64

conflict closely resemble, and actually overlap, the insider-outsider conflict currently occurring within developed societies. (96)

To the extent that this application of elite theory instructs us as to the necessity and inevitability of inequalities, its message is clear: "Western elites and their supporters will again become accustomed to the historically usual need to defend the material and cultural acquisitions of their ... own people," however they might be defined, against the avoidable incursions of others. (127)

Elite theory, as articulated by the theorists discussed in this chapter, concentrates its attention on the causes and consequences of inequality and not on social structures, arrangements, and processes. Political and social structures, in the abstract, are generally not of concern to elite theory. What is central for understanding a given society is not so much its institutional structures as the characteristics and features of its elite or elites. Elite theory would generally maintain that the shape, structures, characteristics, and features of a society will be primarily determined by its elite(s). Political structures and processes will therefore by understandable in terms of the modes of domination chosen by the elite. Pareto's typology of governments was based on this very consideration.

Elite theory, by definition, accepts the inevitability of elites as a fact of life, while offering a variety of reasons for this situation. Human societies, it is argued, have always been, and will always be, characterized by distinctions between the elites and the masses or the rulers and the ruled. As a result, elite theorists tend to hold pessimistic or even negative views of the possibility of democracy or mass participation in complex societies—a possibility of considerable concern to many other political philosophers and theorists.

• FOUR •

PLURALISM

If the key problem for modern political theory and for emerging sociological theory was the problem of order in the context of a class-divided society, twentieth-century pluralism would offer yet another solution. By twentieth-century pluralism we are essentially referring to American political thought: the political theory and concept of the state found in such early U.S. writers as Charles E. Merriam and Arthur F. Bentley, as well as pluralism's most important contemporary apostle, Robert A. Dahl.

English liberalism from Hobbes through Locke, Bentham, and the Mills somewhat begrudgingly accepted the existence of class and other social divisions within civil society, and sought to accommodate these divisions in the structures and operations of the state. In the case of American political theory, such divisions were always accepted as a part of the various theorists' basic assumptions. There are a variety of historical, social, economic, and political reasons for these widely held assumptions, including the structures and relations inherent in the prerevolutionary colonial society. The economic and social differences between the plantation-based southern colonies, the "bread" or mid-colonies, and the New England colonies were all appreciated by those familiar with the region. These differences led one historian to note: "In every one of the thirteen colonies there was a distinct upper class whose superior position was fixed in law and custom" (Bragdon and McCutchen 1954: 14).

In addition to the internal class divisions, there were the distinctions between the native Indian population and those of European ancestry, the presence of a large Black population, many of whom were slaves, and a variety of backgrounds and expectations among the throngs arriving yearly from many places around the world. Added to these social differences were economic and sectional differences between the developing industrial, agricultural, commercial, plantation, and fishery based regions and colonies.

It is not surprising, then, that from its origins in the context of the War of Independence, American political theory recognized the necessity of addressing, in the structures of the state, the multiple divisions of U.S. society. Indeed, the very process of constitutional ratification required extensive discussion, debate, conflict, and ultimately compromise. Amid the debates a number of positions emerged to become the cornerstones of subsequent pluralist theory in the United States.

Perhaps the most important of these statements came from James Madison (1751-1836), an active participant in the constitutional process and later the fourth President. In Madison's work we find an approach to the "problem of order" which extends elements of classical liberalism, while laying the foundation of a pluralistic theory of democracy. For Madison, the root of the problem of order is human nature: "The latent causes of faction are thus sown in the nature of man; and we see them everywhere brought into different degrees of activity according to the different circumstances of civil society" (Madison 1961: 79). Madison notes that there are many bases of factions, "But the most common and durable source of factions has been the various and unequal distribution of property." This conclusion leads Madison to a consideration of the role of the state:

> Those who hold and those who are without property have ever formed distinct interests in society. Those who are creditors, and those who are debtors, fall under a like discrimination. A landed interest, a manufacturing interest, a mercantile interest, a moneyed interest, with many lesser interests, grow up of necessity in civilized nations, and divide them into different classes, actuated by different sentiments and views. The regulation of these various and interfering interests forms the principal task of modern legislation and involves the spirit of party and faction in the necessary and ordinary operations of government.

> No man is allowed to be judge in his own cause because his interest would certainly bias his judgement, and, not improbably, corrupt his integrity. With equal, nay with greater reason, a body of men are unfit to be both judges and parties at the same time; yet what are many of the most important acts of legislation but so many judicial determinations, not indeed concerning the rights of single persons, but concerning the rights of large bodies of citizens? And what are the different classes of legislators but advocates and parties to the causes which they determine? (79)

In contemplating a mode of accommodating these inevitable factions, Madison considered and rejected the possibility of what he termed "pure democracy," meaning "a society consisting of a small number of citizens who assemble and administer the government in person" (81). Under such circumstances there is no way of assuring the protection of the weaker factions. Madison went on to consider some form of a republic in which there would be a delegation of government into the hands of elected officials. The outcome of this process—including heavy debate between federalist and anti-federalist factions—was the U.S. Constitution.

The Constitution, finally ratified in 1788, represented a series of compromises and sought to address the problems of democratic consent in the context of a civil society characterized by a variety of factions and divisions. The separation of state powers among the Congress, the Executive, and the Judiciary was one of the "checks and balances" to protect against "the triple dangers of tyranny, mob rule, and seizure of power" (Bragdon and McCutchen 1954: 107). In addition, the Constitution imposed limitations on the powers of the various levels of government, and internally divided Congress itself between the Senate and the House of Representatives. A Bill of Rights in the form of an initial ten Amendments was ratified in 1791.

In a fundamental way, then, the structure and content of the U.S. Constitution established the framework within which American political theory developed.

ARTHUR F. BENTLEY AND THE PROCESSES OF GOVERNMENT

The century that followed was indeed America's, assuming American refers to the United States. It was a century of unprecedented U.S. geographical expansion and economic growth. Amidst the emergence of industry, geographic expansion south and west, and the Civil War there were some changes in the U.S. political system. The spread of Jacksonian democracy resulted in most states instituting universal male suffrage by 1828, and the Fifteenth Amendment formally extended the vote to Blacks in 1870. However, it was 1920 before the Nineteenth Amendment extended the franchise to women.

During the time of these development there were few systematic theoretical elaborations or expositions of the structures of the system. But the twentieth century brought with it a series of important statements of the theoretical basis of the pluralist problematic. Two of the key theoreticians of the period were Charles E. Merriam and Arthur F. Bentley.

In 1908 Arthur F. Bentley first published his classic work *The Process of Government*. In this work Bentley systematically elaborated a series of basic assumptions upon which his work was predicated and presented a concept of the state and an explanation of its operations that bridges the conceptions of the Founders and modern pluralism.

After setting out about 170 pages of preliminary assumptions, Bentley begins his actual analysis of the processes of government with a consideration of the "raw materials"—human actions or activity. Ultimately he concludes that actions and activities relating to political affairs and governments must be understood in the context of groups. These political groups in turn are tied to the concept of interests:

> It is now necessary to take another step in the analysis of the group. There is no group without its interest. An interest, as the term will be used in this work, is the equivalent of a group. We may speak also of an interest group or of a group interest again merely for the sake of clearness of expression. (Bentley 1935: 211)

Groups, interests, or interest groups are social phenomena and thus must be considered in a social context. At one point Bentley notes: "No group has meaning except in its relations to other groups" (215). When the group is a political group it is assumed to exist in a relationship with other political groups.

The presence of other groups, which can also be defined as other interest groups, obviously implies the presence of other interests. As Bentley summarizes the situation: "Where we have a group that participates in the political process we have always another group facing it in the same plane (to revert to the illustration of the sphere).... There are always some parts of the nation to be found arrayed against other parts" (220). When we examine political questions, therefore:

> We shall always find that the political interests and activities of any given group—and there are no political phenomena except group phenomena—are directed against other activities of men, who appear in other groups, political or other. The phenomena of political life which we study will always divide the society in which they occur, along lines which are very real, though of varying degrees of definiteness. The society itself is nothing other than the complex of the groups that compose it. (222)

Bentley then links group activities to government through a discussion of leadership and public opinion, arguing that once we are able to understand and link human activity, interests, and groups in the context of leadership processes and the role of opinion in group activity, we are in a position to begin an analysis of government.

Bentley asserts: "The phenomena of government are from start to finish phenomena of force." However, since some may find the word "force" objectionable, he states: "I prefer to use the word pressure instead of force, since it keeps the attention closely directed upon the groups themselves" (258). Government then has to do with group pressures and the process of adjustment to these forces. In his definition of government Bentley makes this explicit:

> In the narrowest sense ... government is a differentiated, representative group or set of groups (organ, or set of organs), performing specified governing functions for the underlying groups of the population.... Government in this sense is not a certain number of people, but a certain network of activities. (260-61)

Bentley declines to specify precisely the nature of the functions of government other than by showing government "as the adjustment or balance of interests" (264).

Group interests are so important for government that they can provide the basis of classifying governments. Bentley argues that the essential difference between the city state and the nation is the nature of the interest groups that, to use his words, "wrestle" with each other in government. In the case of a complex, advanced industrial society, there are so many and so complex interest groups that government itself must be complex. Thus in the United States government is organized around at least three separate organs: the President, the Congress, and the Judiciary. Each of these organs of the government plays an essential role in the "wrestling" of interest groups that characterizes the political process.

In order to understand fully the relationship between interest groups and the various branches of government, Bentley introduces political parties into the process. A party is essentially defined as "an organization of voters, brought together to act as a representative of the underlying interest groups in which these voters, and to some lesser extent other citizens, present themselves" (415). Parties ultimately must be considered in the context not merely of interest groups, but of the larger processes of give and take that make up government. In summarizing his conception of government Bentley states:

> It should be clear by this time that in government we have to do with powerful group pressures which may perhaps at times adjust themselves through differentiated reasoning processes, but which adjust themselves likewise through many other processes, and which, through whatever processes they are working, form the very flesh and blood of all that is happening. It is these group pressures, indeed, that not only make but also sustain in value the very standards of justice, truth, or what not that reason may claim to use as its guide. (447)

Government, then, is composed of separate organs that respond in the decision-making process to the multitude of interest groups that arise from the operation of civil society. It is a process that, like the free market, works best when there are no structures of central direction. Bentley summarizes the argument in a powerful statement of pluralist theory:

> In governments like that of the United States we see these manifold interests gaining representation through many thousands of officials in varying degrees of success, beating some officials down now into delegate activity, intrusting representative activity (in the narrow sense) to other officials at times in high degree, subsiding now and again over great areas while "special interests" make special use of officials, rising in other spots to dominate, using one agency of the government against another, now with stealth, now with open force,

and in general moving along the route of time with the organized turmoil which is life where the adjustments are much disturbed. Withal, it is a process which must surprise one more for the trifling proportion of physical violence involved considering the ardent nature of the struggles, than for any other characteristic. (453)

MERRIAM: POWER AND THE PLURALIST DEMOCRACY

A position similar to Bentley's is found in the classical work of Charles E. Merriam. Merriam, the author of a number of influential works on American politics, first published *Political Power* in 1934, and it continues to represent a basic statement of early pluralist thought.

In *Political Power* Merriam defines his purpose as "to set forth what role political power plays in the process of social control" (Merriam 1964: 18). Again, the problem of order emerges—a problem common to the discussion of political power since even before Hobbes. Merriam begins his analysis with a consideration of what he calls the "Birth of Power," arguing in a Hobbesian manner that the "fatherhood of power is found in violence, in the raw will to dominate; in some divine sanction which makes of power a second religion; in some moment of contact between members of the incipient political society" (31). He notes that one must examine social groups, personality types, and the role of leaders—the power hungry—who use group situations and personality types in their quests for power. In the following analysis he clearly emphasizes the nature and role of groups: "Power is first of all a phenomenon of group cohesion and aggregation, a child of group necessity or utility, a function of the social relations among men" (31).

Merriam argues that because the "social situation constantly involves the maintenance of equilibrium between groups, classes, fractions" (32), the accommodation of groups in the social situation is not only an essential feature of group life but also the basis of the emergence of authority. Merriam describes how, in the presence of a number of different groups, a power situation emerges that "involves association for some common purpose, and the emergence of government and the rulers, equipped now with power in the form of violence, or prestige, or interest, that could cut across class lines and individual dispositions" (33):

> The functional situation out of which the political arises is not the demand for force as such, but the need for some form of equilibrium, adjustment, *modus vivendi* between the various groups and individuals of the community, as a substitute indeed for force in many cases. (36-37)

Government, the state, or the political process thus emerges out of a need to establish modes of decision-making, mediation, and social control in a society of power-hungry individuals and competing and conflicting groups of such individuals.

In subsequent chapters Merriam examines different types of power, the role of laws, the negative dimensions of power, and the absence of power. He considers the absence of power through an examination of the process "from below," that is from the viewpoint of those who may lack power, and locates a series of mechanisms available to those who lack power, to aid their efforts to control those with power. He mentions, as available mechanisms, the use of constitutional defences including civil rights, the electoral or "peaceful overthrow of the government," and various types of organized non-violent resistance (176).

In his 1945 volume *Systematic Politics*, Merriam develops a number of these points further, outlining in an even more explicit manner the essential features of the early pluralist approach. The opening chapter of *Systematic Politics*, entitled "The Roots of Government," presents a more institutional approach in which there are none of the earlier references to the will to dominate or the quest for power. To understand the roots of government, he states, "It is essential to explore the nature of the associations or groups with which government is concerned" (Merriam 1945: 6). He continues: "Government is a phenomenon of group cohesion and aggregation, a child of group necessity, a function of the social relations of men." Moreover, since human social relations involve a diversity of groups, classes, and factions, some equilibrium must be maintained and accommodations must be worked out. It is out of this situation that government and political authority operates.

Merriam maintains that governments, within this context, have five essential functions:

> The ends and purposes of government, much discussed by men of all ages, may be simply stated as follows: (i) external security, (ii) internal order, (iii) justice, (iv) general welfare, and (v) freedom. They may be summed up under the term "commonwealth," or the common good. (31)

In a discussion of the "tools" available to government in its efforts to accomplish these ends, Merriam lists: (i) custom, (ii) violence, (iii) symbolism and ceremonialism, (iv) leadership (74). After discussing these various tools Merriam concludes that they are closely related both to the *ends* of government and the *organs* of government. Under organs of government Merriam lists a number of historical alternatives, which range from the organs of headship, through the executive, organs of adjudication, and conciliar types, to managerial organs (119). He examines each case, and introduces the idea of representative government in the context of considering conciliar organs.

A number of key themes emerge in the discussion of the role of representative government, including the question of accommodating special interest needs with the welfare or larger common good. Legislative functions, a function of representative government, include establishing laws, making fiscal allocative decisions, administrating the process, and organizing democratic processes for the solving of social or collective problems.

For Merriam, who believes that the process of government is a group process, it is a logical step at this point to bring groups back into the analysis. Government processes are group processes and thus the state is called upon to perform its "balancing function." We are reminded: "If all interests and pressures settled themselves automatically, there would be no need for government at all" (144). But, as we know, these interests do not necessarily settle themselves and the government is called upon to mediate, which it does in the context of a variety of groups, classes, and factions. Ultimately the common good emerges because, while a number of different groups and individuals attempt to influence the process, "On the whole, one is likely to be balanced by others, and the net contribution is that of a broad discussion of legislative policies" (144). Merriam's conclusion:

> The more highly organized these groups are, however, the smaller their number; and the larger their membership, the more serious the problem becomes, whether these groups are racial, religious, regional, professional, or representative of agriculture, labour, industry, or other social aggregations. In a wide range of groups their very pluralism tends to offset one against another. If, however, these corporate groups are relatively few and prefer their corporate existence and programs to those of the state as a whole, their special goods to the common good, then difficulties arise which are not readily met by any mechanism or formula. The problem under such circumstances is that of creating a genuine community, with priority of common interests over the special. There cannot be any very effective common counsel unless there is an explicit will to provide a common program in the pursuance of common interests. (144)

Merriam thus directs his initial discussion of the organs of government towards an extended consideration of the role of the responsible legislative government in a society characterized by a complex plurality of groups. In the chapter that follows, "Types of Rule," he continues this discussion through an analysis of democracy. While Merriam provides a number of basic principles of democracy, his essential definition comes out as:

> Democracy is a form of political association in which the ends of government are habitually determined by the bulk of the community in accordance with appropriate understandings and procedures providing for popular participation and consent. (199)

Merriam goes on to assert repeatedly that the United States can be considered, as he puts it, "the amplest home of democracy." However, there are trends apparent in American society that will make it even more democratic. Among these trends are the growth of education and increasing economic abundance.

After declaring that "Democracy is the best form of government yet devised by the brain of man," Merriam examines trends in government and future directions. In the context of his final consideration of organs of government he expounds his abiding faith in the future of democratic pluralism.

MODERN PLURALISM: ROBERT DAHL

When considered in the context of the work of Bentley and Merriam, the work of more recent pluralists such as Robert Dahl and D.B. Truman represents more of an extension and an elaboration of the basic tenets of pluralism than original theorizing. To illustrate the point we will use the work of Dahl as representative of the modern pluralist problematic.

A basic understanding of the essential elements of Dahl's position can be gleaned through a reading of his *Pluralist Democracy in the United States: Conflict and Consent* (1967) and his thematic elaborations presented in *Democracy in the United States: Promise and Performance* (1972). Like early pluralists Dahl uses a set of assumptions that link human social existence and political behaviour:

> Thus man's existence as social beings—social animals, if you prefer—is conditioned by a set of contradictory tendencies that, taken altogether, make him a member of some political system:
> 1) His need for human fellowship and the advantages of cooperation create communities.
> 2) But he is unable to live with others without conflict.
> 3) Hence, communities search for ways of adjusting conflicts so that cooperation and community life will be possible and tolerable. (Dahl 1972: 5)

Human communities, Dahl argues, require some form of authority or social power to maintain order. Thus they cannot, and have never, existed without political institutions.

Dahl's work also addresses another important question: What form of political institutions or government is best? Without a detailed treatment of the possible answers, Dahl notes that the United States has chosen a form of government based on political equality and consent. While this form of government represents a concept most would agree with in principle, Dahl notes that achieving such a structure and process presents serious difficulties. After discussing the liberal, humanist, and pragmatic reasons for and principles of consent as a basis of government, Dahl notes:

> But if it is relatively easy to say *why* governments should derive their just powers from the consent of the governed, it is much more difficult to say *how* they can do so. The difficulty stems from that inescapable element of conflict in the human condition: People living together simply will not always agree. When people disagree, how can a decision be based on the consent of all? (Dahl 1967: 16)

In addition to these problems related to securing consent among fractions and conflicting individuals, there are problems with simply postulating the existence of political equality. In reality, Dahl argues, there are a number of causes of political inequality: 1) individual characteristics such as temperament, skills, and endowments; 2) social arrangements such as institutionalized discrimination and inequalities in income or education; and 3) the impossibility of mass participation in large-scale organizations (Dahl 1972: 12-13).

While considering these problems and their solutions, Dahl examines the potentials offered by various forms of government. He concludes, first, that majority rule democracy encounters "serious theoretical and practical problems," including the dilemma of integrating a plurality of minorities into one government. Majority rule in this context refers to a form of government where conflicts and disputes are settled "by a majority of citizens or voters— either directly in public assembly or in a referendum, or indirectly through elected representatives" (23). How, under such a system, can the rights of minorities be assured? Also, majority rule democracy in federal systems encounters problems because by definition the central power in such systems takes on some governing functions for the whole, fractured and divided as it is. How are minority rights to be protected without limiting the powers of the majority and thus undermining a basic premise of majority rule democracy? Furthermore, how can we be assured that the elected leaders, who must make decisions, reflect the wishes of the majority?

After raising these questions Dahl discusses an alternate system: rule by the few or some form of elitist government. Rule by the few is quickly dismissed, not the least reason being that its basic premises violate the more basic principles of the U.S. system: "that the best government for a state is a government of the people based on political equality and the consent of all" (21). Dahl's major focus becomes the system that overcomes the problems related to consent and equality while avoiding the pitfalls of majority rule democracy and rule by the few. The term Dahl applies to what he believes is the best possible system is polyarchy.

Polyarchy, for Dahl, means a system of government that "incorporates certain aspects of both democratic and elitist theories, presents a critique of both, and offers an alternative way of understanding politics in different systems, particularly systems ordinarily called "democratic" (46-47). The polyarchy is a system that recognizes the importance of consent and political equality as processes requiring "that every citizen have unimpaired opportunity to formulate and indicate his or her preferences and have them weighted equally in the conduct of government" (47). Furthermore, the polyarchy requires a number of institutional guarantees to ensure that its principles are upheld in the actual working of government. A polyarchy differs from both majority rule democracy and elite rule in its definition of "the people," guaranteeing of minority rights, modes of addressing inequalities, role allotted to opposition, and reliance on the electoral process for the settlement of conflicts.

Dahl does not provide a concise definition of polyarchy, in part because the term refers to a general structure of government with many possible individual variations in details and specifics (1972: 38-40). Acceptance of the basic premises of polyarchy does recognize the impossibility of, or at least the problems associated with, absolute political equality and consent. In a sense polyarchy is presented as a "realistic" alternative to these conditions. Dahl presents a summary of its essential characteristics (1972: 40-43):

- Citizenship is compulsory. Governments are entitled to use force if necessary to ensure the integrity of national territory from either internal or external threats. A shared sense of nationhood will provide the basis for acceptance of compulsory citizenship.
- Majority rule procedures are restricted by placing some matters outside the legal power of government, developing private and semi-public agencies and organizations to look after certain affairs of the citizens, and by giving citizens a number of opportunities and channels to argue and negotiate their cases.
- Institutional guarantees exist to protect all citizens from arbitrary exercises of power and to ensure their basic rights.

As noted, various concrete, historical forms of government have evolved in different societies; these governments can be characterized as polyarchies because they exhibit the general features outlined above.

The United States, the first nation to develop the polyarchy, is also the country where this form of government has proved to be most durable, according to Dahl. There are, he argues, a number of reasons for this, including a pervasive equality, a shared system of democratic beliefs, and a strong constitutional framework. Dahl later notes that despite the so-called pervasive equality there are substantial inequalities, and despite the commitment to democracy there were, historically, key questions that had to be settled with regard to majority rule; nevertheless the constitutional structures were such as to permit the emergence of polyarchy.

Dahl notes that the political institutions and the nature of the conflict that the constitutional arrangements were designed to accommodate resulted in an "extreme partitioning of political authority" in the United States (50). The partitioning of authority in turn provides one of the essential institutional guarantees for the democratic functioning of the system. The partitioning, of course, refers to the divisions between the Executive, Congress, and the Judiciary, an essential component of the checks and balances in the U.S. Constitution. Pluralists have held up these checks and balances as essential to avoid the concentration of power. Furthermore, since the system is held to be democratic and open, each of these branches of government has certain internal mechanisms to facilitate participation from broad sections of the population.

Between the time of the founding of the Constitution and the twentieth century numerous changes took place in the U.S. system, none more important that the emergence of highly organized and institutionalized political parties. Dahl's analysis of the role of political parties in the political process again reverts to a consideration of the old problems of factions and conflict. This "conflict of views seems to be unavoidable in human affairs," he repeats, so that "political societies have always had to deal somehow with the fact of opposition" (Dahl 1967: 204). Dahl argues that because the Constitution permits freedom of speech, press, and assembly, organized opposition is made easier. He states that political parties, organized factions, interest groups, and representatives of conflict groups inevitably emerge through the interplay of factions and conflicts of civil society and the constitutional provisions for elections and representations (Dahl 1972: 281).

Political parties thus become an essential part of the political process, so essential that Dahl refers to their presence or absence as the litmus test of a democracy. In the U.S. system they have become essential, performing three functions:

- They facilitate popular control over elected officials.
- They help voters to make more rational choices.
- They help in the peaceful management of conflicts. (288-90)

The presence of organized and institutionalized parties within the framework of the U.S. Constitution is for Dahl the key to the success of the political process in the United States. The partitioning of authority, the established system of representation and electoral processes, and the existence of political parties to co-ordinate, organize, and channel factions, interests, and opponents all operate in a functioning polyarchy. In the actual day to day operation of government at all levels, parties and party organizations play a key role, acting as intermediaries between individual citizens and the agencies of government. The intermediary role operates in a dual manner, carrying messages and information from constituents to government and also back from government to constituents.

The picture that emerges in Dahl's analysis is one suggesting the existence of different, and in the long run, more or less equal power centres or constellations. He perceives the state as being a neutral mediator of conflict, receiving "direction" from all of the various power centres, but controlled by none and acting in the best interests of all, at least in the long run. Dahl summarizes this view of society:

> The fundamental axiom in the theory and practice of American pluralism is, I believe, this: Instead of a single center of sovereign power there must be multiple centers of power, none of which is or can be wholly sovereign. Although the only legitimate sovereign is the people, in the perspective of American pluralism even the people ought never to be an absolute sovereign; consequently no part of the people, such as a majority, ought to be absolute.
>
> Why this axiom? The theory and practice of American pluralism tend to assume, as I see it, that the existence of multiple centers of power, none of which is wholly sovereign, will help (may indeed be necessary) to tame power, to secure the consent of all, and to settle conflict peacefully:
>
> • Because one center of power is set against another, power itself will be tamed, civilized, controlled, and limited to decent human purposes, while coercion, the most evil form of power, will be reduced to a minimum.
>
> • Because even minorities are provided with opportunities to veto solutions they strongly object to, and the consent of all will be won in the long run.
>
> • Because constant negotiations among different centers of power are necessary in order to make decisions, citizens and leaders will perfect the precious art of dealing peacefully with their conflicts, and not merely to the benefit of one partisan but to the mutual benefit of all parties to a conflict. (Dahl 1967: 24)

In order to fully understand political power, a pluralist such as Dahl insists that we examine the political processes and political decision-making over time. When we examine a particular instance of decision-making we will usually find one party or interest group victorious or successful. If we look at another instance or issue we would tend to find another interest group victorious. The end result is that no single party, interest group, or faction wins systematically over time; in political contests it is truly a "you win some and you lose some" situation. The essential reason for this outcome is found in the diverse strategies that are open to all those seeking to influence the political process.

Within a polyarchy, political movements and parties have access to the decision-making process and may try to influence government by:

- organizing a political party;
- forming coalitions with others holding similar interests and concerns;
- attempting to nominate and elect candidates favourable to their concerns and interests;
- trying to use their influence within an existing party to have it represent their interests.

Dahl recognizes the existence of differences, even inequalities, in the capacity of individuals and groups to utilize these opportunities. His final conclusions point to the need for, at most, internal reforms to the basic system. Indeed, pluralists in general assume that the U.S. system has a number of basic political problems and that, in an imperfect world, this is as good as citizens can hope to achieve.

PLURALISM QUESTIONED

Henry S. Kariel presents a succinct statement of the basic elements of the pluralist concept of the state:

> Six general propositions are integral to the political theory of pluralism: 1) individual fulfilment is assured by small government units, for they alone are representative; 2) unrepresentative exercise of governmental power is frustrated when public agencies are geographically dispersed; 3) society is composed of a variety of reasonably independent religious, cultural, education, professional and economic associations; 4) these private associations are voluntary insofar as no individual is ever wholly affiliated with any one of them; 5) public policy accepted as binding on all associations is the result of their own free interaction; and 6) public government is obliged to discern and act only upon the common denominator of group concurrence. (Kariel 1968: 164)

Pluralism, as an approach incorporating elements of both the classical liberal and sociological approaches, tends to assume that conflict is an inevitable feature of human social existence. However, unlike classical liberals, pluralists view the state and political institutions as a part of the very fabric of society. In pluralist theory the relationship between the state and society is more akin to functionalist theory than classical liberalism. For the pluralist, the state is not an institution capable of eliminating conflict but rather the arena of legitimate political conflict.

The state, according to pluralist theory, ultimately established the base of social harmony. But this is a harmony based less on shared goals, norms, and values than on collective acceptance of institutionalized mechanism for settling political disputes. Since all parties are assumed to have more or less equal opportunity to utilize the available mechanisms when attempting to influence the political process, there is widespread acceptance of the system as open, democratic, and legitimate.

The harmonious picture of democracy in liberal capitalist society painted by classical pluralist theory has been questioned by writers formerly considered pluralists. Charles Lindblom, who early on was a collaborator with Dahl, argues that there are significant weaknesses in the pluralist approach. In *Politics and Markets*, Lindblom reasons that it is essential to consider the connection between the market and government when examining governments and politics. He opens by declaring: "Aside from the difference between despotic and libertarian governments, the greatest distinction between one government and another is the degree to which market replaces government or government replaces market" (Lindblom 1977: ix). He maintains that the relationship of government to market is central to an understanding of liberal-democratic systems.

The operation of markets is itself a process that requires the recognition of the rights of private property in the form of the "rights to control enterprises; rights to organize and dispose of productive assets, and the rights to income from them" (168). Considering that it has long been recognized that access to property and business enterprises results in the unequal generation and appropriation of wealth, Lindblom asks if it is not possible for those in this position to control the political processes: "The mere possibility that business and property dominate polyarchy opens up the paradoxical possibility that polyarchy is tied to the market system not because it is democratic but because it is not" (168-69).

In his chapter "The Privileged Position of Business" Lindblom examines the political role played by business in "private enterprise market-oriented societies":

> The association between liberal constitutional polyarchy and market is clearly no historical accident. Polyarchies were established to win and protect certain liberties: private property, free enterprise, free contract, and occupational choice. Polyarchy also served the more diffuse aspirations of those elites that established it—"The end is always individual self-help." For both the specific liberties and for the exercise of self-help, markets in which the options can be exercised are required. (164)

Lindblom develops this thesis through consideration of the question of class, the circularity of leadership, and alternate socio-economic systems, and summarizes his findings in a final chapter, "A Future for Democracy?" After reviewing various arguments against and barriers to the spread and extension of democratic institutions, Lindblom takes the central concern of the volume to an ominous and logical conclusion:

> In short, in any private enterprise system, a large category of major decisions is turned over to businessmen, both small and larger. They are taken off the agenda of government. Businessmen thus become a kind of public official and exercise what, on a broad view of their role, are public functions. The significant logical consequence of this for polyarchy is that a broad area of public decision making is removed from polyarchal control. Polyarchal decision making may of course ratify such an arrangement or amend it through governmental equation of business decision making. In all real-world polyarchies, a substantial category of decisions is removed from polyarchal control. (172)

> It has been a curious feature of democratic thought that it has not faced up to the private corporation as a peculiar organization in an ostensible democracy. Enormously large, rich in resources, the big corporations, we have seen, command more resources than do most government units. They can also, over a broad range, insist that government meet their demands, even if these demands run counter to those of citizens expressed through their polyarchal controls. Moreover, they do not disqualify themselves from playing the partisan role of a citizen—for the corporation is legally a person. And they exercise unusual veto powers. They are on all these counts disproportionately powerful, we have seen. The large private corporation fits oddly into democratic theory and vision. Indeed, it does not fit. (356)

Lindblom's analysis and conclusions raise important questions about the fundamental propositions of pluralist theory. In a 1981 Presidential Address to the American Political Science Association, Lindblom draws out some of these implications and points to changes that pluralist theory must be prepared to contemplate. Although in this address he still describes himself as being in the mainstream of the discipline, Lindblom asserts again and again the necessity for reform of pluralist theory, that the lessons of the radical (Marxist) perspective must be heeded. His final words call for a serious consideration of the merits of alternative conceptions of the political process: "My argument has not been that radical thought is a model for all of us. It has been instead, to say it once more, that conventional theory is embarrassingly defective. It greatly needs to call more heavily on radical thought." (Lindblom 1982: 20)

• FIVE •

CLASSICAL MARXISM

The emergence of new social classes was one of the central factors leading first to the revision of classical liberalism in the works of John Stuart Mill and secondly to the disorder that so concerned Comte and Durkheim. This very same process, the emergence of a clearly defined class structure in the context of the development of industrial capitalism, was also a key factor in the social, economic, and political environment that provided the context for the work of Karl Marx.

While Britain was clearly the world leader in the early process of industrialization, by the early and mid-nineteenth century all of Europe was undergoing a transformation. The period of reaction that followed the defeat of the French Revolution was itself followed by the triumph of the bourgeoisie across Europe. The revolutions of 1830 revealed the presence of structural tensions as emerging classes associated with the development of industrial capitalism sought a greater share of political control. The Reform Act of 1832 in Britain and the July Monarchy in France (1830-48) marked the triumph of the bourgeoisie in those nations. In other parts of Europe the process emerged more slowly, but the trend was towards an industrial future.

While the industrial bourgeoisie triumphed economically and politically, part of the process was the development of the industrial working class. Although the industrial working class formed a key element in the political struggles that gave rise to the events of the 1830s, as a force it remained on the margins of society. R.R. Palmer describes the situation of the working class:

> Republicans in France, radical democrats in Britain, felt cheated and imposed upon in the 1820s and 1840s. They had in each country forced through a virtual revolution by their insurrections and demonstrations, and then in each country had been left without the vote. Some lost interest in representative institutions. Excluded from government they were tempted to seek political ends through extra-governmental, which is to say revolutionary or utopian, channels. Social and economic reforms seemed to the workingman far more important, as a final aim, than mere governmental innovations. The workman was told by respected economists that he could not hope to change the system in his own favor. He was tempted therefore to destroy the system, to replace it utterly with some new system conceived mainly in the minds of thinkers. He was told by the Manchester School, and by its equivalent in France, that the income of labor

83

was set by ineluctable natural laws, that it was best and indeed necessary for wages to remain low, and that the way to rise in the world was to get out of the laboring class altogether, by becoming the owner of a profitable business and leaving working people about where they were.

The reigning doctrine emphasized the conception of a labor market. The workman sold labor, the employer bought it. The price of labor, or wage, was to be agreed upon by the two individual parties. The price would naturally fluctuate according to changes in supply and demand. (Palmer 1957: 465)

Palmer suggests two possible solutions, "two means of escape" for the working class. One was to improve its position in the labour market by forming labour unions and engaging in collective bargaining. Unions were still illegal in France and "barely legal" in Britain after 1825, and in both countries it was still illegal to strike. Another means of escape was to leave behind entirely the idea of the market economy and the capitalist system: "It was to conceive of a system in which goods were to be produced for use, not for sale; and in which working people should be compensated according to need, not according to the requirements of an employer. This was the basis of most forms of socialism" (466). The key figure in the emergence of the latter solution was, of course, Karl Marx.

The work and theory of Karl Marx (1818-83), some have argued, were so important to the development of social theory in the west that Marx can be considered a watershed, a point of departure for subsequent sociological and political theory (Zeitlin 1981). While this may be an overstatement, much of the theorizing on the state that has occurred in recent decades has fallen within a Marxian tradition. But any brief consideration of the concept or theory of the state in the work of Marx faces almost insurmountable difficulties, as Martin Carnoy notes:

Since Marx did not develop a single, coherent theory of politics and/ or the State, Marxist conceptions of the State must be derived from Marx's critiques of Hegel, the development of Marx's theory of society (including his political economic theory), and his analysis of particular historical conjunctures, such as the 1848 Revolution in France and Louis Napoleon's dictatorship, or the 1871 Paris Commune. (Carnoy 1984: 45)

In an excellent overview of Marx's thinking on the state, Ralph Miliband notes: "Marx's earliest views on the state bear a clear Hegelian imprint" (Miliband 1965: 279). This is not surprising given Marx's early attachment to Hegelian philosophy, although his treatment of Hegel was to become increasingly critical. One could argue that Marx's first encounters with the state were simultaneously of a direct and philosophical nature. They were philosophical in that he was aware of the key role played by the state and its organs in the overall Hegelian system; and direct because of a number of key state actions that the Prussian government took and that were subsequently influential in the direction of Marx's life and thought.

Upon the completion of his doctoral dissertation Marx had intended to take up a teaching job at Bonn University, but the dismissal of Bruno Bayer from that institution in 1842 left Marx with no hope of an academic career and he became engaged instead in writing as a journalist (McLellan 1970: 97). Again the state intervened in a direct manner as the various journals Marx contributed to became the object of the censor's attention. During 1842 and 1843 Marx was involved with a liberal journal, *Rheinische Zeitung*, for which he wrote a number of articles. In these articles Marx addressed issues ranging from censorship and freedom of the press to a law against the theft of wood and the operation of the Prussian parliament, known as the Estates. While the essays reveal a growing critical stance on the actual operation of the Prussian state, as McLellan points out, "Marx's views were in transition and reveal no systematic framework: it is of the essence of a polemicist to be eclectic, and Marx used expressions and lines of argument drawn alike from Spinoza, Kant, and Hegel" (McLellan 1977: 17).

Following his departure as editor-in-chief of the *Rheinische Zeitung* in the spring of 1843, Marx undertook a detailed examination of Hegel's political philosophy, at the same time attempting to establish his own position on the role of material forces and factors in political society. The result of this activity was a manuscript, the *Critique of Hegel's Philosophy of Right*, in which Marx systematically examined Hegel's political philosophy, at times suggesting alternate conceptions of the state, democracy, and political philosophy. In his introduction to an edition of the *Critique*, Joseph O'Malley suggests that Marx had a number of purposes in preparing the complex and difficult manuscript:

> To summarize the complex character of the *Critique* we can say that it was Marx's first effort to expose and criticize Hegel's philosophy in general and his political philosophy in particular; and through this effort both to criticize existing political institutions and, with the help of research in political theory and history, to clarify the relationship between political and economic aspects of society. (O'Malley 1970, xiii)

HEGEL AND THE BASIS FOR AN ETHICAL COMMUNITY
An understanding of the paragraph-by-paragraph critique of Hegel's political philosophy that makes up the *Critique* requires an understanding of Hegel's

view of the state, in turn based on Hegel's philosophic system, one of the most complex ever produced by a western philosopher.

In brief, Georg Wilhelm Friedrich Hegel (1770-1831) had viewed the whole process of the emergence of civil society as a central aspect of the transition from feudalism to capitalism in western Europe—and the resultant debates about the relationship between civil society and the state—from the vantage point of an early nineteenth-century Prussian. The implications of this vantage point were profound, for, as Shlomo Avineri notes, in Germany there was no imminent emergence of a unified state capable of imposing order on the chaos of civil society:

> The old German Empire at the turn of the eighteenth century was a hodge-podge of kingdoms, principalities, duchies, markgraviates, landgraviates, bishoprics and free imperial cities, all held together by the tenuous semblance of the imperial crown, now firmly established for a couple of centuries in the Habsburg dynasty, bolstered up by legalistic fictions, pious religious humbug about the Universal Empire, and conflicting interests which viewed such an incongruous anomaly as an excellent and convenient arrangement. (Avineri 1972: 36)

The lack of a unified state structure in Germany led, in summary, to a general paralysis of society. Defence of society against external aggression and regulation of the activities within civil society were not possible, and even the enforcement of laws was tenuous (42-43).

The solutions that Hegel ultimately developed for the crisis faced by Germany were much different than those proposed by the classical English liberals and the theorists of the French Revolution. Hegel opposed conceiving of human beings solely in individualistic terms, as Hobbes and even Locke had attempted to do. Hegel, the idealist, was interested at least partly in establishing for political life an ethical basis that would extend beyond the utilitarian individualism of social contract theory. According to Avineri:

> What Hegel is searching for is something not much different from that which, in his theological writings, he had found in the ancient polis: the consciousness of belonging to a community, that feeling which would not view the community in merely instrumental terms. Belonging to such a community, to a people, is for Hegel "absolute ethical life" (*absolute Sittlichkeit*) not because the people represents as such any absolute ethical idea, but because this membership is absolute rather than relative, it is its own end rather than a mere means towards an end determined by self-interest, security or the like. (84)

But how could the basis for an ethical community be established given an individualistic market-based civil society and the political divisions of the Germany of his day? The answer lies in Hegel's conception of the larger institutional organization of human society. He divides modern society into three major realms of human or ethical existence: the family, civil society, and the state.

In the realm of the family, the first sphere of ethical life, human beings do not view themselves primarily as individual persons but rather as part of a collectivity. The collectivity is a limited one, based essentially on a narrow definition of a person's ethical bonds with other family members. As Andrew Gamble notes, "Family relationships were particular not universal, because members felt loyalty and acted altruistically only in relation to the members of their own families, not all families" (Gamble 1981: 95).

In civil society, the second realm of human ethical existence, individuals are emancipated from the bonds of family, religion, and politics as they pursue their own self-interest. Civil society as market society exhibits nevertheless a degree of co-operative and integrated behaviour as individuals compete and focus on self-reliance. Although Hegel views civil society as the sphere of universal egoism, for him it does not degenerate into anything approaching Hobbes' state of nature because not only is there an element of ethical community present in the form of family, but also life in civil society is still based on certain ethical postulates.

The third realm of ethical life, the state, is also the highest and most central. It is the sphere of "universal altruism." In this realm the relationship of human individuals to the state is characterized by relations of unity and harmony, and the state forms the ultimate expression of human social potential in that it represents the interests of all. In each realm—family, civil society, and state—a component of human potential reaches its full development. In the family and civil society the duties of individuals to their families and themselves are realized. In the state the duties of individuals to humanity and society as a whole are realized. The state is the true representation of universal humanity. According to Gamble: "Individuals related to the state altruistically because in obeying its commands and paying its taxes they did not consider their own self-interest, but the objective interest of the whole community" (96-97).

The realm of the political or the state is thus special, "a system of integration aimed at overcoming the atomistic individualism of the economic sphere" (Avineri 1972: 99). Through the state the individual is integrated in a manner not possible in civil society and in a manner more complete than the narrow aggregation of the family. At the same time Hegel feels that a state merely expressing the dominant economic interests is "an abomination." To use Avineri's words: "Hegel's emerging political theory is an attempt to achieve a universality (a 'general will') that would not be, on the one hand, an aggregate of individual wills yet would not appear, on the other hand, as a merely external, coercive antithesis to the individual wills" (99).

As an idealist Hegel arrives at his conception of the state through his understanding of the Absolute Spirit. For Hegel the unfolding of the universe is an unfolding of spirit and rationality; the emergence of modern society and the emergence of the modern state are aspects of the process. In the modern state there is, for the first time, a potential for an extension of rationality in the form of a unity of subjective consciousness and the objective world. Human subjective existence moves out beyond family and economic relations and begins to approach self-realization:

> The rationality which permeates the world of man becomes apparent for the first time in the state, Hegel argues. In the family, it is still hidden behind feeling and sentiment; in civil society it appears as an instrumentality of individual self-interest. Only in the sphere of the state does reason become conscious of itself; in other words, only in the state are the actions of man one with his intentions—man knows what he wants and acts according to it. (178)

Through the state, humans begin to realize freedom in a social, communal way that moves beyond the potentials of family and economic relations. There is a true sense of identity of humans with each other, communally through the state. In Hegel's words:

> The state is actual only when its members have a feeling of their own self-hood and it is stable only when the public and private ends are identical. It has often been said that the end of the state is the happiness of its citizens. This is perfectly true. If all is not well with them, if their subjective aims are not satisfied, if they do not find that the state as such is the means to their satisfaction, then the footing of the state itself is insecure. (quoted in Avineri 1972: 179)

These philosophical conceptions of the state raise a fundamental question: What sort of state did Hegel conceive of as being capable of fulfiling this universal function? Avineri argues that Hegel was setting forth an ideal of the state and therefore any concrete historical example would be difficult to locate. But it is also clear that Hegel did in fact offer quite specific arguments in favour of a specific state structure that would be capable of accomplishing the task his philosophy had set for it.

The state form that Hegel elaborates in *The Philosophy of Right* and which Marx subsequently criticized was a form of constitutional monarchy. For Hegel, such a state would contain the necessary structural characteristics to facilitate the development of its role as universal representative of humanity.

As O'Malley notes, Hegel's thought develops a specific state form:

> Hegel's task in The *Philosophy of Right* is to demonstrate how the unity of social and political life is effected within the modern state despite the apparent duality of civil and political life which this achievement of the modern world implies. His claim is that this unity is effected within and by means of an institutional framework whose principle features are: (1) a monarch who comes to the throne by birth, and thus independently of political factions; (2) an extensive bureaucracy of salaried civil servants, who constitute an estate or class whose aims are identical with those of the state itself; and (3) an Assembly of Estates, in which representatives of the crown and the executive power meet with representatives of the civil estates to deliberate and determine the way in which the aims of the state and of civil society shall be reconciled, and to translate their decisions into law. (O'Malley 1970: x/viii)

Marx was to examine critically each of these three aspects of the state: the monarchy, bureaucracy, and assembly.

Hegel identifies the assembly as "the agency *par excellence* for the achievement of socio-political unity in the modern state" (O'Malley 1970: 1). His view of its role springs from his understanding of civil society as having a definite class structure, including a variety of occupations, professions, and classes with common interests and concerns. These groups, associations, and classes tended to be organized into corporations, which came to serve a useful political purpose. The membership of the assembly would be made up of representatives of the various corporations as well as representatives of those with private property, along with the bureaucracy and the crown. Hegel maintains that within the assembly there is the potential to create the unity necessary for the state to assume its universal role. The assembly would determine the course of state policy and consider the overall interests of the body politic. According to O'Malley, Hegel describes the assembly as:

> a complex system of mediations within which is achieved the desired synthesis between the particularism of civil society and the universality of the state. As an institution it embodies and brings to fruition all the particular mediations between private and public interest already implied in the bureaucracy as universal class, the corporation-structured acquisitive class, and the substantial class subsisting on entailed landed property. It is in no sense, according to Hegel, to be construed as a body antagonistic to the crown, or to the executive's power in general; rather the Estates and the government-*qua*-executive are "complementary organs of one and the same body politic." (1970: 1)

The various components of the state would ensure the universal unity of its operation. Hegel sees the bureaucracy as being above the sectional interests of civil society and with interest identical to the state, that is, universal in its interests and concerns. The head of the state, the monarch, is essentially a figurehead, the universal representative and part of the state but not conceivable in isolation from the other aspects of the state. Avineri explains:

> Herein lies the paradox of Hegel's theory of the monarchy. While keeping the traditional form of the monarchy, Hegel divests the monarch himself of any real power by making the Crown into the symbol of self-determination. Hegel, it seems, thought that the only effective way of combating the old absolutist idea of the monarchy and the legitimist theories of the Restoration would be to keep the form of the monarchy as a symbol for the modern political idea of subjectivity and self-determination. (Avineri 1972: 187)

MARX'S CRITIQUE OF HEGEL

In 1843 Marx set out to critique Hegel's "Philosophy of Right." Although Marx did not yet have an alternate concept of the state, he was to develop one as he critically examined the Hegelian position in philosophical terms while simultaneously examining the empirical operation of the Prussian state.

The notes that make up the *Critique* are a paragraph-by-paragraph discussion of Hegel's analysis of the state and its relationship to the family and civil society. The work displays Marx's growing dissatisfaction with what he refers to as "the theological, pantheistic mysticism" of the Hegelian system (Marx 1970a: 7).

In his brief comments on the nature of the constitution Marx continues to develop his critique of the idealist basis of Hegel's analysis. Hegel's system, Marx declares, imposes the logical form of its argument onto reality and the state is moulded not in reality but in philosophical terms to conform to the Hegelian system. Marx declares: "Thought is not conformed to the nature of the state, but the state to a ready-made system of thought" (19). The implications of this idealist philosophical determinism are apparent in the entire Hegelian system, Marx argues, as he focuses his attention on Hegel's concept of the crown. It is only in philosophy that the crown can be characterized as a universal representative of the entire society, because in the real, empirical, historical world the crown has a persona. The crown or sovereign is a real human being existing in history, with an existence structurally located in a broad set of human social relations. Marx writes:

> The activities and agencies of the state are attached to individuals (the state is only active through individuals), but not to the individuals as physical but political; they are attached to the political quality of the

individual.... Hence the absurdity of Hegel's conceiving the activities and agencies of the state in the abstract, and particular individuality in opposition to it. He forgets that particular individuality is a human individual, and that the activities and agencies of the state are human activities. (21-22)

Marx concludes that for Hegel the crown can only exist as a universal at the level of an idea, and that such a concept of monarchy is possible to maintain only at the expense of a developed concept of *democracy*.

For Marx this introduction of the concept of democracy leads to a further critique of the Hegelian position. Marx sees democracy as a necessary precondition for the full realization of human social life. Humans are by nature, Marx argues, social and thus political, and the full development of this aspect of their existence as human beings demands some form of democratic institutions. Marx states:

In monarchy the whole, the people, is subsumed under one of its modes of existence, the political constitution; in democracy the constitution itself appears only as one determination, and indeed as the self-determination of the people. In monarchy we have the people of the constitution, in democracy the constitution of the people. Democracy is the resolved mystery of all constitutions. Here the constitution not only in itself, according to essence, but according to existence and actuality is returned to its real ground, actual man, the actual people, and established as its own work. The constitution appears as what is, the free product of men. (29-30)

Further:

Democracy is *human existence*, while in other political forms man has only *legal* existence. That is the fundamental difference of democracy.

All remaining forms of the state are certain, determined, particular forms of the state. In democracy the formal principal is simultaneously the material principle. For that reason it is the first true unity of the universal and the particular. (30)

In a *Resumé* of his critique of Hegel's concept of the crown, Marx notes that Hegel's idealism was responsible for the errors in his political philosophy. In a statement that previews many of the arguments that were to unfold in the *1844 Manuscripts* and *The German Ideology*, Marx explains the basis of the errors in Hegel's position:

But Hegel conceives of society, family, etc., the artificial person in general, not as the realization of the actual, empirical person but as the *real* person which, however, has the moment of personality in it only abstractly. Whence also comes his notion that it is not actual persons who come to be state but the state which must first come to be an actual person. Instead of the state being brought forth, therefore, as the ultimate reality of the person, as the ultimate social reality of man, a single empirical man, an empirical person, is brought forth as the ultimate actuality of the state. This inversion of subject into object and object into subject is a consequence of Hegel's wanting to write the biography of the abstract Substance, of the Idea, with human activity, etc., having consequently to appear as the activity and result of something other than man; it is a consequence to Hegel's wanting to allow the essence of man to act for itself as an imaginary individual instead of acting in its actual, human existence, and it necessarily has as its result that an empirical existence is taken in an uncritical manner to be the real truth of the Idea, because it is not a question of bringing empirical existence to its truth but of bringing the truth to empirical existence, and thereupon the obvious is developed as a real moment of the Idea. (39)

Having criticized Hegel's notion of the crown in both philosophical and empirical terms, Marx addresses the concept of the executive, which is responsible in the Hegelian system for carrying out the decisions of the state. The executive's central component is the bureaucracy, the universal class. Marx summarizes Hegel's position:

Hegel has the state proper, the executive, move into the management of the state's universal interest and of legality, etc. within civil society via holders [of the executive power]; and according to him these executive office holders, the executive civil servants, are in reality the true representation of the state, not "of" but "against" civil society. The opposition between state and civil society is thus fixed; the state does not reside within but outside of civil society; it affects civil society merely through office holders to whom is entrusted the management of the state within this sphere. The opposition is not overcome by means of these office holders but has become a legal and fixed opposition. The state becomes something alien to the nature of civil society; it becomes this nature's otherworldly realm of deputies which makes claims against civil society. The police, the judiciary, and the administration are not deputies of civil society itself, which manages its own general interest in and through them. Rather, they are office holders of the state whose purpose is to manage the state in opposition to civil society. (49-50)

As in his discussion of the crown, Marx argues here that in fact, in reality, in the concrete world, this philosophical position breaks down. The executive turns out, Marx remarks, to be composed of real humans with real interests, real concerns, capable of—as the state censors have already shown Marx— real caprice. Far from being a universal class acting in the universal interest, the executive both mirrors the particularity of the entire state structure and possesses interests of its own. As O'Malley points out, "Marx dismisses Hegel's claim that the bureaucracy represents the identify of the universal interests with the interest of a particular social class: in the bureaucracy this identity is imaginary and contradictory" (O'Malley 1970: iii). Marx will locate his own universal class in an "Introduction to the Critique" written after the main text was completed.

The final element of the Hegelian state system that Marx examines is the assembly. For Hegel the assembly is the central political organ, ensuring participation by all the people, all citizens, in the political process. In the assembly or legislature the crown and the people are joined and classes are united. Indeed, for Hegel the legislatures are, as O'Malley puts it, "the mediating organ, the middle term between the crown and the people, the government and the private citizen, the political and civil spheres of modern life; they are the medium *par excellence* for the abolition of the dualism of state and civil society" (ix). Again, Marx offers both a philosophical and an empirical critique of this concept.

Indeed, the major portion of the *Critique* is dedicated to a discussion of the concept, construction, and role of the legislature or assembly. In a wide-ranging analysis of the contradictions and inconsistencies of the Hegelian account of the assembly, Marx argues that the legislature is dominated by bureaucrats and representatives of the state. Moreover, its medieval origin and structure make it inappropriate for handling modern social problems and, perhaps most importantly, the members of the assembly simply continue to represent the manifold interests of civil society, which "placed" them in the assembly in the first place (Marx 1970a: 122). This final point relates to the key element of restricted voting rights, which Marx addresses near the end of the discussion. If the legislature, as an institutional arrangement, makes a claim to universality, it must be a legislature based on the universal franchise:

The vote is the actual relation of actual civil society to the civil society of the legislature, to the representative element. In other words, the vote is the immediate, the direct, the existing and not simply imagined relation of civil society to the political state. It therefore goes without saying that the vote is the chief political interest of actual civil society. In unrestricted suffrage, both active and passive, civil society has actually raised itself for the first time to an abstraction of itself, to political existence as its true universal and essential existence. But the full achievement of the abstraction is at once also the transcendence [*Aufhebung*] of the abstraction. In actually establishing its political existence as its true existence civil society has simultaneously established its civil existence, in distinction from its political existence, as inessential. And with the one separated, the other, its opposite, falls. Within the abstract political state the reform of voting advances the dissolution [*Auflösung*] of this political state, but also the dissolution of civil society. (121)

It is thus apparent that in Marx's first systematic effort at political analysis there is no emerging problematic or theoretical concept of the state. The *Critique* is what its name implies, a critique of the Hegelian system, but one that fails to postulate an alternative approach. Although Marx makes plain his commitment to democracy and political emancipation as essential to human development and realization, he does not yet articulate the form and structure of a democratic society. The *Critique* was, we must keep in mind, a notebook, an effort to work through key issues in political philosophy. As such it was vital in the emerging materialist position that Marx was developing.

THE GERMAN IDEOLOGY

In the early fall of 1843 Marx moved to Paris, where be began the detailed studies of political economy that would occupy the remainder of his life. At the same time he continued to develop his critique of Hegel and the Young Hegelians, and to study French socialist thought. The key work of his early days in Paris is the *Economic and Philosophical Manuscripts of 1844*, which contain further critiques of Hegel, evidence of the fruits of his first systematic economic analysis, and key comments regarding his emerging concepts of species being and alienation. The *Manuscripts* do not, however, contain any new or systematic comments on the state.

In Paris Marx met Friedrich Engels, who was to become his lifelong collaborator, friend, and supporter. Between November 1845 and October 1846 they completed a manuscript that was to become *The German Ideology* (1846). Massive in size, *The German Ideology*, in the guise of a wide-ranging critique of the Young Hegelians, contained many of the basic positions and assumptions that were to become the essence of Marx's and Engels' materialist approach to the investigation of human society and politics.

The concept of the state that emerges in *The German Ideology* must be understood in the context of the overall philosophical, epistemological, and political approach that Marx and Engels were developing. In the *1844 Manuscripts* Marx has started to develop his materialist approach, arguing that

94

modern, capitalist society must be understood in relation to the revolutionized productive capacities and social relations of production characterized by alienation, exploitation, and domination. *The German Ideology* contains a much more systematic statement of the materialist approach, laying out the well-known "First Premises of Materialist Method," which argue for an examination of human productive activity and conditions as the point of departure in all social investigation.

The first systematic statement regarding the state locates it in the context of productive activities:

> The fact is, therefore, that definite individuals who are productively active in a definite way enter into these definite social and political relations. Empirical observation must in each separate instance bring out empirically, and without any mystification and speculation, the connection of the social and political structure with production. The social structure and the State are continually evolving out of the life-process of definite individuals, but of individuals, not as they may appear in their own or other people's imagination, but as they *really* are; i.e. as they operate, produce materially, and hence as they work under definite material limits, presuppositions and conditions independent of their will.
>
> The production of ideas, of conceptions, of consciousness, is at first directly interwoven with the material activity and the material intercourse of men, the language of real life. Conceiving, thinking, the mental intercourse of men, appear at this stage as the direct efflux of their material behaviour. The same applies to mental production as expressed in the language of politics, laws, morality, religion, metaphysics, etc. of a people. Men are the producers of their conceptions, ideas, etc.—real, active men, as they are conditioned by a definite development of their productive forces and of the intercourse corresponding to these, up to its further forms. Consciousness can never be anything else than conscious existence, and the existence of men is their actual life-process. (Marx 1970b: 46-47)

Marx and Engels then elaborate their position of the essential nature of human productive activities in the development of human history, the relationship of production to consciousness, and the process by which a division of labour and private property emerges. Within the context of a division of labour, divisions of interest between individuals and the community emerge, and this contradiction gives rise to the development of the state:

> And out of this very contradiction between the interest of the individual and that of the community the latter takes an independent form

as the *State*, divorced from the real interests of individual and community, and at the same time as an illusory communal life, always
based, however, on the real ties existing in every family and tribal
conglomeration—such as flesh and blood, language, division of labour on a larger scale, and other interests—especially, as we shall
enlarge upon later, on the classes, already determined by the division
of labour, which in every such mass of men separate out, and of
which one dominates all the others. It follows from this that all
struggles within the State, the struggle between democracy, aristocracy, and monarchy, the struggle for the franchise, etc. etc. are merely
the illusory forms in which the real struggles of the different classes
are fought out among one another. (53-54)

The argument moves quickly, as the division of labour is tied to the
emergence of classes, domination, and the postulation of political struggles as
class struggles. The concept of the state ties the structures and organization of
the state to productive forces, productive relations, and the larger structures of
society. Indeed, in a letter written in 1846 Marx articulates his general view of
the structures of human society in clear terms:

What is society, whatever its form may be? The product of men's
reciprocal action. Are men free to choose this or that form of society?
By no means. Assume a particular state of development in the productive faculties of man and you will get a particular form of commerce and consumption. Assume particular stages of development in
production, commerce and consumption and you will have a corresponding social constitution, a corresponding organization of the
family, of orders or of classes, in a word, a corresponding civil
society. Assume a particular civil society and you will get particular
political conditions which are only the official expression of civil
society. (McLellan 1977: 192)

The essence of this position is clearly an emphasis on the need to examine
first the material basis of society. Although Marx will later use more determinist explanations of the relationship of the economic structures and practices to
other aspects of society, in *The German Ideology* there are clear statements of
a non-determinist materialist position.

This conception of history thus relies on expounding the real process
of production—starting from material production of life itself and
comprehending the form of intercourse connected with and created
by this mode of production, i.e. civil society in its various states, as
the basis of all history; describing in its actions as the state, and also

explaining how all the different theoretical products and forms of consciousness, religion, philosophy, morality, etc., etc., arise from it, and tracing the process of their formation from that basis; thus the whole thing can, of course, be depicted in its totality (and therefore, too, the reciprocal action of these various sides on one another). (Marx 1970b: 58)

Since the forces, practices, and relations of material production are so vital in structuring the entire range of social and political practices that make up civil society and the state, the character of "the economic" comes to pervade the entire society. In capitalist society in particular the centrality of class relations as relations of domination has an impact on the structure, role, and function of the state:

Through the emancipation of private property from the community, the State has become a separate entity, beside and outside civil society; but it is nothing more than the form of organization which the bourgeois necessarily adopt both for internal and external purposes, for the mutual guarantee of their property and interests.... Since the State is the form in which the individuals of a ruling class assert their common interest, and in which the whole civil society of an epoch is epitomized, it follows that the State mediates in the formation of all common institutions and that the institutions receive a political form. (80)

While there are other references to the state through the remainder of *The German Ideology*, there are no further significant theoretical or conceptual elaborations.

MARX'S LATER WORK (1848-79)

In Paris Marx and Engels became actively involved in politics through the actions of the Communist League, and as part of their activities they formulated a clear statement of principles (both analytical and political) and objectives. The result was one of their key polemical works, *The Communist Manifesto* (1848). In the *Manifesto* Marx and Engels sought both to popularize the mode of analysis they had been developing to present a political program based on this analytical approach. They conceptualized the state in this well-known passage:

Each step in the development of the bourgeoisie was accompanied by a corresponding political advance of that class. An oppressed class under the sway of the feudal nobility, an armed and self-governing association in the medieval commune; here independent urban republic (as in Italy and Germany), there taxable "third state" of the monarchy (as in France), afterwards, in the period of manufacture proper, serving either semi-feudal or the absolute monarchy as a counterpoise against the nobility, and in fact, corner-stone of the great monarchies in general, the bourgeoisie has at last, since the establishment of Modern Industry and of the world-market, conquered for itself, in the modern representative State, exclusive political sway. The executive of the modern State is but a committee for managing the common affairs of the whole bourgeoisie. (Marx and Engels 1952: 43-44)

The actual course of events in Europe during 1848 and after was much different than that which Marx and Engels had hoped for, and as a result of the unsuccessful rebellions Marx and his family were forced to move to England. There Marx plunged into an analysis of the complex structures of capitalist society, a work that would occupy the remaining three decades of his life. One of the central tasks he also undertook was a detailed analysis of the political events that had taken place in France during the late 1840s. The results of these efforts are *The Class Struggles in France* (1850) and *The Eighteenth Brumaire of Louis Bonaparte* (1852).

Both of these texts, originally written as a series of articles, illustrate at his best Marx the social scientist and Marx the political activist. *The Class Struggles in France*, described by Engels in his introduction to the book as "Marx's first attempt to explain a section of contemporary history by means of his material conception, on the basis of a given economic situation," presents an analysis of the 1848 Rebellion in the context of the key economic and political forces (Marx 1972a: 5). Rich in detail, the text destroys all arguments that Marx maintained a simplistic conception of class, class power, and political power. Its contribution in theoretical terms is less easy to assess.

The second empirical and historical work, *The Eighteenth Brumaire*, is also a detailed account of events in France, this time the coup d'état of Louis Napoleon. It again examines the concrete social and economic factors behind the political events. Here the focus is on an illustration of the complexities of social class factions and the state as well as on the role of religion, tradition, and custom in political behaviour.

In *The Communist Manifesto*, Marx and Engels had presented a simple picture of the state, especially the executive. *The Eighteenth Brumaire* talks of "government power, the army and the legislative body, in short, of the whole power of the state" (Marx 1972b: 458). In examining the at times independent operations of these three branches of the state, Marx pictures the state as much more than the executive committee for the management of the affairs of the bourgeoisie. The state is indeed the site of considerable class conflict as various classes and fractions attempt to influence its actions and policies. As

Marx traces through the intricacies and intrigues of the events, one clear theme emerges: In a crisis situation, when the bourgeoisie is internally divided and facing a variety of other classes and fractions, political developments are volatile and uncertain. Under such conditions, in a literal sense, anything can happen and in a sense the coup of Louis Napoleon was just that, the coup of a "princely lumpenproletarian" (487).

In the years following his arrival in London, dedicating his life to his work on political economy, Marx ultimately produced the major texts that make up the *Grundrisse* (1859), *Capital* (1867-79), *The Theories of Surplus Value*, (1862-63), and others. In 1857 he outlined a program of studies and writings that was to include a study of the state, but he did not complete the tasks outlined (Marx 1973: 108). As a result there is no systematic theoretical statement or perspective on the state in his own works. There are, however, a series of what Martin Carnoy terms "analytical fundamentals," which Carnoy suggests frame subsequent debates among Marxists regarding the nature of the state.

Carnoy provides a succinct summary of several key points in Marx's views of the state. First, there is the materialist basis of Marx's analysis of society: "Marx viewed the material conditions of a society as the basis of its social structure and of human consciousness" (Carnoy 1984: 46). In a capitalist society the class-based relations of power and domination that characterize the relations of material production influence the structures and operation of the state. As Carnoy notes, Marx does not view the state as "the trustee of the society as a whole" (47). Carnoy summarizes Marx's position:

> Once he came to his formulation of capitalist society as a class society, dominated by the bourgeoisie, it necessarily followed that the State is the political expression of that dominance. Indeed, the State is an essential means of class domination in capitalist society. It is not above class struggles, but deeply engaged in them. (147)

Lastly, there is the related issue of the repressive role of the state in capitalist society. Given the conflict and tension inherent in a class-based society, some means of repressing class conflict becomes essential. The state takes on this role, serving the dominant class, the bourgeoisie, and taking over a primary function of community: the enforcement of laws. In doing this, as Carnoy puts its, "According to Marx and Engels, the State appears as part of the division of labor, that is, part of the appearance of differences among groups in society and the lack of social consensus" (50).

FOLLOWING MARX: ENGELS, LENIN, AND GRAMSCI

In considering the "classical Marxist" position we should also note the contributions of Engels and Lenin. Friedrich Engels (1820-95) is best known in this regard for the analysis presented in *The Origin of the Family, Private Property and the State*, first published in 1884. In this text, based primarily on a reconsideration of the work of anthropologist Lewis Morgan, Engels restates the basic elements of the simpler concept of the state found in his and Marx's earlier writings. Engels actually takes the analysis back to the Grecian constitution, tracing the acquisition of individual and family wealth and linking that process to the need for and emergence of institutions to protect wealth. The need for an institution to protect accumulated wealth is the basis, Engels argues, of the invention of the state (1948: 106-107).

This general frame of reference provides the groundwork for Engels' subsequent arguments concerning the state in capitalist society. Once class relations emerge to the point of becoming "insoluble contradictions" and "irreconcilable antagonisms," a position is reached that requires "a power seemingly standing above society that would alleviate the conflict, and keep it within the bounds of 'order'" (166). That power emerges, of course, in the form of the state.

The state, Engels argues, arises not only in the midst of class conflict, but also within the context of the existence of a dominant class. The state's efforts to address and "solve" class conflict thus turn out to be undertaken in the interests of the dominant class. The state is not therefore some neutral institution operating to solve conflict in the interests of the society as a whole. Rather it is "the state of the most powerful, economically dominant class" and becomes that class's new means of holding down and exploiting the oppressed class (168).

It is worth noting that Engels did foresee the possibility of exceptional circumstances emerging when "warring classes balance each other so nearly that the state power, as ostensible mediator, acquires, for the moment, a certain degree of independence of both" (168). Under such circumstances unusual political developments and state forms may emerge; however, a phenomenon such as Bonapartism will tend to be the exception, not the rule.

Engels also comments on the future. He argues that because the economic structures and contradictions of societies based on private property and private appropriation of wealth gave rise to the state, the transformation of these societies will subsequently result in the transformation of the state:

> The state, then, has not existed from all eternity. There have been societies that did without it, that had no idea of the state and state power. At a certain stage of economic development, which was necessarily bound up with the split of society into classes, the state became a necessity owing to this split. We are now rapidly approaching a stage in the development of production at which the existence of these classes not only will have ceased to be a necessity, but will become a positive hindrance to production. They will fall as inevita-

bly as they arose at an earlier stage. Along with them the state will inevitably fall. Society, which will reorganize production on the basis of a free and equal association of the producers, will put the whole machinery of state where it will then belong: into the museum of antiquities, by the side of the spinning-wheel and the bronze axe. (170)

A final "Marxist classic" that is on occasion referred to in the context of Marxist theories of the state is Lenin's *The State and Revolution*. Written essentially as a political polemic, the text contributes little to the further systematic extension of Marx's theoretical thinking, but does reiterate a number of basic positions. Indeed, Lenin makes the purpose of the text crystal clear: "In view of the unprecedentedly widespread distortion of Marxism, our prime task is to *re-establish* what Marx really taught on the subject of the state" (Lenin 1965: 6). He goes on to specify what he considers the essence of Marx's teaching on the historical role and meaning of the state:

> The state is the product and the manifestation of the *irreconcilability* of class antagonisms. The state arises when, where and to the extent that class antagonisms objectively *cannot* be reconciled. And, conversely, the existence of the state proves that class antagonisms are irreconcilable.

It is here, Lenin argues, that the "distortion of Marxism" begins:

> On the one hand, the bourgeois and particularly the petty-bourgeois ideologists, compelled under the weight of indisputable historical facts to admit that the state only exists where there are class antagonisms and the class struggle, "correct" Marx in such a way as to make it appear that the state is an organ for the *reconciliation* of classes. According to Marx, the state could neither arise nor maintain itself if it were possible to reconcile classes. According to the petty bourgeois and philistine professors and publicists it appears— very frequently they benignantly refer to Marx to prove this—that the state does reconcile classes. According to Marx, the state is an organ of class *rule*, an organ for the *oppression* of one class by another; it is the creation of "order," which legalizes and perpetuates this oppression by moderating the conflict between the classes. (7-8)

The theme identified here—state oppression—becomes the central point of Lenin's analysis. Following the writing of Engels on the issue of power, Lenin redefines state power largely by discussing the role of force, and concludes by asking: "A standing army and police are the chief instruments of state power. But can it be otherwise?" (10). He answers this question himself:

> It is impossible, because civilized society is split into antagonistic and, moreover, irreconcilably antagonistic classes, the "self-acting" arming of which would lead to an armed struggle between them. A state arises, a special power is created, special bodies of armed men, and every revolution, by destroying the state apparatus, clearly demonstrates to us how the ruling class strives to restore the special bodies of armed men which serve it, and how the oppressed class strives to create a new organization of this kind, capable of serving not the exploiters but the exploited. (11)

The State and Revolution discusses at length Marx's historical analysis and the lessons that the proletariat can draw from history, and offers polemical critiques of contemporaries whose positions Lenin disagreed with. Lenin also makes efforts to elaborate on the structure of the state, noting that there are two essential components to the centralized power of the modern state: the bureaucracy and the standing army. "In their works, Marx and Engels repeatedly show that it is the bourgeoisie with whom these institutions are connected by thousands of threads" (34).

A recurring theme of the text is the essentially undemocratic nature of the state in capitalist society. Even under the best conditions real democracy and capitalism are deemed to be incompatible:

> In capitalist society, providing it develops under the most favourable conditions, we have a more or less complete democracy in the democratic republic. But this democracy is always hemmed in by the narrow limits set by capitalist exploitation, and consequently always remains, in reality, a democracy for the minority, only for the propertied classes, only for the rich. Freedom in capitalist society always remains about the same as it was in the ancient Greek republics: freedom for the slave-owners. Owing to the conditions of capitalist exploitation the modern wage slaves are so crushed by want and poverty that "they cannot be bothered with democracy, they cannot be bothered with politics"; in the ordinary peaceful course of events the majority of the population is barred from participation in public and political life. (103-104)

Because of these conditions the establishment of a democratic society would not be an easy task. Lenin was, above all, a revolutionary who recognized that the transformation of capitalist structures would not immediately bring about a new democratic society. The achievement of true democracy would require a transitional period during which the state would be vital:

> The essence of Marx's teaching on the state has been mastered only by those who understand that the dictatorship of a *single* class is necessary not only for every class society in general, not only for the *proletariat* which has overthrown the bourgeoisie, but also for the entire *historical period* which separates capitalism from "classless society," from Communism. The forms of bourgeois states are extremely varied, but their essence is the same: all these states, whatever their form, in the final analysis are inevitably the *dictatorship of the bourgeoisie*. The transition from capitalism to Communism certainly cannot but yield a tremendous abundance and variety of political forms, but the essence will inevitably be the same: *the dictatorship of the proletariat*. (41)

The transitional phase in human society itself, by definition, will pass. With the development of socialism human relations, human capacities, indeed "human nature," will change, giving rise eventually to the famous "withering away" of the state (Engels' expression, not Marx's) (McLellan 1971: 212). Lenin comments:

> From the moment all members of society, or even only the vast majority, have learned to administer the state *themselves*, have taken this work into their own hands, have "set going" control over the insignificant minority of capitalists, over the gentry who wish to preserve their capitalist habits and over the workers who have been profoundly corrupted by capitalism—from this moment the need for government of any kind begins to disappear altogether. The more complete the democracy, the nearer the moment approaches when it becomes unnecessary. The more democratic the "state" which consists of the armed workers, and which is "no longer a state in the proper sense of the word," the more rapidly does *every form* of state begin to wither away.
>
> For when *all* have learned to administer and actually do independently administer social production, independently keep accounts and exercise control over the idlers, the gentlefolk, the swindlers and suchlike "guardians of capitalist traditions," the escape from this popular accounting and control will inevitably become so incredibly difficult, such a rare exception, and will probably be accompanied by such swift and severe punishment (for the armed workers are practical men and not sentimental intellectuals, and they will scarcely allow anyone to trifle with them), that the *necessity* of observing the

simple, fundamental rules of human intercourse will very soon become a *habit*.

And then the door will be wide open for the transition from the first phase of communist society to its higher phase, and with it to the complete withering away of the state. (Lenin 1965: 121-22)

The title of this Chapter, "Classical Marxism," seeks to differentiate the original works, ideas, and political analyses of Marx (and those who immediately followed in his path) from those who were to remould these ideas after the middle of the twentieth century. Disputes and differences as to what Marx *really* meant began to occur even before his death, and by the turn of the century there was an unfortunate but persistent tendency to see Marx as an economic determinist. Russell Jacoby (1971) argues that the regrettable fate that befell many of the Marx's ideas and arguments during the first two decades of the Twentieth century was the outcome of two different forces. First, there were the political configurations of the time characterized by the collapse of the International Socialist Movement, compounded by the dismal picture of workers killing each other in the trenches of Europe, and the suppression of the post-World War I uprisings in many parts of Europe. There was, it seems, little space or time for theoretical reflection or innovation. Secondly, there was the failure of many so-called Marxists to follow the complex and sophisticated methods and modes of analysis pioneered by Marx, resulting in what John Merrington (1977) describes as an intellectual malaise. He notes that "the ossification of bureaucratic structures of organization went hand in hand with an 'official Marxism' based on a rigid set of categorical doctrines, 'laws of social development' of the natural-scientific type" (1977: 140).

There were, however, some thinkers who attempted to remain true to the complex nature of Marx's approach with its emphasis on a non-determinist dialectical analysis of the social totality. Jacoby notes two important exceptions in the title of his 1971 essay, "Towards a Critique of Automatic Marxism: The Politics of Philosophy From Lukacs to the Frankfurt School." As he explains, the official Marxism that emerged in the post-World War I period was a Bolshevized interpretation, one in which Russian interests and needs came to dominate the so-called international socialist movement (Jacoby 1971: 122).

While Jacoby focuses on the work of Georg Lukacs and some of the thinkers associated with the Frankfurt School, there were others active during the same era who sought to remain true to the principles of Marx while becoming increasingly critical of official Marxism. Predominant among these was the Italian scholar, journalist, and political activist Antonio Gramsci. Born in Sardinia in 1891, Gramsci studied linguistics at university, became a journalist, later an activist in the Turin factory council movement, and then an official in the Italian Communist Party before being arrested in 1926 by the fascists. By all accounts Gramsci, who was never physically strong, suffered tremendously in jail after being sentenced to a twenty-year term; however, he was still able to study and write. After his death in jail at the age of forty-six his relatives were able to salvage hundreds of pages of his writings, some of which are now widely available as the *Prison Notebooks* (Gramsci 1975).

The *Prison Notebooks*, as one might expect, are not a tightly organized volume that systematically develops a readily identifiable and coherent set of themes. This point notwithstanding, the volume is one of the most important tracts of any post-World War I Marxist, containing analyses and commentary on topics as diverse as the role of intellectuals, education, Italian history, Machiavelli's Prince, and Fordism/Taylorism in America. Among the most interesting is his critique of vulgar Marxism in a section entitled "Problems of Marxism."

Gramsci was determined to put to rest any simplistic notion that the state and politics can somehow be understood as simply corresponding to the needs of a given mode of economic production at a given moment in time. He wrote:

> The claim, presented as an essential postulate of historical material-ism, that every fluctuation of politics and ideology can be presented and expounded as an immediate expression of the structure, must be contested in theory as primitive infantilism, and combated in practice with authentic testimony of Marx, the author of concrete political and historical works. (Gramsci 1975: 407)

Gramsci packs an amazing number of points into this one sentence. In addition to stating that politics and ideology must be analyzed independently from other structures, he reminds us that much official historical materialism has become a perversion of Marx, and that ultimately Marxian analysis is about using theory to guide political practice. For Gramsci, one of the many errors wrought by economic determinism was the predominance of structure over human agency. In a rather convoluted passage he (1975: 191) wrote:

> The historical "automatism" of certain premises (the existence of certain objective conditions) is potentialised politically by parties and by men of ability: absence of inadequacy (quantitative and qualita-tive) of these neutralises the automatism itself (which anyway is not really automatic); the premises exist abstractly, but the consequences are not realised because the human factor is missing.

The introduction of the "human factor" means the introduction of thinking, conscious actors, and while this may not seem like a particularly innovative notion to the Twenty-first century mind, in the context of the Marxism of the

1920s it was! As Gramsci went on to explain, humans are complex creatures because we carry and formulate complex systems of ideas about the world and our place in it:

> Each man [sic], finally, outside his professional activity, carries on some form of intellectual activity, that is he is a "philosopher," an artist, a man of taste, he participates in a particular conception of the world, has a conscious line of moral conduct, and therefore contributes to sustain a conception of the world or to modify it, that is, to bring into being new modes of thought. (9)

Thinking, conscious actors must be understood as being imbued with ideas, beliefs, intellectual conceptions, and understandings all of which must be taken into account and understood because of the fact "that 'popular beliefs' and similar ideas are themselves material forces" (165).

A consideration of conscious intelligent actors focuses our attention on one of the central concepts associated with Gramsci's work—hegemony. Anne Showstack Sasson (1983: 201) says that "most commentators agree that hegemony is the key concept in Gramsci's *Prison Notebooks* and his most important contribution to Marxist theory." As Sasson points out, Gramsci uses the term in several different contexts implying slightly different definitions thus making it somewhat difficult to understand his precise meanings, nevertheless we will risk adopting the fairly straightforward definition provided by Julia and David Urry. Hegemony is "the ideological/cultural domination of one class by another, achieved through 'engineering consensus' through controlling the content of cultural forms and major institutions" (Urry and Urry 1995: 279).

It is clear that Gramsci recognized the reality of differing modes of domination and control by the dominant class in capitalist society. One, more indirect, was accomplished by controlling consciousness and knowledge, and another, more direct, was in the use of state power:

> What we can do ... is to fix two major superstructural "levels": the one that can be called "civil society," that is the ensemble of organisms commonly called "private," and that of "political society" or "the State." These two levels correspond on the one hand to the function of "hegemony" which the dominant group exercises throughout society and on the other to that of "direct domination" or command exercised through the State and "juridical" government. (Gramsci 1975: 12)

The distinctions that Gramsci makes here between civil society and the state are an important theme in his work. Indeed one of the major sections of the *Prison Notebooks* is entitled "State and Civil Society." This section deals with a number of concrete historical descriptions of what can and has occurred when ruling classes face crises of hegemony that threaten the stability of an existing order. In an oft quoted subsection, "Political Struggle and Military War," he compares a social revolution to a First World War battlefield in which the state can be compared to an outer defensive ring, encircling civil society, just like a series of outer trenches might protect a military headquarters. The mere act of seizing state power would not necessarily result in the transformation of society as a totality any more than capturing the first line of defences would mean that a military campaign is over. Because Gramsci eschewed abstract and excessively theoretical intellectual endeavours, his discussion of the relationship of the state to civil society is laced with historical examples that illustrate the importance of historical and national variations in the precise arrangement of social institutions into the complex totality we call society.

Needless to say, given that the material was written while Gramsci was imprisoned for his political views and activities, for him there was little doubt about the nature of the state. In a discussion of Italian history, he begins with this observation: "The historical unity of the ruling classes is realised in the State, and their history is essentially the history of States and groups of States" (Gramsci 1975: 52). In an earlier 1919 piece, (Gramsci 1977: 73-74) which he wrote as a practising journalist, he noted:

> In fact, the laws of historical development were laid down by the property-owning class organized in the State. The State has always been the protagonist of history. In its organs the power of the propertied class is centralized. Within the state, the propertied class forges its own discipline and unity, over and above the disputes and clashes of competition, in order to keep intact its privileged position in the supreme phase of competition itself: the class struggle for power, for pre-eminence in leadership and ordering society.

Despite the fact that for Gramsci understanding the state was literally a life and death situation, he was never able to articulate a clear-cut and definitive theory of the state. He did however leave us with some important directions to follow. First, we should see the state as a complex entity characterized by both a unity and a separation of powers:

> Unity of the state in the differentiation of powers: Parliament more closely linked to civil society; the judiciary power, between government and Parliament, represents the continuity of the written law (even against the government). Naturally all three powers are also organs of political hegemony, but in different degrees: 1. Legislature 2. Judiciary; 3. Executive. (1975: 246)

Second, there are two primary functions of the state as illustrated in the role of law. The first function is clear: "The Law is the repressive and negative aspect of the entire positive, civilising activity undertaken by the State" (247). The second function referred to in this sentence—"civilising" activity of the state—has to do with the state providing education and basic knowledge to its citizens. For Gramsci, this role is contradictory because such knowledge typically includes the elements of a hegemonic ideology which serves to benefit the dominant class:

> The cultural state, is this: every State is ethical in as much as one of its important functions is to raise the great mass of the population to a particular cultural and moral level, a level (or type) which corresponds to the needs of the productive forces for development, and hence to the interests of the ruling class. (1975: 258)

So what then can we learn about the state in capitalist society from Gramsci? First, Gramsci theorized in the Marxian tradition, meaning that he made particular assumptions about the dynamics of and the relationships between the class structure and the state. He was clear, however, that these abstract assumptions were not to be confused with analytical or historical analysis because the precise nature and dynamics of the relationship between the class and state structures was never predetermined. This relationship needed to be concretely understood in each national context if it was to guide political practice. One last quote will serve to summarize Gramsci's contribution and analytical instruction:

> The conception of the State according to the productive function of the social classes cannot be applied mechanically to the interpretation of Italian and European history from the French revolution throughout the nineteenth century. Although it is certain that for the fundamental productive classes (capitalist bourgeoisie and modern proletariat) the State is only conceivable as the concrete form of a specific economic world, of a specific system of production, this does not mean that the relationship of means to ends can be easily determined or takes the form of a simple schema, apparent at first sight. (1975: 116)

In the end, then, in Marx's works there is no single consistent theoretical position regarding the state. David Held, in his book *States and Societies*, published in 1983, argues that Marx's study of the relation between classes and the state carried two strands of thought, although these strands "are by no means explicitly distinguished by Marx himself" (Held 1983: 25). The first strand, according to Held:

stresses that the state generally, and bureaucratic institutions in particular, may take a variety of forms and constitute a source of power
which need not be directly linked to the interests, or be under the
unambiguous control of, the dominant class, in the short term. By this
account, the state retains a degree of power independent of this class:
its institutional forms and operational dynamics cannot be inferred
directly from the configuration of class forces—they are "relatively
autonomous."

The second strand that Held "disentangles" is that "the state and its bureaucracy are class instruments which emerged to co-ordinate a divided society in
the interests of the ruling class." According to Held this second strand is
dominant in Marx's writing, but the first "is certainly a more complex and
subtle vision" (25-26).

Given that Engels and Lenin failed to elaborate on the theoretical initiatives offered by Marx, it follows that the "classical Marxism" position failed to
offer a clearly articulated theoretical approach to the state. The position ties the
state to the dominant economic class, but does not systematically analyze the
precise modes of domination that help to translate economic power into
political power. It is not surprising, then, that the revival in interest in Marx's
works and Marxian analysis that emerged in the 1960s should lead to an effort
to develop a more systematic theoretical approach within the Marxian tradition.

• SIX •

NEO-MARXIST THEORIES

As the twentieth century unfolded, numerous social, economic, and political developments occurred that led to a critical re-examination of many of the positions of the "classical Marxists." The twentieth-century maturation of capitalism brought no prolonged economic crises or revolutionary situations in the advanced industrial centres. Clearly there were periodic serious depressions and the rise of fascism in Europe but the post-World War II economic boom meant a continuation of rising standards of living in most western nations, a development underway since the turn of the century. In addition, the late nineteenth and twentieth centuries brought extensions of citizenship and democratic rights in most advanced capitalist nations. A broad range of social reforms, increased public funding of education, and the range of social services commonly characterized as the welfare state seemed to alleviate the worst hardships imposed by market relations. In many nations concessions were made to the working classes through the legalization and growth of trade unions and collective bargaining rights. There was also the emergence of what some have termed "mass culture" and a concomitant decline in class conflict.

As these developments occurred, the inability of "classical Marxism" to explain them became apparent. It was clear to many that the state was not merely acting as an executive committee managing the affairs of the bourgeoisie. Nor was the state merely acting as a repressive agent of the bourgeoisie, using rigid force to maintain the capitalist system. In many of the social and political developments the state took a leading interventionistic role, and conceiving of it as a class instrument of the bourgeoisie became more and more difficult.

The ultimate outcome of this situation was not the abandoning of the Marxian tradition but a series of ongoing efforts to revise and reformulate the Marxian approach to the study of the state. As a result, beginning primarily in the 1960s, scholars influenced by Marx produced a mass of new interpretations, concepts, and theories of the state. Numerous volumes, articles, and papers discussed the issue, postulated the basis of *the* Marxist approach, and criticized alternate conceptions. This massive production contrasts sharply with the 1930 to 1960 era, when there were few systematic and substantial efforts to re-evaluate Marx's thought. The key exceptions were scholars working with and associated with what became known as the Frankfurt School, and they contributed little directly to the literature on theories of the state *per se* (Held 1980; Jay 1973).

In the United States there was a renewed interest in the reformation of some of Marx's economic analyses led by Paul Sweezy, Leo Huberman, and Paul Baran and centring around the publication *Monthly Review*. In 1942 Sweezy produced a major introduction to and revision of Marxian political economy in the form of *The Theory of Capitalist Development*, which included a simple and cursory treatment of the state. For the most part Sweezy's work fares better as a descriptive effort than as an analytical study.

In his chapter "The State," Sweezy comments on the key role of the state in advanced capitalist society, and notes the essential difference between what he terms a class-domination view of the state and the more conventional approach:

> As against the class-mediation theory of the state, we have here the underlying idea of what has been called the class-domination theory. The former takes the existence of a certain class structure for granted and sees in the state an institution for reconciling the conflicting interests of the various classes; the latter, on the other hand, recognizes that classes are the product of historical development and sees in the state an instrument in the hands of the ruling classes for enforcing and guaranteeing the stability of the class structure itself. (Sweezy 1942: 243)

Sweezy emphasizes that for capitalist society the expressions "class domination" and "protection of private property" are virtually synonymous: "Hence when we say with Engels that the highest purpose of the state is the protection of private property, we are also saying that the state is an instrument of class domination."

Sweezy examines historical and empirical data relating to state actions, concluding with a summary of the principles governing the economic role of the capitalist state:

> In the first place, the state comes into action in the economic sphere in order to solve problems which are posed by the development of capitalism. In the second place, where the interests of the capitalist class are concerned, there is a strong predisposition to use the state power freely. And, finally, the state may be used to make concessions to the working class provided that the consequences of not doing so are sufficiently dangerous to the stability and functioning of the system as a whole. (249)

This statement raises a number of key questions, including precisely how are the state and capitalist class "connected"? How do those in the state know what concessions should not be granted lest they be viewed by the ruling class as a threat to the system? How does the working class make its demands for concessions known, that is, how does the state know when it is necessary to act?

It was to be some time after Sweezy's 1942 volume before neo-Marxists were to attempt to elaborate a theory of the state capable of addressing these questions. But, with the predominance of the pluralist perspective during the post-World War II period, it is not surprising that one of the first systematic attempts to elaborate a Marxian position in the late 1960s was also a systematic attack on pluralism.

MILIBAND'S CRITIQUE OF PLURALISM

In 1969 Ralph Miliband published *The State in Capitalist Society*, and started by noting the pervasive acceptance by western political scientists of the pluralist approach. He states: "One of the main purposes of the present work is in fact to show that the pluralist-democratic view of society, of politics and of the state in regard to the countries of advanced capitalism, is in all essentials wrong—that this view, far from providing a guide to reality, constitutes a profound obfuscation of it" (Miliband 1973: 6). He suggests that an alternate concept of the state may be found in Marxist analysis, in a Marxist approach which he argued was as yet undeveloped and required further elaboration. Miliband states that his volume will, in addition to criticizing the pluralist position, "make a contribution to remedying that deficiency."

The initial goal, a criticism of pluralism, occupies a dominant position in the book. Utilizing a Marxian concept of class, Miliband demonstrates that concentration and centralization of capital had resulted in a substantial concentration of power in the "hands" of the capitalist class and that the trend towards concentrated wealth was increasing, rather than decreasing as some had argued. According to Miliband this trend further reinforced the concentration of power in capitalist society. He argues that the owners and controllers of this private wealth can indeed be designated as a ruling elite.

Miliband admits the possibility of differences among those who have wealth and power; that is to say, there may be a number of different "elites." This fact does not undermine his argument, for, as he illustrates through the use of data on the class origins, educational backgrounds, and political opinions of the elite members, the various elites are homogeneous enough to be considered a ruling class:

> This "elite pluralism" does not, however, prevent the separate elites in capitalist society from constituting a dominant economic class, possessed of a high degree of cohesion and solidarity, with common purposes which far transcend their specific differences and disagreements. (45)

According to the pluralist approach, however, the presence of an economic elite, or even of a powerful economic class composed of the owners and controllers of large-scale capital, is not sufficient evidence to refute the existence of a pluralist society. Centres of power, pluralists argue, might be countered by other competing power centres. To critique this argument Miliband dissects the state into its various components—the government, the administration, the military, the police, and so on—and illustrates that the dominant economic class in turn dominates most of the decision-making posts in these major state structures. He notes, "The evidence conclusively suggests that in terms of social origin, education, and class situation, the men who have manned *all* command positions have been largely, in many cases overwhelmingly, drawn from the world of business and property, or from the professional middle class" (61).

Miliband presents additional evidence to illustrate the extent to which the ideology of the holders of the top command posts in state agencies such as the police and military is congruent with that of corporate capitalism. In addition, he suggests that there are other important state agencies whose function it is to promote the ideological justification of the present socio-economic system; these are controlled by the dominant economic class or its representatives as well.

On the basis of these arguments and the data he presents, Miliband concludes that the pluralist approach is inadequate as an analytical approach for explaining political power in capitalist society. Despite this conclusion it is essential to note, however, that he neglects the second task set forth in his introduction, the further development of a Marxian position or concept of the state.

POULANTZAS: POLITICAL POWER AND SOCIAL CLASS

During the period when Miliband was preparing his volume, a major theoretical work on the state from a Marxian position, by Nicos Poulantzas, was being published in France. While it did not receive widespread attention in the west until after its English translation, published in 1973, the Poulantzas volume *Political Power and Social Classes* (1968), stimulated further interest in the study of the state.

Poulantzas' point of departure was to also note a weakness in the "classic" Marxist texts as they relate to the state: that is that the classics do not contain a systematic theoretical treatment of the state. In *Political Power and Social Classes* Poulantzas attempts to outline the general theoretical and methodological contours of a Marxist problematic for understanding and explaining the state in capitalist society. According to Poulantzas, the basic concept to be used is that of the mode of production:

> By mode of production we shall designate not what is generally marked out as the economic (i.e., relations of production in the strict

114

sense), but a specific combination of various structures and practices which, in combination, appear as so many levels or instances, i.e., as so many regional structures in this mode. A mode of production ... is composed of different levels or instances, the economic, political, ideological and theoretical.... The type of unity which characterizes a mode of production is that of a *complex whole* dominated in the last instance by the economic. The term determination will be reserved for this dominance in the last instance. (Poulantzas 1972: 13-14)

Here Poulantzas suggests the existence of four distinct levels, regions, or instances in a mode of production: economic, political, ideological, and theoretical. In taking this approach he utilizes the epistemological suggestions of the French Structuralists Louis Althusser and Etiénne Balibar (1970).

An integral aspect of capitalist society is, Poulantzas argues, the class nature of that society. For Poulantzas the concept of class is a complex formulation. In a capitalist mode of production the concept is ultimately determined by relations of production, but it can be influenced by the "political and ideological regions" as well. Thus social class in a social formation must be understood by looking at its complex economic, ideological, and political determinations. Second, in elaborating his concept of class, Poulantzas introduces the concepts of fractions, category, and strata to assist understanding of the actual dynamics of class relations and struggle in a capitalist social formation. The concept of fractions is crucial for his work on the state, because he suggests that fractions are divisions within classes (broadly defined by relations of production) based on economic interests (for example, industrial, financial, and commercial capital).

Finally, Poulantzas suggests that power can be located in a power bloc which "constitutes a contradictory unit of *dominant* classes or fractions, a unity dominated by the hegemonic class or fraction" (296-97). The basis of the position of the hegemonic class or fraction cannot be abstractly postulated, beyond noting that it seeks to fulfil "the double function of representing the general interest of the people/nation and of maintaining a specific domination among the dominant classes and fractions" (141).

What Poulantzas attempts to do is utilize these various concepts in the formulation of a theoretical approach that can be used to understand and explain the state in capitalist society. He suggests that in a capitalist mode of production, the various instances or levels are relatively autonomous, although in the last instance the determinant role is played by the economic. As far as the political, the realm of the state, is concerned, in a capitalist mode of production it has the particular role of "constituting the factor of cohesion between the levels of a social formation" (44). Elsewhere he expands this theme, noting, "The state is precisely *the factor of cohesion of a social formation and the factor of reproduction of the conditions of production of a system"* (1972: 246). The fact that the state acts as a cohesive factor, basically attempting to ensure the continuance of the society's relations of production, does not mean that it is a neutral mediator of conflict, ensuring continuity and equilibrium. The concept of class, structurally determined, and the notion of power are important in this regard. For Poulantzas, capitalist society is a class society, characterized by a system of production which results in the expropriation of wealth produced by one class by another class, so that any mechanism which has as its function the maintenance of those relations, is not a "neutral" phenomenon.

Poulantzas thus suggests that the state's role is to attempt to ensure the continuing overall maintenance of capitalist relations of production. In this task he suggests that the state is not simply "governed" by *the* capitalist class, because often a *fraction* of that class might have hegemony and be able to control the state. The fact that in the long run the state seeks to maintain capitalist relations of production does not mean that in particular instances it cannot act against the interests of fractions of the ruling class to attain that long-term goal.

THE MILIBAND-POULANTZAS DEBATE

The neo-Marxist discussion of the role of the state moved further along with the 1969 publication by the *New Left Review* of a Poulantzas review of Miliband's book.

Arguing from the standpoint of French Marxist structuralism, Poulantzas begins by locating Miliband on the terrain of empiricist epistemology and criticizes him for a failure to develop a Marxist theory of the capitalist state. Regarding the overall position of the text, Poulantzas argues that Miliband's attempts to use empirical concepts to criticize the pluralist approach sacrifice the project because the "concepts and notions" of the adversary are legitimized by their use (1972: 241).

Because Miliband made this serious error, Poulantzas argues, his analysis is seriously compromised throughout. In a detailed criticism Poulantzas attacks Miliband's discussion of the role of managers, the bureaucracy, his analysis of the state branches, the forms of the capitalist state, and the role of the ideological apparatuses. In the process of developing this critique Poulantzas reiterates his position that an adequate analysis of the state should take into account the existence of the state as a specific instance in a capitalist mode of production with relative autonomy. In essence, Poulantzas accuses Miliband of developing an analysis that characterizes the state as merely being an instrument of the dominant class.

Poulantzas' criticisms were answered by Miliband in the following issue of the *New Left Review* (Miliband 1972). In his reply Miliband began by confronting the criticism of his method. In response to the criticism regarding his failure to develop an alternate theory, Miliband states that he indeed did develop a Marxian theory, briefly in the book and also in an earlier essay. As for the concern over his use of empirical data to criticize the pluralist position, Miliband argues that it was the only way to address the issue at hand, and again points out that there was a problematic implicit in his work. Miliband refers to Poulantzas' own volume, noting that in his study Poulantzas "errs in the opposite direction" by not providing sufficient empirical support for his theoretical concepts. Miliband notes a general propensity among the structuralists to give the empirical world less attention that it deserves. Miliband raises this point again, later on in the article, accusing Poulantzas of "structural superdeterminism" (259). In the rest of the review Miliband replies to the major specific criticisms. However, the essential focus of the debate, which revolved around the respective epistemological positions of the protagonists, had been established.

The debate between Miliband and Poulantzas was further developed with the English translation of Poulantzas' volume, an occasion that prompted a review by Miliband, again in the *New Left Review* (Miliband 1973b). In the review Miliband presents his major contribution to the debate in the form of a criticism of the approach adopted by Poulantzas. Miliband attacks the difficult language and abstract nature of the study, indicating again that these problems are symptomatic of the Althusserian structuralist approach adopted by Poulantzas. The lack of concrete analysis and the fact that the abstract analysis is based on a particular reading of Marx weakens the analysis, Miliband argues. The approach of Poulantzas, which Miliband had earlier termed "structural super-determinism," is now referred to as structuralist abstraction. The difference in terminology is important as structuralism generally refers to an epistemological position that is not necessarily the same as structuralist analysis.

In the review Miliband utilizes his general criticism of Poulantzas' approach as the basis for his major specific criticisms. The approach, structuralist abstractionism, is found wanting in its capacity to address the issue of the relative autonomy of the state, an issue that Miliband states "may be taken as the starting-point of Marxist political economy" (87). Miliband sees the errors of structural abstraction as being responsible for Poulantzas' failure to distinguish between state and class power, a problem that Miliband says results in the complete stripping of the state of any autonomy and a turn to "complete instrumentalism." Structuralist abstraction results in Poulantzas assuming that a relationship exists between class and state, something Miliband argues "has to be *explained*" in an analysis of a capitalist mode of production (89).

After Poulantzas had criticized *The State in Capitalist Society* Miliband had immediately responded, but after Miliband's review of Poulantzas no immediate response was forthcoming. Indeed, it was not until after a third party entered the debate that Poulantzas replied.

In an essay published in *Economy and Society* in 1975, Ernesto Laclau summarizes the debate up to that point and adds his own criticism of both positions (Laclau 1975). Regarding the debate over the respective epistemological positions, Laclau agrees that Miliband does not adequately and explicitly develop a Marxist theory of the state. However, regarding the suggestion that Miliband thus placed himself in the empiricist "camp," Laclau states: "On this point, however, I feel that Poulantzas' critique has gone a little too far" (96). Laclau criticizes Poulantzas' method and, although disagreeing at the same time with some of Miliband's analysis, agrees with Miliband's argument that Althusserian structuralism tends to lead to structuralist abstraction and formalism. Laclau argues that these problems are inherent within the Althusserian structuralist position and that its stress on theoretical practice—in which the creation of concepts is the basic operation—leads to taxonomy and formalism. The result is that concepts and symbols are developed at a level of abstraction which ultimately makes it impossible to determine their logical relations, and more importantly inhibits their capacity to explain the real world.

Laclau's criticism sparked a response from Poulantzas in which he replies to both Miliband and Laclau (Poulantzas 1976). Here Poulantzas directly confronts the epistemological criticisms of both Miliband and Laclau in a way that indicates a substantial shift from his position in *Political Power and Social Classes*. Poulantzas begins by noting that the debate is not one between Miliband and instrumentalism versus Poulantzas and structuralism. This view, he argues, is simply incorrect. There are, however, important differences between their theories, and Poulantzas criticizes Miliband's work as lacking a theoretical problematic and being rooted in an "empiricist or neo-positivist approach" (65).

First, with regard to his Althusserian structuralist epistemological position in *Political Power and Social Classes*, Poulantzas acknowledges that although this was once his position, it no longer remains so. He now rejects the central notion of theoretical practices as the source of scientific knowledge, and points out how the "concrete real" has re-entered his understanding of the production of knowledge:

> What we failed to see at the time was that, while firmly upholding the specificity of the theoretical process in relation to the "concrete real," we should have perceived the particular way in which the theory-practice relation functions throughout the entire theoretical process. (66)

What is the relationship between "theory-practice"? In the practice of research, Poulantzas says, "Real facts give rise to the creation of these concepts." "These concepts" are of course the concepts that one uses in theoretical explanation of the "real." This thought indicates a dramatic shift from his former structuralist position.

Poulantzas goes on to note that in his earlier study the only role for concrete data was its usage to illustrate theoretical concepts. Poulantzas now agrees with the criticism of his formalism, noting that it developed out of his battle with empiricism, an event that caused him to overreact. On the matter of his structuralism, Poulantzas notes that there are two distinct usages of the term; one that is general and encompasses all those approaches that tend to focus on the structural features of human society, viewing human existence as being influenced by forces beyond free will and choice; and another that refers to structuralism as characterizing an analysis that ignores class struggle in its critique of human society and history. Poulantzas argues that neither describes his current position, and to demonstrate this he addresses Miliband's specific criticisms regarding his view of the relative autonomy of the state, his understanding of class and state power, and his analysis of forms of the state. In each case Poulantzas seeks to demonstrate that his is not an Althusserian structuralist position *emphasizing* the impossibility of general answers and the necessity of concrete social analysis. The role of the general concepts is clearly to assist concrete analysis of specific social formations.

Near the end of the essay Poulantzas addresses Laclau's criticism, again agreeing that his past work was too formal. In assessing the reason for these problems, he again cites his former Althusserian epistemological position. He notes that this position even led him to consider the possibility of developing a general theory of the state, adding that he did not attempt the task at the time, but for the wrong reason. He now understands that the task is impossible because the state and class can ultimately be fully understood only with regard to specific analysis of various developing and changing capitalist social formations.

While Poulantzas devotes a good deal of the essay to his response to Miliband and Laclau at the epistemological level, he also further clarifies his theoretical position on the capitalist state, stressing a number of basic points. First, Poulantzas addresses the question of the relative autonomy of the state, indicating that in his opinion the precise degree of this relativity cannot be specified theoretically since the state can only be fully understood in an analysis of a specific social formation. In discussing the issue of how relatively the autonomy of the state is constructed, Poulantzas writes:

> I can give no *general answer*—not, as Miliband believes because I take no account of concrete individuals or the role of social classes, but precisely because the term "relative" in the expression "relative autonomy" of the State (relative in relation to what or to whom?) *here* refers to the relationship between the State and dominant classes (i.e., relatively autonomous in relation to the dominant classes). In other

words, it refers to the class struggles within each social formation and its corresponding State forms. (72)

Poulantzas notes that there are negative limits to this autonomy in that the state "can only correspond to the political interests of the dominant class or classes." He again argues that the question required specific empirical investigation to be fully answered:

> Yet, within these limits, the degree, the extent, the forms, etc., (*how* relative, and *how* is it relative) of the relative autonomy of the State can only be examined (as I constantly underline throughout my book) with reference to a given capitalist state, and to the precise *conjuncture* of the corresponding class struggle (the specific configuration of the power bloc, the degree of hegemony within this bloc, the relations between the bourgeoisie and its different fractions on the one hand and the working class and the supporting classes on the other). (71)

Poulantzas also restates his position on the role of the state in a capitalist society, noting that the capitalist state has "a precise role as political organizer and unifier, and as a factor for the establishment of the 'unstable equilibrium of compromises,' which role is constitutively connected with its relative autonomy" (71). Poulantzas explicitly rejected a structuralist explanation for the basis of state power, noting that when the structuralist understanding of power as located in institutions and organs is incorporated into Marxism a key aspect of the Marxist position is lost, and that being "the primordial role of classes and class struggle by comparison with structures" (75). For Poulantzas class struggle is "prime" and it is only in the context of class struggle that we understand the state. He notes, "The state should be seen (as should capital according to Marx) as a relation, or more precisely as the condensate of a relation of power between struggling classes." As an institution the state itself may structurally be "shot through and constituted with and by class contradictions" (76). The point is, Poulantzas maintains, that at the level of theory we cannot specify what these class struggles may involve, what form of the state they may influence, and thus the analysis at the level of theory is limited. We are merely to understand the state in capitalist society as operating to maintain capitalist relations of production, as being relatively autonomous from capital or any fraction thereof, and as being influenced and shaped by class struggle. There are a number of possible forms of state that one might find. The precise nature of each can be specified only in concrete analysis.

MILIBAND'S *MARXISM AND POLITICS*
Miliband made no further direct contributions to the debate, but in 1977 published a new book which elaborated on his approach to the study of the

state (Miliband 1977). In *Marxism and Politics*, Miliband makes it evident that the perspective that maintains that there are two Marxist positions on the state (his own instrumentalism and Poulantzas' structuralism) is incorrect. Poulantzas, having altered his position ("rectified" it in his own words), cannot now be considered an Althusserian structuralist. In *Marxism and Politics* Miliband develops a theoretical position on the state, thus making it evident that he is not an empiricist and, given the position he adopts, not an instrumentalist.

In his development of a Marxist approach to the state in capitalist society Miliband is systematic. His point of departure is a restatement of the basic Marxian premise that capitalism is a class society and therefore any notion of a community of interest or "national interest" has to be rejected. Since the class nature of capitalist society results in the existence of contradictory and fundamentally different interests among the classes, the notion of a state representing all interests also has to be rejected. The state is therefore not the universal representative, nor is it a neutral mediator. It is, rather, directly involved in the class structures and class struggles.

> It is not "above" class struggles but right in them. Its intervention in the affairs of society is crucial, constant and pervasive; and that intervention is closely conditioned by the most fundamental of the state's characteristics, namely that it is a means of class domination— ultimately the most important by far of any such means. (67)

The argument that the state is related to class and class struggle is not new in Miliband's analysis. However, in the passages that follow he elaborates his *new* analysis of how that relationship should be understood. First, Miliband notes that it is not a simple matter of the state serving the interests of the dominant class, because in a capitalist society the bourgeoisie itself may contain important internal differences or cleavages. The state must therefore not be understood as an instrument of a monolithic dominant class. Miliband notes therefore that the state, by necessity, "must have a certain degree of autonomy in relation to the 'ruling class'" (68). He discusses in more detail the theoretical position that understands the state as an instrument of the dominant class, noting three basic arguments that might support this concept. Each argument deserves consideration.

A powerful argument for considering the state to be merely an instrument of the dominant class can be developed on the basis of an analysis of the personnel of the various state agencies. If one conducts such an analysis, Miliband notes, it will be determined that in many cases there are definite class, educational, kinship, personal, and ideological "connections" between and among many of the personnel of the state and the dominant class. This evidence of personal and other direct affiliation between the dominant economic class and the personnel of the state can be convincing: "The bourgeois state has tended to be run by people very largely of the same class as people who commanded the 'private sector' of the economy of capitalist societies (and for that matter the 'public sector' as well)" (69). Despite evidence supporting this approach, Miliband argues that it is inadequate because it is possible to amass counter-evidence, instances in which the dominant class has not "staffed" the state, while the state has continued to serve the dominant class. In summary he writes: "In other words, the class bias of the state is not determined, or at least not decisively and conclusively determined, by the social origins of its leading personnel" (71).

Another argument developed to support the concept of the state as an instrument of the dominant class is based on analysis of the economic power of the dominant class. This argument holds that the owners of the means of production in a capitalist society are the group with the greatest amount of power. Thus they are clearly the most effective pressure group and are able to control or use the state to serve their needs. This argument, Miliband maintains, is also not adequate in that it simplifies the process of decision-making. As well, the argument is predicated on the notion that the dominant class is relatively homogeneous. In conclusion Miliband states:

> Capitalist enterprise is undoubtedly the strongest "pressure group" in capitalist society; and it is indeed able to command the attention of the state. But this is not the same as saying that the state is an "instrument" of the capitalist class; and the pressure which business is able to apply upon the state is not in itself sufficient to explain the latter's actions and policies. (72)

Finally, Miliband notes a third argument often presented to support the "state as instrument" position. This argument is totally different from the other two in that it involves conceiving of the state in capitalist society as an objective structure, impersonal and with a specific task given the nature of the mode of production. Miliband summarizes the position:

> In essence, the argument is simply that the state is the "instrument" of the "ruling class" because, given its *insertion in the capitalist mode of production*, it cannot be anything else. The question does not, in this view, depend on the personnel of the state, or on the pressure which the capitalist class is able to bring upon it; the nature of the state is here determined by the nature and requirements of the mode of production. (72)

Miliband notes that although the argument has a certain strength, as the basis of an entire approach it has serious weaknesses. Among the problems associated with adopting a strict structuralist approach is the tendency towards simplistic analysis—actions are explained simply as resulting from the larger structural role of the capitalist state. As well, Miliband sees in this argument a tendency towards determinism in that the analysis "deprives 'agents' of any freedom of choice and manoeuvrability and turns them into 'bearers' of objective forces which they are unable to affect" (73).

After examining these possible bases of an instrumental analysis Miliband rejects any approach that understands the state as simply an instrument. The state, Miliband maintains, is not merely an instrument in that it is a class state with an important feature: It has relative autonomy from the dominant class.

> While the state does not act, in Marxist terms, on behalf of the "ruling class," it does not for the most part act at its behest. The state is indeed a class state, the state of the "ruling class." But it enjoys a high degree of autonomy and independence in the manner of its operation as a class state, and indeed must have that high degree of autonomy and independence if it is to act as a class state. The notion of the state as an "instrument" does not fit this fact, and tends to obscure what has come to be seen as a crucial property of the state, namely its relative autonomy from the "ruling class" and from civil society at large. This notion of the relative autonomy of the state forms an important part of the Marxist theory of the state and was, in one form or another, much discussed by Marx and Engels. The meaning and implication of the concept require further consideration. (74)

After expanding on the theme of the relative autonomy of the capitalist state and offering evidence from other Marxist writings to support the argument, Miliband offers an analysis of the role of this relatively autonomous state in capitalist society.

> The main points concerning the forms of the capitalist state and its relative autonomy may be illustrated by reference to the functions which it performs. Briefly, four such functions may be distinguished, even though there is much overlap in practice between them: (a) the maintenance of "law and order" in the territorial area or areas over which the state is formally invested with sovereignty—the repressive function; (b) the fostering of consensus in regard to the existing social order, which also involves the discouragement of "dissensus"—the ideological-cultural function; (c) the economic function in the broad sense of the term; and (d) the advancement so far as is possible, of what is held to be the "national interest" in relation to external affairs—the international function. (90)

In this later and major work on the state, then, it is clear that Miliband takes a theoretical approach. The state is not merely an instrument of the dominant class but rather is a relatively autonomous institution. The state is tied to class and its major tasks are performed in a manner that seeks both to assure the continuation of capitalist relations of production and to benefit capital as a whole. For Miliband no analysis of the state that merely focuses on its personnel, the role of business as a pressure group, or the state's objective structure is totally adequate. Although these issues will be a part of any analysis of the state, for Miliband the issue of relative autonomy is more important.

What we find then in the more recent writing of both Miliband and Poulantzas is a considerable level of agreement. When their work is viewed in its entirety it is apparent that many of the basic differences in their earlier positions are eliminated as each "rectified" his position. In their earlier works each scholar was guilty of some of the charges directed at the other: Poulantzas of sacrificing concrete analysis in building his Althusserian structuralist position; Miliband of failing to elaborate a theory of the state. In the course of the debate, however, the mutual criticisms that the protagonists put forward were indeed taken seriously. In this regard the reply of Poulantzas to Miliband and Laclau, and Miliband's *Marxism and Politics,* are major works.

The state is to be understood as an institution with various components which operate in a number of ways to facilitate, promote, and maintain capitalist relations of production. The class structures of capitalism require an understanding that not only are there major divisions between the major classes, but also that internally there may be important divisions within classes. Given this latter fact, the state must be understood as having relative autonomy, capable of mediating the internal differences within the dominant class in such a manner as to ensure the continued existence of capitalist relations of production.

Since much of the earlier debate was over the respective epistemological positions of the protagonists it is useful to examine the more recent epistemological positions. In his reply essay, Poulantzas clearly moves away from the Althusserian structuralist position. In his more recent volume Miliband, in developing a comprehensive theoretical position regarding the state, demonstrates that his position cannot be characterized as empiricist. Both authors maintain that social scientific analysis must involve work that ranges over several levels of abstraction. The "concrete-real," the object of investigation, is understood and explained through the usage of theory. In this process concepts, which are the products of processes of abstraction, are used to develop theoretical analysis and explanations. General abstract theories apply at the level of the mode of production. However, the ultimate purpose of these theories is to assist in the analysis and understanding of the real world. Social analysis must therefore use these general theoretical systems in actual research, investigation, and empirical explanation at the level of the social formation. In summary, a theoretical explanation of the state in capitalist society is developed in order to facilitate an understanding of the state in a specific social formation.

ERIK OLIN WRIGHT: THE TESTING OF THE MARXIST THEORY

Miliband and Poulantzas both suggest that the state is to be understood as being relatively autonomous. Yet their arguments—perhaps due to the high level of abstraction—failed to answer a fundamental question: Why does the state in capitalist society, with its relative autonomy, tend to operate or function in the interests of capital?

Miliband and Poulantzas reject a structuralist explanation for this question and, similarly, both reject any simple "instrumentalist" explanation that would conceptualize the state as an instrument of the capitalist class. The state is not capital's instrument because of lobbying, personal or personnel connections, or the social background or ideological disposition of the state personnel. We are left, then, with a relatively autonomous state serving the general interests of capital, but we are not shown how this apparent insight can be used to develop a concrete empirical analysis.

Other Marxists have explicitly addressed these problems of using empirical research and "linking Marxist theory to data" that are apparent in the work of Poulantzas and the later work of Miliband. Erik Olin Wright's important book *Class, Crisis and the State* is a good example of this (Wright 1979).

Wright begins his study with a "Methodological Introduction" in which he argues that Marxist theory must be capable of being "tested" and of guiding empirical research: "It is also important to develop a more systematic way of understanding the causal relations between the structural categories of Marxist theory and the level of appearances tapped in empirical investigation." In his efforts to contribute to this task Wright develops a "differentiated schema of structural causality compatible with Marxist theory" (14-15).

Wright's explanation of structural causality is located in his various "modes of determination." There are six basic interdependent modes of determination, and he argues that these modes of determination explain the linkages and relations among the key aspects, categories, or elements of the structural processes of human society. The six modes of determination are: structural limitation, selection, reproduction/nonreproduction, limits of functional compatibility, transformation, and mediation. The key aspects of the social structure that he seeks to link via these modes of determination are the economic structures, state structures, state policies, and class struggles.

Wright's elaboration of the six basic modes of determination is, however, less straightforward in stimulating and assisting empirical research than his introductory comments would seem to indicate. The first two modes are relatively straightforward. He argues that some social structures establish limits within which other structures and processes can vary (structural limitation). He states that there are "social mechanisms that concretely determine ranges of outcomes, or in the extreme case specify outcomes, within a structurally limited range of possibilities" (selection). The mode of determination he refers to as reproduction/nonreproduction is more complex (even according to Wright); it refers to "a kind of limiting process" that "maintains the reproduced structure within certain limits of variation" (18-19). The limits in this case are important because Wright assumes that without the reproduction effect there could be fundamental changes in the structures—change that might threaten the entire system.

The last three modes of determination are even more difficult to use in empirical research because they refer to processes that determine whether a given state structure will be reproductive or nonreproductive (limits of functional compatibility), and to the manner "by which class struggle (practices) directly affect the process of structural limitation, selection and reproduction/ nonreproduction" (transformation) (21). Wright maintains that the limits of functional compatibility mode of determination is essential because it leads to an understanding of the complex dialectical relationship between, for example, class struggles and social structures. He notes that class struggle, "itself structurally limited and selected by various social structures, simultaneously reshapes those structures" (23). Although, as Wright notes, the efforts of classes to change or transform structures through class will not always be successful, the potential for transformation through class struggle must be recognized in social analysis.

He refers to mediation as "the most complex mode of determination" in that it involves the manner by "which a given social process shapes the consequences of other social processes." Wright explicitly points out that a mediating variable is different from an intervening variable in that the concept of mediation implies an impact or effect on the entire process, including all relationships involved. To illustrate he specifies schematically how class struggle mediates the relationship between state structures and state interventions.

While these modes of determination do not dominate all aspects of Wright's book, they are his basic concepts. Wright attempts to illustrate and expand some of the essential aspects of Marxian analysis; however, the volume ultimately suffers from the very problems he refers to in the introduction. The modes of determination that he elucidates have theoretical significance for an exposition of the difference between Marxian and non-Marxian analysis. But in the end they prove of little assistance in attempting to answer actual empirical questions.

LEO PANITCH ON THE CANADIAN STATE

While the theory of the state that one is able to extract from the Miliband-Poulantzas debate is extremely general, it has been useful enough so that others studying the state have taken and developed a similar approach. In a volume on the state in Canada published in 1977, Leo Panitch argues that an adequate Marxist theory of the state must accomplish three tasks:

> It must clearly delimit the complex of institutions that go to make up the state. It must demonstrate concretely, rather than just define abstractly, the linkages between the state and the system of class inequality in the society, particularly its ties to the dominant social class, and it must specify as far as possible the functions of the state under the capitalist mode of production. (Panitch 1977: 5)

A theory of the state capable of accomplishing these tasks, Panitch notes, will not only assist analysis, but will also actually "use" analysis in a manner "that will illuminate empirical and historical circumstances" (6). In his essay Panitch elaborates on his understanding of each of the three tasks.

On the question of the state's components Panitch writes: "The state is a complex of institutions, including the government, but also including the bureaucracy (embodied in the civil service as well as public corporations, central banks, regulatory commissions, etc.), the military, the judiciary, representative assemblies, and (very important for Canada) what Miliband calls the sub-central levels of government, that is, provincial executives, legislatures, and bureaucracies, and municipal government institutions" (6).

As for the problem of establishing linkages, Panitch notes that a theory of the state must avoid the structuralist abstraction apparent in the work of Poulantzas. Panitch states that the relationship between the state and the dominant class must be demonstrated in an empirical and historical context. Finally, with regard to the functions of the state Panitch refers to James O'Connor's work and his argument that the state has two general sets of functions, one related to accumulation, the other to legitimization (O'Connor 1973). Panitch notes that actually there are three sets of functions, those relating to ensuring that accumulation remains possible, those relating to the establishment and maintenance of "harmony" and a more direct coercive function. In the remainder of the essay Panitch demonstrates his understanding of the general adequacy of the Marxist approach by using it to analyze aspects of Canadian social development.

In stating that a theory of the state must specify "linkages between the state system and the class structure," Panitch demands that the essential problem left unanswered by both Miliband and Poulantzas be addressed. He notes that the essential question "of the *extent* to which the state is acting on behalf of the dominant class" is an issue that must be established empirically in each instance (7-8). Panitch himself proceeds to establish these linkages largely by examining the various personnel of the state agencies, finding that it has been historically common in Canada for people with direct connections to capital to staff the state. He concludes:

> The point to be drawn from all this is not that the state in Canada would be independent of the capitalist class without these specific linkages, given the balance of class forces within which the state operates. It certainly does suggest, however, "a confraternity of power" of such dimensions as to permit the clear employment of the term "ruling class" in the political as well as the economic sense in the Canadian case. It suggests, above all, an ideological hegemony emanating from both the bourgeoisie and the state which is awesome, which is reflected in the sheer pervasiveness of the view that the national interest and business interests are at one, and which certainly ensures the smooth functioning of the relationship between the state and the capitalist class. (13)

In his work Panitch does identify a central weakness in the thought of both Miliband and Poulantzas: namely, their failure to provide a satisfactory answer to the key question: Why does the state in capitalist society tend to serve the interests of capital? The answer to this question requires, perhaps, a more systematic elaboration of what Panitch refers to as the "linkages between the state system and the class structure."

SZYMANSKI: MODES OF CONTROL

A Marxist scholar who has addressed the question of the linkages between the capitalist class and the state is Albert Szymanski (1978). In his study *The Capitalist State and the Politics of Class* (1978), Szymanski argues that it is important not to assume that the dominant class is absolutely dominant in all ways. He maintains that while the capitalist class clearly is dominant, possessing as it does the major wealth of capitalist society, it would be mistaken to argue that this class can merely have the state do what it desires.

Szymanski argues that there are two fundamentally different means—direct and indirect—by which the dominant class influences the state and has it act in its own interests. The direct means or linkages are:

1) Direct involvement in the operation of the state by members of the dominant class.
2) Dominance through lobbying. Szymanski maintains that the capitalist class is able to finance the massive expenditures required to lobby the various state institutions.
3) Dominance through public policy formation. Szymanski argues that the

128

capitalist class controls and even operates public policy organizations that influence state policy. (23-24)

In addition to these direct means of control or linkages, Szymanski argues that there are four important indirect means of control:

1) The dominant class is able to influence the overall ideological development of the larger society; thus it influences the social environment in which the state operates. The dominant class is able to convince many that its interests are the national interest and thus actions against it by the state would be opposed by others not in the capitalist class.
2) The capitalist class makes the important decisions regarding economic development and thus it has the power to curtail or relocate production if the state does not act in its interests or if the state acts against its interests. The capitalist class generally controls the sources of financing that the state requires for its normal operations.
3) The dominant class has access ultimately to the military, either domestic or foreign, and in a crisis this mechanism may be used.
4) The dominant class finances the major political parties and controls the mass media and this facilitates control over parties and even governments. Since the withdrawal of financing of parties or massive negative public relation campaigns can result in a government or administration failing, these means of control are important. (24-25)

Although Szymanski's discussion of modes of direct and indirect control is important, his book shows a certain lack of theoretical consistency. Szymanski does not attempt to incorporate his insights into a larger theoretical framework such as that developed by Miliband and Poulantzas, and thus downplays the concept of relative autonomy to the point where his summary of the major points in a Marxian theory includes only "three essential ideals":

> (1) the idea that the state is dominated, and basic state policies structured by the capitalist class; (2) the idea that state policies normally facilitate and advance the interests of the capitalist class, although there are contradictions between what the state is required to do and the various capital class interests; and (3) the ideas of the class basis of politics. (32)

CAPITAL-LOGIC AND THE JESSOP CRITIQUE
One additional perspective that has emerged during the last two decades comes out of the work of a group of German scholars. Referred to as the "capital-logic school" or the "derivationists," these scholars have developed a critique of Miliband and Poulantzas, arguing that neither addresses the core

issue, which is the capital-labour connection. In their introduction to the collection *State and Capital*, John Holloway and Sol Picciotto summarize the capital-logic critique of other Marxian positions, arguing that there has been "an inadequate theorization of the relation between the economy and the political as discrete forms of capitalist social relations" (Holloway and Picciotto 1978: 3). The editors state the capital-logic solution to this problem: "The only way forward, we shall suggest, is ... by developing an adequate theory of this relation, a theory which founds both the specificity of the political and the development of political forms firmly in the analysis of capitalist production" (3).

At the core of this approach, then, is the assumption that by investigating the nature of capitalist production it is possible to develop an adequate theory of the state. Holloway and Picciotto summarize this central argument:

> The "state derivation" debate, receiving much of its inspiration from a revival of interest in *Capital* in the late 1960s, sees in Marx's great work not an analysis of the "economic level" but a *materialist critique* of political economy, i.e. a materialist critique of bourgeois attempts to analyse the "economy" in isolation from the class relations of exploitation on which it is based; consequently the categories elaborated in *Capital* (surplus value, accumulation, etc.), are seen not as being specific to the analysis of the "economic level" but as historical materialist categories developed to illuminate the structure of class conflict in capitalist society and the forms and conceptions (economic or otherwise) generated by that structure. From this it follows that the task is not to develop "political concepts" to complement the set of "economic concepts," but to develop the concepts of *Capital* in the critique not only of the economic but also of the political form of social relations. (4)

Proceeding from these assumptions, the capital-logic approach postulates that the central task of a theory of the state is the examination and elaboration of "how and to what extent the nature of 'the system' ... brings about an 'objective coincidence' between the 'functions of the state' and the 'interests of the dominant class' and how and to what extent changes in the system affect both the interests of the dominant class and, hence, the functions of the state" (5).

It is apparent from the terminology used here—state function and interest of dominant class—that this approach does not differ radically from that of Poulantzas. The essential criticism that the school directs at Poulantzas relates to his separation of the state from the economic. The capital-logic position centres on the fundamental intimacy of the productive process and political actions. Indeed, an understanding of the state can be "derived" from an analysis of the nature of production, especially via an analysis of the problems and contradictions inherent in capitalist production. The basic thesis locates and theorizes the state in the context of functions that must be performed if the contradictions of the capital-labour relation are not to destroy the system. In his essay in *State and Capital*, Elmer Altavater make this explicit:

> What then are these functions which the state assumes inside capitalist society, due to the impossibility of their being performed by individual capitals? There are essentially four areas in which the state is primarily active, namely: 1. the provision of general material conditions of production ("infra-structure"); 2. establishing and guaranteeing general legal relations, through which the relationships of legal subjects in capitalist society are performed; 3. the regulation of the conflict between wage-labour and capital and if necessary the political repression of the working class, not only by means of law but also by the police and army; 4. safeguarding the existence and expansion of total national capital on the capitalist world market. While all these functions may be called general characteristics of the bourgeois state, they nevertheless develop on the *historical* basis of the accumulation of capital. (42)

Bernhard Blanke, Ulrich Jurgens, and Hans Kastendiek—other contributors to *State and Capital*—criticize this statement to some extent, but restate the functionalist element in terms of state functions vis-à-vis the needs of capital and its reproduction. They argue that the state's functions must be not understood as state functions *per se*, but as necessary functions that must be performed for capital. The state, its form, and functions are to be clearly derived from capital's logic and problems (137).

The abstract and essentially functionalist nature of this position has been widely criticized. One of the most detailed critiques comes from Bob Jessop in his book *The Capitalist State* (1982). Jessop develops a detailed substantive and methodological critique of this approach, arguing that there is a tendency to take for granted a certain functionalist point of departure. Having accepted this point of departure, these theorists, Jessop argues, encountered difficulties because their "approaches are marred irredeemably by essentialism and functionalism due to their reduction of the form of the state to an essential expression of certain functional needs of the self-reproduction of capitalism" (Jessop 1982: 121). In his methodological critique Jessop elaborates a point that captures the essential basis of the capital-logic approach:

> In short, despite their methodological self-awareness and stress on a careful adherence to the methods of Marx, the proponents of form

derivation have failed to provide a fully coherent account of the nature of derivation. It is not a simple logical process of unfolding more concrete concepts from an abstract starting point along a single (albeit ramified) plane of analysis. (139)

Social analysis, Jessop argues, must produce concepts capable of being used and understood at various levels of abstraction. Concepts that cannot be used in empirical analysis, investigation, and explanation have little heuristic value. Jessop, explaining social analysis and conceptualization, notes: It involves the differential articulation of concepts of varying degrees of abstraction situated in different planes of analysis to reproduce the concrete as the complex synthesis of multiple determination" (139).

This brief survey indicates the richness and diversity of approaches in the recent development of the neo-Marxist tradition. Indeed, there are any number of additional theorists who could have been considered. If there is a central point that clearly emerges, it is that there is no single neo-Marxist approach to, or theory of, the state. The differences apparent among even the few theorists considered here are fundamental and significant enough to prevent any identification of a single neo-Marxist approach.

• SEVEN •

THE ANARCHIST CRITIQUE

All of the various theorists, theories, and schools of thought, in spite of their many and radical differences, do in fact have something in common. Because they are primarily concerned with explaining the nature, structure, and character of politics and the polity, none of them seriously questions the very need for organized political structures and relations of authority.

Without doubt these theories do assist our efforts to understand and explain the nature, operations, and structures of power, authority, and the state apparatus in capitalist society. They provide radically different analyses of the political process in capitalist society, ranging from the essentially positive pluralist endorsement of liberal democracy to the Marxist and neo-Marxist critical analysis of how class domination is reinforced through the various branches of the state. The theories all essentially assume the need for some degree of organized political activity, and to the extent that this need involves relations of power and authority and systems of administration they are willing to accept that it is a part of the human condition. While they may disagree about which organizational structures are the most appropriate and democratic, they do accept the need for formal political structures.

But not all political thinkers agree that formally organized political structures and systems of political power are necessary and inevitable. Indeed, various theorists have questioned this premise, since at least the time of the Greek philosophers (Kropotkin 1989: 88-89). The term most commonly associated with thinkers who have sought to challenge the assumption that structured relations of authority and power are necessary is anarchism.

As Frank Harrison (1983) argues in his important book, *The Modern State*, anarchist thought defies simple summation because it is "open-ended, thematic rather than systematic" (13). Yet thinkers who identify themselves as anarchists have raised important fundamental questions concerning the nature of the polity. In her classic definition of anarchism Emma Goldman notes that all forms of government rely on some measure of violence and are therefore inappropriate for the development of a fully human existence. She notes that anarchism is "the philosophy of a new social order based on liberty unrestricted by man-made law" (1970: 37). For Goldman, anarchism introduced the possibility of having a human society without formal government and laws, and without legal and repressive systems to enforce those laws.

One point remained uncontested within the liberal, Marxian, pluralist, and elite perspectives: whether the state was made necessary by human nature, or whether it was necessary to protect natural right or to ensure equal access for all to whatever would bring pleasure and happiness, the state was a given; it was seen as an essential part of the human condition. In the liberal tradition, for example, there was an assumption about the individual as the basic and ultimate unit of society and about social and political arrangements centring around that unit; individual development and happiness without a formally organized and structured polity were never an option. Anarchists and anarchist theory, however, have addressed not only the possibility of but also *the necessity of* removing all constraints to human development.

PIERRE-JOSEPH PROUDHON

One of the best-known anarchists, partly because of his long and sometimes bitter conflicts with Karl Marx, is Pierre-Joseph Proudhon (1808-65), born in France as the son of a cooper and tavern-keeper, a man, therefore, of "peasant stock" (Woodcock 1970: 378). In 1840 he published his famous tract *What is Property?*, a book containing one of the first systematic presentations of several key anarchist arguments in the modern era. In subsequent years Proudhon became a political activist, helping to organize the International Workingmen's Association or, as it came to be called, the First International. It was in connection with the political activities of the First International that Proudhon came into serious conflict with Marx. As Woodcock (1977) points out, Proudhon distrusted all grand theoretical systems and structures, believing instead that social and political thought had to develop and evolve along with the real world of social and political events it claimed to explain. Though Proudhon eschewed organized political party activity because he felt such activity tended to produce structures that hampered freedom, he was elected to the French Assembly during the 1848 revolution. In the Assembly he voted against the proposed constitution because, in his words, "it was a constitution" (1977: 14).

Proudhon believed there was a supreme principle that must inform all human actions, namely, a concern with justice. In his words, "Justice is the inviolable yardstick of all human societies." (1960: 44) While noting that all societies claim to operate under the principle of justice, Proudhon points out that in societies governed by the principles of either property or communism, true justice is not possible. Communist societies seek equality and the rule of law while property-based societies highly value what Proudhon called independence and proportionality. "But communism, mistaking uniformity for law, and levelism for equality, becomes tyrannical and unjust. Property, by its despotism and encroachments, soon proves itself oppressive and anti-social" (1977: 67). It is only when we establish a society on the basis of all four principles—equality, law, independence, and proportionality—that justice becomes possible.

Equality, in Proudhon's view, refers to equality of condition or latitude for action. All individuals must have the same opportunity to act, though, as

Proudhon notes, it is clear that not all individuals will end up with the same degree of "comfort," because the degree of comfort that our efforts produce will vary according to our individual achievements. For Proudhon laws are those limits on our action that are rooted in nature and in our knowledge of natural laws. But laws must be few in number and never violate individual independence, that is, individual autonomy. The recognition of individual intellectual and emotional differences is what Proudhon calls proportionality. The simple recognition of individual differences must not lead to the violation of basic precepts of justice and social equality.

A society constructed on these principles, Proudhon states, would be a synthesis of communism and property and would be called *liberty*. A libertarian society would be the result of adopting organizing principles that are "true, and in harmony with the laws of Nature and society" (1977: 68). Proudhon lists eight principles that a new social order would be based upon:

1. The indefinite perfectibility of the individual and of the race;
2. The honourableness of work;
3. The equality of fortunes;
4. The identity of interests;
5. The end of antagonisms;
6. The universality of comfort;
7. The sovereignty of reason;
8. The absolute liberty of the man and the citizen. (1977: 293)

Proudhon argues that the development of a social, economic, and political system based on these principles is the end result of a developmental process. Indeed, he states that the more ignorant a person is, the more obedient, and thus the degree of authority of some people over other people is proportional to their state of intellectual development. The more intellectually developed people are, the less authority is needed, because people who are intellectually developed will readily understand that: "All men are equal and free; society, by nature and destination, is therefore autonomous and ungovernable.... Whoever puts his hand on me to govern me is an usurper and a tyrant; I declare him my enemy" (1977: 166).

Proudhon makes powerful statements about the nature of political power in liberal-democratic societies and states. When describing his experiences in parliament he declares that the meetings left him "exhausted with fatigue and disgust." He states that in parliament he lost touch with the outside world and the masses, finally realizing that "the men who are most completely ignorant of the state of the country are almost always those who represent it" (1977: 111). The precise form of government is not the problem, as Proudhon argues: "In whatever form it may appear, monarchial, oligarchic, democratic—royalty, or the government of man by man, is illegal and absurd." The problem is the very notion of humans governing humans based on human systems of laws, because "The government of man by man is slavery" (1960: 47).

MICHAEL ALEXANDROVICH BUKUNIN

Proudhon was a contemporary of Michael Bukunin (1814-76), another theorist well known for his differences and disputes with Karl Marx, and it is clear that Proudhon's work had a great influence on Bukunin. Indeed, Bukunin referred to Proudhon as "The Master of us all" (1977: 378). Bukunin's background was much different, coming as he did from a wealthy, land-owning Russian family. It seems as if Bukunin engaged in rebellious acts all his life. He travelled to Europe to learn philosophy in the 1840s and became familiar with the works of Hegel, Fichte, and Proudhon. After becoming involved in the 1848 revolutions, he was arrested and transported back to Tsarist authorities, who kept him in prison for years. He finally escaped and went to the United States via Japan, eventually ending up back in Europe where be became involved in further uprisings in the 1870s, just before his death. Bukunin was a member of the First International but was expelled along with other anarchists in 1872.

The conventional wisdom regarding Bukunin's writings is that they tend to be disorganized and difficult to summarize and discuss in a systematic manner. Nevertheless, Bukunin developed a number of important themes. One idea he seems to have taken over from Proudhon relates to the evolution of human society and in particular its political dimensions. He links the evolutionary process to the idea of progress, writing that human society "moves in a constantly ascending line" (1960: 79). Originally the human being is "a wild beast, a cousin of the gorilla" but the historical process changes this bestial nature (1960: 80). The process of evolutionary change, Bukunin argues, involves a period of being in slavery to God, when we come to believe that God is the cause, centre, and source of life; however, we develop beyond this phase. The process is not easy, as Bukunin notes: The "historical negation of the past takes place now slowly, sluggishly, sleepily, but now again passionately and violently" (1960: 80). Besides illustrating a significant Hegelian influence, this argument focuses attention on the idea that humanity does indeed develop, progress, and move forward. The ultimate trajectory of humanity's development is clear as Bukunin declares, "Freedom must be understood in its fullest and widest sense as the destination of man's historic progress" (1977: 84).

Bukunin theorizes that the full development of human freedom must take place within a society: "We are convinced that all the richness of human intellectual, moral and material development, as well as man's apparent independence, is the product of life in society" (1977: 84). Elsewhere he notes that "the human race is the most social of all races of animals on earth" and outlines the ultimate end that humanity and society must attempt to move towards:

It is the triumph of humanity, it is the conquest and accomplishment of full freedom and the full development, material, intellectual and moral, of every individual, by the absolutely free and spontaneous organization of economic and social solidarity as completely as possible between all human beings living on the earth. (1966: 81)

Much of Bukunin's work, it seems, aimed at showing that this envisioned triumph of humanity and of all humanity's potentials was not possible without a radical change in the existing social, economic, and political relations. For Bukunin, people are naturally sociable. The failure to understand this simple fact has led some thinkers, Bukunin postulates, to proclaim the necessity for a state and the enactment of laws to control human behaviour (1977). On the contrary, innate human sociability means it is possible to hold society together on the basis of contracts freely entered into by people whose freedom is acknowledged and respected. Indeed, a free society can only be maintained by members entering into free, non-coercive contractual arrangements with each other. Bukunin summarizes this argument: "The liberty of man consists solely in this: that he obeys natural laws because he has *himself* recognized them as such, and not because they have been externally imposed upon him by an extrinsic will whatever, divine or human, collective or individual" (1977: 310-11).

Bukunin sees serious flaws in the existing state structures. For instance, regardless of the various philosophical arguments and political rhetoric that has been produced to justify the existence and structures of states, political power is a negative factor in human affairs. In powerful prose Bukunin links political power and domination:

Whoever talks of political power talks of domination; but where domination exists there is inevitably a somewhat large section of society that is dominated, and those who are dominated quite naturally detest their dominators, while the dominators have no choice but to subdue and oppress those they dominate. (1977: 109)

In addition to expressing his firm opposition to political power and domination in a general sense, Bukunin was also concerned about the nature of political power in capitalist society. Bukunin comments on the situation in Switzerland, where "As elsewhere, the ruling class is completely different and separate from the mass of the governed." Further, "Here, as everywhere, no matter how egalitarian our political constitution may be, it is the bourgeoisie who rule, and it is the people—workers and peasants—who obey their laws" (1977: 109).

Bukunin argues that the precise form of the government is not the issue. Even universal suffrage, the presumed basis of real democracy and freedom, is not a solution, because it creates an illusion "that a government and a legislature emerging out of a popular election must or even can represent the real will of the people" (1977: 109). Because political domination itself is unacceptable and the bourgeoisie necessarily comes to dominate the state, the universal franchise must remain an illusion. Indeed, Bukunin argues that there is something intrinsic to the holding of power that seems to corrupt people, for no matter how "democratic may be their feelings and their intentions, once they achieve the elevation of office they can only view society in the same way as a schoolmaster views his pupils, and between pupils and master equality cannot exist" (1977: 109). He discusses the feelings of superiority that follow and that make relationships of equality impossible, no matter how the rulers are chosen and the rules created. Elsewhere Bukunin's language is even more forceful on this issue:

> It is characteristic of privilege, and of every privileged position, that they poison the minds and hearts of men. He who is politically or economically privileged has his mind and heart depraved. This is a law of social life, which admits no exceptions and is applicable to entire nations as well as to classes, corporations, and individuals. It is the law of equality, the foremost of the conditions of liberty and humanity. (1960: 83)

For Bukunin, the obvious solution is to completely replace the formal structures, with their inevitable domination and despotism. This is a truly radical suggestion, but for Bukunin it is the logical outcome of the evolutionary process. Such a move is predicated on the expansion of mass education, which will aid the development of a truly free society in which humans understand their moral and social obligations to each other and act accordingly. The free society Bukunin advocates will be based on the "natural needs, inclinations and endeavours" of all people and involve the "free union of individuals into communes, of communes into provinces, of provinces into nations" and finally of nations into a world system (1960: 85). There is a clear utopian element in this thinking, but Bukunin does examine the practical side of political theory. In a critical assessment of Marx's ideas about post-capitalist society he refers to Marx as the Bismark of Socialism. For Bukunin a central problem in much of Marx's thought is its tendency to be associated with what he calls the cult of the state (1966: 84-85). He issues a dire warning: A future free society can only be created by the masses of people themselves, and we must avoid "the organization and the government of a new society by Socialistic scientists and professors—the worst of all despotic government!" (1966: 97).

PETER KROPOTKIN

Bukunin shared something of a common background with Peter Kropotkin (1842-1921). Both of them had been born into the Russian nobility and both had been expected to undertake careers in the Russian military (Shatz 1971: 184). Like Bukunin, Kropotkin was also influenced by the ideas associated with evolutionary theory, though he came to disagree with the thinkers who argued that the evolutionary process favours those best able to compete for survival. It is in fact mutual aid and co-operation, Kropotkin says, that have allowed the human species to survive and prosper, and future society should be constructed with an eye to further facilitating these processes.

For Kropotkin one of the most important developments in humanity's intellectual development was the articulation of the law of evolution. An understanding of how the evolutionary processes unfold is an essential first step to ensuring that humans conduct their activities in accordance with this basic law of nature. Interestingly, this argument was made by many other thinkers with diverse outlooks; thinkers as different as Hobbes, Locke, Comte, and even Marx. In the hands of Kropotkin the application of the principles of evolution to human society and history merely shows that the current stage of development is inadequate, inappropriate, and passing. What we need to understand, he says, is that our current social, economic, and political arrangements will soon pass and be replaced by more adequate ways of social organization. Human society must be organized in a manner that will "establish the best conditions for realizing the greatest happiness of humanity" (1960: 97). This logically raises the question: What are these conditions?

Though ultimately Kropotkin does not provide a precise picture of the social, economic, and political conditions that would prevail in the new society, he describes how that new order will be different from the society of his day. To establish a social, economic, and political order that would facilitate the fullest development of human potentials, all the various laws that have been enacted by humans over the years will have to disappear. Because human society has developed and evolved, most enacted laws have not only lost their purpose, but they have also turned into their opposite. Kropotkin states: "The law which first made its appearance as a collection of customs which serve for the maintenance of society, is now merely an instrument to keep the exploitation and domination of the industrious masses by wealthy idlers. It has now no longer any civilizing mission; its only mission is to protect exploitation" (1960: 99).

Kropotkin argues that there are three basic categories of laws: "The millions of laws which exist for the regulation of humanity appear upon investigation to be divided into three principle categories: protection of property, protection of persons, protection of government" (1977: 111). Kropotkin engages in an examination and critique of each of these types of laws, arguing that none of them serves the interests of the majority of people. The laws serving to protect property, for example, are unjust because they protect, for instance, a particular piece of property that has been appropriated by the law to a certain person at the expense of those who actually contributed the labour or produced the wealth that went into the property. Such laws "serve no other purpose than to maintain this appropriation, this monopoly for the benefit of certain individuals against the whole of mankind" (1977: 112). There are no equivalent laws ensuring that working people, the producers, are guaranteed the benefits of their activity.

Laws relating to the protection of government must be understood in the context of the central purpose of government. For Kropotkin the chief purpose of government is to protect the class that has economic power. Laws serving to protect government thus have nothing to do with serving the interests of all members of society, because governments do not and cannot serve the interest of the majority. In Kropotkin's words:

> We know very well—anarchists have often enough pointed out in their perpetual criticism of the various forms of government—that the mission of all governments, monarchial, constitutional, or republican, is to protect and maintain by force the privileges of the classes in possession, the aristocracy, clergy and traders. (1977: 113)

The other category of laws, those protecting individuals, must also be considered to be "as useless and injurious as the preceding ones" (1977: 114). This is because most laws, which are supposed to be about protecting people, are really about protecting their property and possessions. What is needed instead of the many repressive laws is a system of education and equal possessions, both of which would go a long way towards eliminating the various so-called crimes against people.

Though Kropotkin advocates mutual aid and co-operative social structures based on free and sociable individuals, he recognizes that humanity still harbours anti-social traits and is capable of anti-social behaviour. The problem with government and laws is that they exacerbate these tendencies instead of encouraging humanity's growth beyond them. As Kropotkin put it:

> The main supports of crime are idleness, law and authority; laws about property, laws about government, laws about penalties and misdemeanours; and authority, which takes upon itself to manufacture these laws and to apply them.
>
> No more laws! No more judges! Liberty, equality, and practical human sympathy are the only effective barriers we can oppose to the anti-social instincts of certain among us. (1977: 117)

Perhaps more than any of his contemporaries, Kropotkin had first-hand experience with the law, judges, and the penal system from being imprisoned in both Russia and France. In reflecting on his prison experiences Kropotkin described the debilitating effects, both mental and physical, and the complete loss of will to the point where the human becomes a machine. According to Kropotkin, there is no punishment more inhuman and devastating than the complete loss of liberty, and such treatment destroys the person, ensuring that he will never be a fit member of society (1977: 126).

In discussing the future Kropotkin again refers to the process of evolution. He sees anarchism as the next stage of human social evolution, a stage in which humans will live together in a free association. Kropotkin refers to the Red Cross as an example of the type of free association he envisions, noting that it came into being partly to deal with the calamities caused by states engaging in war (1960: 105). Working together, humans in free association will develop their potential and capacities in ways that are unimaginable for people living under the yoke of state domination (106). Kropotkin provides a glimpse of what he hopes will be the future:

> Suppose there is a need for a street. Well, then the inhabitants of the neighboring communes come to an understanding about it, and they will do their business better than the Minister of Public Works would do it. Or a railroad is needed. Here too the communes that are concerned will produce something very different from the work of the promoters who only build bad pieces of track and make millions by it. Or schools are required. People can fit them up for themselves at least as well as the gentlemen at Paris. Or the enemy invades the country. Then we defend ourselves instead of relying on generals who would merely betray us. Or the farmer must have tools and machines. Then he comes to an understanding with the city workmen, who supply him with them at cost in return for his product and the middleman, who now robs both the farmer and the workman, is superfluous. (1960: 107)

ANARCHIST THOUGHT: MORE RELEVANT THAN EVER?

These anarchist thinkers—Proudhon, Bukunin, and Kropotkin—represent only a small fraction of the large number of individuals who have contributed to anarchist thought. There are many others, including Leo Tolstoy, Emma Goldman, Murray Bookchin, William Godwin, Paul Goodman, Benjamin Tucker, Noam Chomsky, and Frank Harrison, whose work warrants careful analysis. Here we will have to be content with summarizing the essential tenets of anarchist thought and of its critique of the other state theories.

Although both liberalism and anarchism share a concern for the interests of the individual (Shatz 1971: xiv; Harrison 1987: 101B-102B), anarchist thinkers tend to see the role of human nature very differently. The very possibility of humans existing in a social environment that does not include formally constructed and organized political structures requires a human animal quite different from the individualistic, egocentric, competitive creatures that stalk through liberal theory. William Hocking describes "human nature" as including a "bent to goodness" that "gives the best account of itself when unfettered by artificial requirements" (1970: 116). But, while anarchists do not attempt to provide "blueprints" for a world without systems of formally organized political coercion, for many of them such a world could not be devoid of all organization. Indeed, the polity might very well be predicated on free association and co-operation among many different people who would be organized on the basis of many different characteristics, including professional and territorial considerations (Kropotkin 1989: 85; Novak 1970: 28). What people could share in common is the commitment to develop a mode of human social organization that would aid a more complete development of the full range of human capacities and potentials than does any other mode of social organization that has yet emerged.

By postulating the possibility of the development of a mode of social organization and existence radically different from what exists in most parts of the world, the anarchists share common ground with streams of Marxist and socialist thought. Both Marxists and anarchists might argue that the capacity to extend our vision of humanity beyond current conditions is an essential part of our continuing effort to better ourselves. An essential tenet of Marxist thinking is the necessity of not being bound by the appearance of phenomena and current or actual modes of existence. Anarchists and Marxists alike have critiqued the role of private property. For most anarchists, the existence of individually owned and controlled productive property is incompatible with the notion of a free co-operative society in which individuals live and develop unfettered by elaborate and formal systems of law. April Carter notes that for many anarchists the necessity of protecting property requires an extensive network of laws and regulations, In addition, the existence of individually owned private productive property entails the accumulation of personal power and authority by some individuals and organizations, a condition incompatible with a truly egalitarian society. For a number of reasons, then, the personal or individual ownership of society's productive resources could indeed be deemed to be incompatible with free and equal individuals existing in mutual freedom, security, and peace.

In stressing the primacy of the autonomous individual whose development must occur under conditions of maximum freedom and liberty, unfettered by the arbitrary authority of property and government, anarchists again share certain concerns with Marxist or socialist thinkers about the role of property and the state in capitalist society. Within the Marxist tradition the state in capitalist society is directly tied to property relations: The central functions of the state are related to maintaining and protecting private property and the larger system of capital accumulation; and both the legal system and the repressive and ideological apparatus of the state operate primarily in the interests of private property. For Marxists the abolition of private property will come about, in part, through the use of state power by those opposed to the prevailing relations of production. Moreover, in the period following the transformation of the systems of property relations that characterize capitalist society, the state will continue to play an important role. For example, in the period immediately following a radical reorganization of the productive relations in a capitalist society the state will, some Marxists have maintained, need to undertake whatever measures are necessary to protect itself against counter-revolution. Put slightly differently, those whose positions of wealth, power, and privilege within capitalist society have been destroyed will surely attempt to undo the changes. A certain vigilance will be required in the society to guard the gains of the revolution.

For Marxists, in the longer run in complex advanced industrial societies the state will continue to play important co-ordinating and organizing roles, especially given the abandonment of the formal structures of the market. While such a role for the state is different from its essentially repressive role in an immediate post-revolutionary period, relations of authority, power, and perhaps even domination are still involved. It is out of a concern with the possibility that the state in a noncapitalist society will become yet another centre of political power, controlling and dominating economic production and producers, that anarchists have come to define their position as non-Marxian socialism (Harrison 1987: 101B-104B).

Despite some similarities, the anarchist attitude towards the human individual, property, and the role of the state in creating a free and democratic society is radically different from the approach of most Marxist thinkers. Contemporary anarchist thinking is very much concerned with issues surrounding the creation of a society in which individual people have the opportunity to develop their capacities to the fullest, all within the context of a community that limits as little as possible a person's autonomy and freedom. For anarchists, human happiness, freedom, and full development are not ensured by the unfettered capitalist market, the bureaucratic welfare state, or centralized economic planning. It is only through interacting in a free community of equals that freedom and happiness can be realized.

In considering the arguments developed by anarchist thinkers it is important to avoid the misrepresentation of anarchists as advocates of chaos and violence. It is also important not to assume that anarchists are opposed to organization *per se*. Most anarchists recognize that some form of organization is necessary; however, they insist that all organizations be based on relationships among equals, and that the relationships be voluntary and non-hierarchical, usually with some system of rotational delegation among all members. Implicit in such a conception of human organization is the assumption that all

143

people are capable of assuming responsibility for their own lives and of controlling their own development.

The issues raised by anarchists and anarchist thought over the centuries are compelling. The anarchist critique of prevailing modes of thought is made even more poignant by the fact that anarchist theorists are at the forefront of the efforts to develop new insights into two fundamental issues of the 1990s, namely the environmental crisis and the continuing efforts to understand patriarchal and other systems of sex and gender relations. Ever since Emma Goldman, anarchist thinkers have drawn our attention to the fact that true freedom for all of us means more than the alteration of existing state and government structures. True freedom cannot be deemed to exist for anyone if one sex or gender continues to experience relations of violence, domination, oppression, and inequality. Among the many writers developing anarchist feminist thought is Marsha Hewitt, who notes that feminists and anarchists have shared much in common for many years (1986: 173). Surely one of the most important theoretical and practical tasks in the future will be the integration of feminist and anarchist thought and political practice.

If anarchist thought does nothing else, it should force us to critically evaluate the basic assumptions that underlie the traditions of political thought that characterize the intellectual legacy of western thought; and thereby lead us all to develop a critical appraisal of those approaches.

• EIGHT •

CAPITALISM, GLOBALISM, AND THE NATION-STATE

As we begin the new century and millennium the task of theorizing the precise nature, structure, and role of the state in capitalist society remains incomplete. The situation is further compounded and complicated given that for more than a decade powerful and influential voices have theorized, called for, and worked for the virtual abolition, or at least dramatic shrinkage, of the state. What are we to make of these new approaches to the role of the state? Is the era of the nation-state really over? How do the approaches fit with what is happening in the real world.

A theme throughout this book has been the necessity of attempting to connect the process of theorizing the state in capitalist society with the unfolding and development of the capitalist system. In Chapter One we looked at the economic, social, and political context for the emergence of the ideas associated with classical liberalism. We argued that the very emergence of capitalism as an economic system required an active and interventionist state to establish the necessary preconditions for the emergence of the market as the dominant force in shaping society. We subsequently noted that, as a discipline, sociology emerged within the chaos and turmoil that accompanied the triumph of the market as the organizing mechanism for society. It was partly its historical context that resulted in sociology's concern with seeking alternative ways of addressing the Hobbesian "problem of order." As capitalism matured in North America and the class structure took on its distinctive American form, new political and sociological theories and ideas emerged to explain and justify the operation of a liberal-democratic polity within societies character-ized by significant class and other inequalities. As capitalism continued to change and develop, the insights of Marx were deemed to be, even by many sympathetic to his method and critical insights, in need of revision. As a result, new Marxism(s) emerged, determined to revitalize the critical approach to questions of the state and rescue it from the years of theoretical neglect brought on by the taint of its alleged association with Stalinism and the Soviet system.

As we undertake to understand the changing role of the state in what is being termed the global era, we need once again to remind ourselves about the essential nature of capitalism and review how capitalism has unfolded, and is continuing to unfold. To do this we need to consider, briefly, some key developments of the modern era, that is to say, of the past several centuries.

Over the past decade much has been made of how capitalism is a global or world system. It is interesting that this observation is being touted as a new insight even though scholars since Adam Smith and Karl Marx have understood this simple fact. Thinkers as diverse as Smith ([1776] 1969), Marx (1973), Immanuel Wallerstein (1974), W.W. Rostow (1965), Karl Polanyi (1944), and Eric Wolf (1982) agree about one characteristic of the capitalist system: it is a world system. As for the dynamics that drive the system, that too has long been well understood.

THE RISE AND FALL OF THE WELFARE STATE

The Canadian philosopher and theologian George Grant (1965: 47) summarized the essence of the capitalist system: "Capitalism is, after all, a way of life based on the principle that the most important activity is profitmaking." In his essay "The Drive for Capital," Robert Heilbroner (1992: 32) uses the phrase "the rage for accumulation" to describe the inner logic of the system. He notes that the ceaseless accumulation driving the system is the central dynamic that leads to the continual changes that characterize capitalism:

> Capital thus differs from wealth in its intrinsically dynamic character, continually changing its form from community into money and then back again in an endless metamorphosis that already makes clear its integral connection with the changeful nature of capitalism itself. (Heilbroner 1992: 30)

Thinkers such as E. K. Hunt (1990), Broadus Mitchell (1967), Paul Baran and Paul Sweezy (1966), S.B. Clough and C.W. Cole (1967), and Heilbroner (1968) all argue that capitalism has passed though a series of distinct phases or stages, each marked by different forms and levels of technical development and social relations of production, and each characterized by different forms and roles for the state. Although the schemas employed by these writers vary, a periodization schema can be distilled from their writings:

1500–1770s	Mercantilism or Merchant Capitalism
1770s–1860s	Industrial Capitalism
1860s–1930s	Corporate Industrial Capitalism
1930s–1970s	Keynesian State/Corporate Capitalism
1970s–Present	Neo-Liberal/Corporate Capitalism

Cough and Cole (1967) use the term "mercantilism" to describe the initial phase of modern capitalism, although "merchant capitalism" is also appropriate given that trade and commerce were the central means of accumulating capital. The era witnessed the rise of nation-states across western Europe via a union of merchants and monarchs. During the mercantilist era colonies, as a source of wealth and power, were important for both merchants and monarchs, and the era of mercantilism was one of feverish colonialism. Various European states and their merchant allies explored and invaded almost every part of the world. The successful capital accumulation of the mercantilist era produced the conditions that gave rise to its transformation into the next stage of capitalist development.

In the period between the late 1770s and the 1850s a revolution occurred that transformed, among other things, the class structure, conceptions of wealth, the manner by which wealth was produced and appropriated, and the role of the state in facilitating capital accumulation. The industrial revolution, which ushered in the second stage of capitalist development, brought further radical changes as factory-based mechanized production came to dominate wealth creation. The new technologies and modes of organizing production resulted in productivity and output increases that would have been unimaginable just fifty years earlier. As Thomas and Hamm (1947: 566) point out, during the fifty years following the Napoleonic wars, for a variety of reasons "there was little interest in colonies" and a concomitant lessening of the importance of the state. Indeed, this was the era that would witness the emergence of laissez-faire, with its emphasis on the necessity of a free market, unrestrained by state regulation.

In his discussion of the development and dynamics of this first period of industrial capitalism, E.K. Hunt (1990) indicates that this "classical" phase of industrial capitalism was relatively short-lived. He writes: "The period from the mid-1840s to 1872 ... has been called the golden age of competitive capitalism." However, he points out that it contained the seeds of its transformation:

> Just as competitive capitalism seemed to be achieving its greatest successes, the forces Marx had predicted would lead to the concentration of capital began to show themselves. Improvements in technology were such that largersized plants were necessary to take advantage of the more efficient methods of production. Competition became so aggressive and destructive that small competitors were eliminated. Large competitors, facing mutual destruction, often combined themselves in cartels, trusts, or mergers in order to ensure their mutual survival. In the United States the competition was particularly intense. (Hunt 1990: 98-99)

Heilbroner (1968: 109) makes a similar point: "A system originally characterized by large numbers of small enterprises was starting to give way to one in which production was increasingly concentrated in the hands of a relatively few, very big and very powerful business units." Clough and Cole (1967: 639) also describe this process as one that "was definitely away from individual ownership to corporate ownership." Numerous scholars have argued that we can date the emergence of the modern corporation from the post-Civil War period (Baran and Sweezy 1966: 218; Mitchell 1967: 155; Heilbroner 1968: 109). Hunt (1990: 121) comments on the important changes that occurred during this period:

> During the late nineteenth and early twentieth centuries, capitalism underwent an important and fundamental transformation. Although the foundations of the system—the laws of private property, the basic class structure, and the processes of commodity production and allocation through the market—remained unchanged, the process of capital accumulation became institutionalized in the large corporation.

Most scholars acknowledge that the emergence of the modern corporation transformed the capitalist system and brought forth a series of new tendencies and dynamics. The large-scale production made possible by the concentration and centralization of capital soon encountered obstacles of its own making as raw-material supplies began to decline. In addition, the productivity of the modern corporation soon meant that domestic and local markets became saturated, and as a result profitable local or domestic investment outlets became harder and harder to find, especially in more industrialized nations such as Britain and the United States. According to Hunt (1990: 121), this change in the basic structures of the accumulation process saw "the accumulation process rationalized, regularized, and institutionalized in the form of the large corporation," and it was accompanied by a further important change, namely "the internationalization of capital."

These changes to the structures and dynamics of capitalism led to the emergence, within the period of corporate industrial capitalism, of what is commonly referred to as the age of the "New Imperialism." The geographical expansion associated with this new imperialism differed from mercantile colonialism in that it involved an unprecedented internationalization of capital as the corporations competed on a global scale for raw materials, markets, and investment outlets. Clough and Cole (1967: 618) note that after about 1875 a number of factors produced a renewed interest in colonial expansion:

> There was a need for new markets to absorb the goods produced by Europe's ever expanding productive equipment. There was a need for raw materials to satisfy the maws of European industry and of foodstuffs to feed Europe's ever growing population. There was a need, so it was believed, for places to invest capital where the return would be high and the danger of default for political reasons would be slight. And there was thought to be a need for colonies to relieve the pressure of population—of overpopulation—in Europe.

Thomas and Hamm (1944: 571) summarize the characteristics of the new imperialism: "These, then—markets for manufacturers, sources of raw materials, above all, places for investment of surplus capital—are the main reason for imperialism."

The internationalization of capital and the global competition for raw materials, markets, and investment outlets were key factors leading to the First World War. That war proved to be a turning point in global relations, marking the beginning of the end for the British Empire and the emergence of the United States as the hegemonic world economic and military power. Despite the unimaginable tragedy of the war, western Europe and North America experienced prosperity and economic growth throughout the first three decades of the twentieth century. Indeed, it is possible to argue that the boom period from the turn of the century to the Great Depression of the 1930s was a kind of golden age of corporate capitalism, although some scholars, such as Baran and Sweezy, maintain that this prosperity was based on a series of unique historical contingencies. In any event, in 1929 the system suffered a nearly total collapse as the international capitalist system entered a severe worldwide crisis.

The Depression wrought many changes, but perhaps none was as important as the revolution that occurred in economic theory and the role of the state. Keynesian economics ushered in a new era of capitalism that included a widespread acceptance of the notion that state intervention in the economy is both legitimate and essential during periods of crisis. Government expenditures as a means of increasing aggregate demand were coupled with increased government regulation designed to smooth out some of the contradictions and excesses of the market, producing what Heilbroner refers to as "guided capitalism." The potential impact of government expenditures on the economy was demonstrated by the very fact that the Depression did come to an end and was replaced by prosperity as a result of massive state spending associated with the preparation for, and the conduct of, the Second World War. Students of history use various terms such as "warfare economy" and the "military industrial complex" to describe the new institutional structures and economic arrangements characterizing the intimate relationship that formed between large industry and the state.

The eventual Allied victory did not bring an end to government economic intervention, as the Bretton Woods Conference of 1944 and the postwar Marshall Plan established a framework for sustained government expenditures geared to rebuilding shattered economies and keeping them firmly within the capitalist fold. The bulk of the financial and other resources used in the massive postwar rebuilding process originated in the United States, now the unchallenged leader of the capitalist world. The outbreak of the Korean War in 1950, the emergence of the Cold War, the massive expenditures necessary to provide an infrastructure for the postwar baby boom, the spread of suburbia, and the growing space race all contributed to two decades of prosperity. In addition to, and perhaps more important than, these specific expenditures was the emergence of what has become known as the welfare state. Gary Teeple (2000: 15) provides an excellent explanation:

> Although sometimes used as a generic term for government intervention "on many fronts," the welfare state can also be seen as a capitalist society in which the state has intervened in the form of social policies, programs, standards, and regulations in order to mitigate class conflict and to provide for, answer, or accommodate certain social needs for which the capitalist mode of production in itself has no solution or makes no provision.

Teeple argues that the typical welfare state involved state intervention in four distinct areas, all of them vital to the maintenance of the overall system and the postwar boom. According to Teeple (2000: 15), these areas included, first, actions and policies in the areas of education and health care to facilitate "*the physical propagation of the working class and its preparation for the labour market.*" The second area of activity involved "regulations on the minimum wage, hours of work, child labour, retirement age, education/training, injury insurance, immigration," and other dimensions of labour-market control. The state's third major focus was attempting to minimize labour-capital conflict in the actual arena of production through the provision of an "institutional framework for class conflict (collective bargaining) and to protect the workers from the worst effects of the exploitation by capital." The fourth and last form of state intervention was the "provision of income assurance for the '*unproductive' and after-productive life*" (2000: 15), a reference to pensions, social assistance, and the like.

Stephen McBride and John Shields refer to the same set of policies as the "Keynesian Welfare State," arguing that in the aftermath of the Great Depression and the Second World War it was essential to humanize capitalism, and the state undertook to "provide a better integration of the working class into a reconstituted capitalism" (McBride and Shields 1993: 9). They note that the provision of direct social benefits, regulation of labour and the economy, and the provision of a range of welfare benefits, while often secured only after forms of class struggle, was actually "part of the terms of a peace formula including labour and other previously socially disenfranchised groups" (14).

Just as there was something in the logic of the system of competitive capitalism that led to its transformation to corporate capitalism, so too did the logic of the era of Keynesian state/corporate capitalism arguably contain the seeds of its own transformation. Among the contradictions was the fact that the prosperity and stability of the postwar welfare state were predicated on high levels of government spending and an associated growth in government deficits. In addition, by the end of the 1960s the success of the Marshall Plan had begun to create problems and tensions in the international market as western European and Japanese corporations started to challenge the traditional markets of U.S.-based multinational corporations. Added to this were the problems associated with growing government debts—debts, to be sure, that had in large part been incurred as a result of spending in areas that directly benefited the corporate sectors, as in the expansion of the military and the space race. Other international events, such as the emergence of OPEC, accentuated the instability of the international system, so much so that by the 1970s another crisis was looming.

The growing international competition that accompanied the fiscal crisis of the state in many western nations gave rise to a sustained and well-articulated critique of Keynesian economics and the state practices that had sustained the system since the Great Depression. The growing popularity of supply-side and monetarist economics and ascendancy of governments committed to state cutbacks under the banner of neo-conservative (actually neo-liberal) philosophies ushered in a new era of capitalist development.

While the terms neo-liberal and neo-conservative have both been used to describe the destruction of the Keynesian welfare state, as Joyce Green (1996: 112) points out, these two descriptors refer to slightly different phenomena:

> "Neoliberalism" is an ideology that advocates an economic arena free of government regulation or restriction, including labour and environmental legislation, and certainly free of government action via public ownership. It advocates retreat from welfare's publicly funded commitments to equity and social justice. It views citizenship as consumption and economic production. This, not coincidentally, is compatible with and advances in tandem with "neoconservatism," an ideology advocating a more hierarchal, patriarchal, authoritarian and inequitable society.

The rhetoric of deregulation, fiscal responsibility, and freeing the market from the fetters and burdens of government intervention and interference began to dominate the actions and policies of more and more governments. As they undertook massive withdrawals from previous responsibilities and initiatives, governments also faced restrictions and limitations on their actions as a result of the terms and conditions of international agreements such as GATT (General Agreement on Tariffs and Treaties) and the ongoing authority and power of agencies such as the International Monetary Fund, the World Bank, and the World Trade Organization. The power of nation-states and capital with a regional or national base paled in the face of global capital supported by transnational international accords. The accumulation strategies and plans of giant multinational corporations became increasingly based on calculations concerning inputs, labour supplies, and markets that were truly global in scope. Teeple (2000: 5) describes the emerging era and how is it distinguishable from the previous period:

> We have entered a transitional era between two phases in the development of capitalism. In this period there has been a profound shift from a mode of production based on semi-automated processes, sometimes referred to as advanced Fordism, to a more automated mode based on microelectronics and computer applications. In this transition, in which nationally based economic development has been more or less transfigured into a self-generating global economy, all the social and political institutions associated with the national economy come into question and indeed begin to undergo a commensurate transformation.

Capitalism, then, has indeed passed through a series of distinctive stages or epochs as it has evolved. Throughout these various stages of development the inner logic or *raison d'être* of the capitalist system has remained unchanged: the system is driven by the pre-eminent drive of capital to accumulate. While the goal of capital has remained constant, its precise form and structure have changed as a result of the unmistakable tendency towards the concentration, centralization, and internationalization of capital.

BEYOND THE WELFARE STATE?

Is there still a role, then, for the contemporary nation-state in the so-called global era? As one could surmise, given the historical context, some critics would argue that the nation-state is a relic of the past and has become largely irrelevant. For example, several speakers at a 1996 symposium on the future of Canada succinctly summarized the prevailing opinion that Canadians have little choice but to adjust our public policy for the global era. One of them noted, "The success of the current globalization experiment depends on many factors which are not guaranteed. First, developed nations must maintain open borders to imports from developing nations. This is best ensured by an economic system which is not susceptible to political pressure within those countries" (Brown 1996: 114). As astounding for placing deliberate limitations on democracy as this justification is (with its recognition that this is an "experiment" without controls), it was still more qualified than another claim made at the conference: "The Canada that we have come to know and love no longer exists! There is no viable status quo! We have to remake our nation and society in the light of irreversible external forces of globalization and of the knowledge/information revolution" (Courchene 1996: 45).

Politicians of a neo-conservative inclination and the mass media have also popularized the general notion that we are in a global era in which nation-states are somehow impelled by the constraints and strictures of a global market. The periods around the presentation of government budgets seem to provide the media with an opportunity to warn politicians that they are no longer really in control. For example, at the time of the 1995 Canadian federal budget the *Globe and Mail* ran a column in which the president of a Chicago investment house asked rhetorically, "Is Moody's the newest superpower?"(March 6, 1995), less than a week after running a commentary from the *New York Times* entitled "Don't Mess with Moody's" (*Globe and Mail*, February 27, 1995). Between the time that these articles ran, in another commentary headlined "Dollar shows what world thinks of budget," Terence Corcoran reminded Canadians that the really important measure of the budget was the reaction of international finance markets (*Globe and Mail*, March 3, 1995). Writing in the *New Left Review* Linda Weiss (1997: 4) summarized the message of these spokespersons of inevitable and unfettered globalization:

> According to this logic, states are now virtually powerless to make real policy choices; transnational markets and footloose corporations have so narrowly constrained policy options that more and more states are being forced to adopt similar fiscal, economic and social policy regimes. Globalists therefore predict convergence on neoliberalism as an increasing number of states adopt the lowtaxing, market based ideals of the American model.

Academics have also argued that we are in a new era in which the traditional role and power of the nation-state have been radically altered. For example, although he operates at a much more sophisticated theoretical level, in *The Global Age* Martin Albrow takes the point one step further by suggesting that a new global state is emerging. He writes:

> The global shift leads necessarily to a reconceptualization of the state. It desegregates the linkage of nation and state which national elites managed to effect and focuses attention on the development of institutionalized practices operating at the transnational level, and on the operation of global relevancies in the day-to-day activities of ordinary people. (Albrow 1997: 172)

Albrow argues that the emergence of a world society is accompanied by the emergence of a world state, but he fails to provide conceptual clarity for either concept.

Several other scholars have argued that the nation-state is losing its efficacy to govern. In his important study of the decline of the welfare state, Teeple sounds a warning about the potential political implications of globalization. He says: "For the state the consequences of economic globalization are above all those of erosion of its functions and redefinition at the international level" (Teeple 2000: 73-74). After commenting on how the nation-state is being made somewhat unnecessary or redundant because transnational capital has superseded and/or replaced national capital, he adds:

> Without fear of exaggeration, it can be said that the national state has lost and continues to lose much of its sovereignty, although the degrees of independence vary with the degree of remaining integrity to national economic and military formations. It is not so much that a political state cannot act independently because of the erosion or usurpation of its powers, but that its *raison d'être*—the existence of a nationally defined capitalist class—has been waning. Taking its place has been the rise of an international capitalist class with global interests. (2000: 75)

In *When Corporations Rule the World,* David Korten (1995: 94) sounds a similar warning: "Corporations have emerged as the dominant governance institutions on the planet." He notes that among the problems we face as a result of the growth of transnational corporations is that the marketplace (which governs more and more dimensions of our existence) is itself governed by a special kind of "democracy": "In the market, one dollar is one vote, and you get as many votes as you have dollars. No dollar, no vote" (66). Korten aptly summarizes his concerns and warnings: "The greater the political power of the corporations and those aligned with them, the less the political power of the people, and the less meaningful democracy becomes" (140).

AN ALTERNATIVE VIEW: THE STATE IS STILL RELEVANT
While some theorists claim that the state has lost virtually all its power, and scholars such as Teeple and Korten are concerned that the nation-state is losing power, others have maintained that it is erroneous to place too much emphasis on the new globalization and the apparent attendant loss of national state power. Perhaps the most vigorous proponents of this view are found in the pages of *Monthly Review*. The title of William Tabb's article, "Globalization Is *An* Issue, The Power of Capital Is *The* Issue" (his emphasis), tells the story as he warns that it is defeatist for workers to accept that the power of global capital is supreme (Tabb 1997: 21). In their articles and debates with others, Harry Magdoff and Ellen Meiksins Wood repeatedly argue that while capitalism is changing, as it always has, it remains capitalism, and as such the nation-state remains essential to its continued functioning. Meiksins Wood (1998: 42) states:

> Besides I don't accept the premise of the "globalization thesis" ... that the importance of the state and political power declines in pro-

portion to globalization. On the contrary, I think (as I have been repeating far too often, and as Harry Magdoff explains in this issue's Review of the Month more clearly than I have ever been able to do) that capital now needs the state more than ever to sustain maximum profitability in a global market.

In their analysis of the possibilities of worker resistance to globalization, Judy Fudge and Harry Glasbeek (1997: 220) concur, noting, "We observe that despite repeated assertions about nation-states being outmoded political units, the very roles that governments of nation-states are asked to play on behalf of the forces that favour the development of a differently structured capitalism— a globalized one—make them a pertinent and vital site of struggle." In an analysis of the role of the nation-state in regulating banking and financial transactions, Ethan Kapstein (1994: 2) states the objective of his study: "If I can show that states are responding to the challenges posed by globalization in this area and that they remain the single most important actors, then we will expect to find them playing a key role in governing other sectors of the global economy as well." In his conclusions Kapstein notes that his findings support the initial contention that what is emerging are nation-states with a two-level structure, "with international cooperation at the upper level and home country control below" (177-78).

Robert Boyer and Daniel Drache bring together an important set of essays in *States against Markets: The Limits of Globalization*. The collection contains several well-articulated arguments for the need to continue paying close attention to the state. In his essay Boyer concludes that free markets simply have not been able to provide the goods required by the majority of the population, and therefore "The state remains the most powerful institution to channel and tame the power of the markets" (Boyer 1996: 108). In her analysis of the impact of deregulation in the public and private spheres, Janine Brodie (1996a) convincingly argues that it is not that the state that has lost its relevance and power; it is rather that states have adopted quite radically different policies. Her argument meshes with the approach of Claus Offé in his "Aspects of the Regulation–Deregulation Debate," in which he argues that deregulation is itself a form of state intervention. Offé notes: "To be sure … invocations of a market–liberal pathos of freedom fail to notice that a politics of deregulation, no less than one of regulation, has a character of massive state 'intervention.' For both cases involve a decisive change in the situations and market opportunities brought about by public policy" (Offé 1996: 75).

B. Mitchell Evans, Stephen McBride, and John Shields have also argued that, while the nation-state's role and function are being transformed by globalization, it is a mistake to underestimate its continued importance. The position that claims the nation-state is irrelevant or has lost most of its power serves "to mask the active role the state has played in establishing the governance mechanisms and the new state form congruent with a system of neo-liberal regionalised trading and investment blocks" (Evans, McBride, and Shields 1998: 18). They buttress their claim that "nation-states, however, are far from irrelevant" (19) with a variety of arguments concerning the new roles that the nation-state must take on in the global era.

David Held, who remains one of the most important political thinkers of our day, has in recent years added to his impressive contribution with one of the most systematic and thoughtful theoretical treatises on globalization and the state yet produced. The book, *Democracy and the Global Order: From the Modern State to Cosmopolitan Governance* (1995) builds on his outstanding capacity to summarize difficult and complex arguments. He begins by tracing the origins and history of the nation-state and liberal-democratic theory, but the real focus of the study is the fate of the nation-state in the global era. While offering an innovative model of global governance, Held notes that the nation-state has not become totally irrelevant. He argues: "If the global system is marked by significant change, this is perhaps best conceived less as an end of the era of the nation-state and more as a challenge to the era of 'hegemonic states'—a challenge which is as yet far from complete" (Held 1995: 95). Later he repeats the theme: "Global processes should not be exaggerated to represent either a total eclipse of the states system or the simple emergence of an integrated world society" (136). The task that Held undertakes, so important to current political theory, is to examine the consequences and implications of the rise of international and intra-state entities for democratic theory and the state. He notes that his efforts are "motivated by the necessity to rethink the theory of democracy to take account of the changing nature of the polity both within pre-established borders and within the wider system of nation-state and global forces" (144).

In a sense, the gauntlet that Held throws down is almost as sharp a challenge as feminism presents to existing theory. Held suggests that we have no choice other than to think our way through and around the existence of global structures and relations of power. Such centres and relations of power now exist; it is just that we do not theorize them, control them, understand them, or even realize they exist (Held 1995: 138-39). Held encourages us to engage in democratic thought experiments in order to conceive of new ways of understanding the multi-dimensional relations of power that characterize the contemporary era. He argues that there are seven essential sites of power ranging from the personal level of our bodies through our cultural and civic associations to the legal and regulatory agencies that formulate and control law (Chapter 8). In his final chapter he outlines what he terms a cosmopolitan model of democracy and postulates the possibility of radically new international governance structures and processes that would integrate democratic governance principles into what must be termed the structures of a global polity.

While there are many more contributors to this debate, the current literature addressing the issue of the relevance (or irrelevance) of the nation-state contains at least three problems. Firstly, there are too few empirical historical studies that might cast light on what is actually happening with regard to state policy and action. Secondly, in the heat of the debate positions become polarized, and as a result little or no attention is paid to the merits and strengths of the various positions, and synthesis and development are given short shrift. Lastly, the proponents on both sides of the debate—for both a strong and weak globalization thesis (terms borrowed from Weiss)—have not attempted to demonstrate how their positions impact our understanding of the state, in either its weakened or normal condition. In short, where do we find ourselves in terms of the development of state theory? What, if any, advances have been made over the last decade in our capacity to understand and explain the development and implementation of state policy and action? Beore attempting to offer final critical comments and suggestions for new directions, we need to review the current situation in pluralist and Marxian thought.

RECENT DEVELOPMENTS IN EXISTING PERSPECTIVES: PLURALISM

In all the attempts to understand the operations of the polity, government, and the state over the course of the past century, the pluralist perspective has been the most commonly adopted approach in North America, both among the intelligentsia and the public at large. Pluralism's appeal rests in its emphasis on western social and political systems as being basically stable, democratic, and open (Rossides 1968: 157; Tumin 1967: 45-46). The core thesis of the perspective is that western liberal democracy represents a political system that prevents obvious individual inequalities from being translated into systematic social or political inequalities. Liberal democracies are deemed to recognize the necessity and functional value of individual inequalities, but these individual inequalities do not impinge on the overall process of social decision-making.

According to Tumin, the essential features of a pluralist, democratic political order are the opportunities that all members of a society have to utilize formally established electoral procedures in order to select the personnel who operate the political institutions. In addition, all members of society can compete to influence the decision-making process between elections, through actions such as lobbying the decision-makers (Tumin 1967: 44-45). The most important aspect of Western democracies, a pluralist functionalist would argue, is the extent to which all members of society have an opportunity to participate in attempting to influence government policies through these activities. The income levels or class positions of individuals may well vary considerably, and the amount of status someone enjoys can vary according to occupation, ethnic group, or gender. But in the social decision-making process, all people are equal. In all liberal-democratic societies the creed is "one person, one vote," and thus on election day all eligible voters are essentially equal: people with high incomes and people on social assistance are equal in the polling booth. The same basic structural situation exists in lobbying the government, because regardless of a person's class or status position, all people are equal in having the right to make their opinions known to the decision-makers. There are no rules preventing anyone, regardless of income level or status, from engaging in this activity. Through lobbying, each individual and interest group has an opportunity to attempt to influence those who have been democratically elected to operate the political institutions.

Although in theory all individuals have the opportunity to influence the polity through the electoral process and lobbying, the pluralist approach tends to pay more attention to the activities of organized groups in the political process than it does to the actions of individuals. People tend to find that they can be more influential if they organize themselves and act collectively, and thus it is common in liberal-democratic societies to see the emergence of organized groups representing different sectors and interests in society. However, none of these groups are typically dominant over any extended period of time, and thus the outcomes of policy formation do not systematically favour any particular individual or group. As individuals and groups compete with each other to influence the decision-making process, over time, supposedly, no one group wins all the time or loses all the time. The phrase "you win some, you lose some, and some are draws" summarizes the expectations of this approach. Political power and influence are scattered throughout the society in the myriad of interest groups and individuals competing through elections and lobbying tactics to influence the social decision-making process.

In a recent spirited defence of pluralism, *Reconstructing Political Pluralism*, Avigail Eisenberg warns that groups in a liberal democracy represent a double-edged sword. Eisenberg (1995: 5) writes:

> On the one hand, groups are the means to sort out self-development often identified as the *raison d'être* of democracy. On the other hand, groups can stifle and distort development through socialization processes that seek to control and oppress the individual.

She goes on to note that because groups are essential to the fabric of society, while being both a means to political power and important for personal development, they continue to be a core concept in contemporary pluralism. Eisenberg's book is a conservative reconstruction of pluralism that devotes considerable time and attention to developing a critique of the communitarian side of what she terms the liberal-communitarian debate. While the study provides insights into new and classical debates within the circles of pluralist and liberal theory, its overriding concern is with individual or personal development and the extent to which pluralism and liberal democracy provide the most effective means for facilitating that growth.

Eisenberg's conclusion presents nine lessons drawn from the extensive discussions of core pluralist ideas that form the bulk of the text. Among the lessons is the need to understand that political power plays an important role in facilitating personal development; but she reminds us that pluralism must always keep in mind that it "aims at securing individual well-being and, as such, is individualistic" (Eisenberg 1995: 187). Other lessons include the stricture that pluralism must be explicitly normative, that it must recognize the plurality of group contexts in which individuals are involved, and that it seeks to "avoid state intervention in shaping substantive values that define communities" (188). Additional lessons include acknowledging that healthy individual development is predicated on the realization that individuals are the best judges of what is good for their self-development. The final lessons include warnings about the need to maintain pluralism among groups requesting special protections in "the cultural marketplace," and to watch for external forces that might impose values on the collectivities to which we belong, values that might result in individuals finding themselves "hostage to the standards of others which aim to determine" key aspects of ourselves (191).

While Eisenberg's reconstructed pluralism seems not to be excessively concerned with the obvious presence of enormous and growing disparities in wealth and income that we witness in most western societies, one of Robert Dahl's later works looks at pluralism in the context of the post-Soviet world and the collapse of Soviet-style communism. In *After the Revolution? Authority in the Good Society,* Dahl offers a sympathetic, yet realistic and even critical, re-examination of the contemporary status of pluralist theory. After reviewing some possible bases for authority in modern society, Dahl theorizes that his analysis demonstrates two conclusions: "that no single form or authority is the most desirable in all associations and that possible combinations of various forms in any concrete association must be nearly endless." He states, "Consequently, it would be folly to think that a single mass-produced model stamped out according to eternal patterns can possibly fit all the kinds of associations we need in order to cope with our extraordinarily complex world" (Dahl 1990: 44).

Dahl describes this complex world as one involving enormous and politically significant structured inequalities. He examines the significant inequalities of resources (wealth and income) in U.S. society, as well as the domination of the economy by "corporate leviathans" that represent a form of public authority but are under the control of private rulers (Dahl 1990: 96-101). Although he pauses to lament the lack of tradition of socialist thought in America, Dahl ends up concluding that in the world we live in polyarchy offers the nearest thing to a system capable of providing some measure of democracy—even if it is only because he sees no alternatives:

Although polyarchy shows up badly compared with unrealized ideal forms, it looks very much better when it is compared with other political systems that have actually existed to the present. In particular, when it is placed alongside rival political forms that have been tried out this century—waves of the future that swept people overboard—polyarchy looks to be not only incomparably closer to genuine rule by the people but much more humane, decent, tolerant, benign, and responsive in dealing with citizens.

Here, then, is a pluralist who continues to argue that a reconstructed pluralism or a realistic polyarchy or both represents the best option for a democratic polity in the modern era.

We must ask, however, if this view of power and the state is realistic in the face of what we know about the plight of the homeless, the Third World, and the systematic attacks on the marginated and underclasses witnessed over the past two decades. Arguments that there are no dominant centres of power and that all members of society have anything close to an equal chance to influence state policy and action are without empirical or theoretical basis in the face of the brutal realities of class and power differentials. Are there other options with other intellectual traditions, such as critical theory? Let us see what is new in the intellectual tradition that supplied the most compelling critiques of pluralism: Marxism.

BEYOND NEO-MARXISM

As we've seen, for a major part of the last half of the twentieth century the works of Nicos Poulantzas and Ralph Miliband were central to the neo-Marxian attempts to offer an alternative to pluralism. What tended to emerge was a form of Marxian functionalism: that is, a study of the state based on its functions for the capitalist class. As is generally the case with functionalist logic, these theories could not facilitate empirical research and actual explanations of state action and policy that were not circular and even teleological. An exception is the approach of Albert Szymanski, which represents an important attempt to develop a theoretical model capable of facilitating historical and empirical research.

While Miliband, Poulantzas, Szymanski, and many other critics sought to understand the relationship between various classes and the state in capitalist society, a number of scholars, including Eric A. Nordlinger and Theda Skocpol, were engaged in a developing an approach to the state in capitalist society that went beyond merely articulating a certain degree of relative autonomy for the state. Although it would not be appropriate to place these thinkers all within the Marxian tradition, they all do accept that "the state is a force in its own right and does not simply reflect the dynamic of the economy and/or civil society" (Jessop 1990: 279). The "state-centred" approach obviously directs our analytical attention to the structures and operation of the state as an independent "actor" in the complex interplay of economic, social, and political forces. Such an approach does not assume that the state is tied to or will reflect any class forces. Skocpol summarizes the argument: "States conceived as organizations claiming control over territories and people may formulate and pursue goals that are not simply reflective of the demands or interests of social groups, classes or society" (Skocpol 1985: 9). She notes, "Bringing the state back in to a central place in analyses of policy making and social change does require a break with some of the most encompassing social-determinist as-sumptions of pluralism, structural-functionalist developmentalism, and vari-ous neo-Marxisms" (20). The question of determining whether the state is pursuing a policy objective or direction that originates within its structures and personnel, or whether it is reflecting the priorities of some class or group, becomes a historical and empirical matter, subject to historical and empirical investigation. The key point that emerges from this approach is the necessity of recognizing the possibility and even the probability, that the state itself may be acting as an independent and fully autonomous actor.

In his 1990 book Jessop offers a substantial critique of the "state-centred" theorists; but he also argues that the work of scholars such as Ernesto Laclau and Chantal Mouffe represents an even more serious challenge to current thinking and theorizing about the state. According to Jessop, Laclau and Mouffe do not just question the manner by which scholars operating from a variety of perspectives have understood the state; the logic of their work challenges the very existence of the state as the central site of struggles over power. There are at least two different reasons why Laclau and Mouffe question the prevailing orthodoxies concerning the centrality of the state. The first has to do with Laclau and Mouffe explicitly referring to themselves as post-Marxists. As such, they reject a number of tenets of classical Marxism including the notion that the working class is somehow a universal class with a privileged position in future emancipatory political processes. They note that our current situation is one in which new forms of social conflict and opposi-tion have emerged, forces that include:

> the rise of the new feminism, the protest movements of ethnic, national and sexual minorities, the anti-institutional ecology strug-gles waged by marginalized layers of the population, the anti-nuclear movement, the atypical forms of social struggle in countries on the capitalist periphery—all these imply an extension of social conflictuality to a wide range of areas, which creates the potential, but no more than the potential, for an advance towards more free, democratic and egalitarian societies. (Laclau and Mouffe 1985: 1)

They go on to note that abandoning the notion of a universal class is essential if we are to make progress in understanding the complexities of the contemporary world:

> Is it not the case that, in scaling down the pretensions and the area of validity of Marxist theory, we are breaking with something deeply inherent in that theory: namely, its monist aspiration to capture with its categories the essence or underlying meaning of History? The answer can only be in the affirmative. Only if we renounce any epistemological prerogative based upon the ontologically privileged position of a "universal class," will it be possible seriously to discuss the present degree of validity of the Marxist categories. (1985: 4)

Secondly Laclau and Mouffe also reject the notion that society can be understood as a complex totality whose essential character and shape is determined by the nature of the mode of production. There are some determining processes, what they call nodal points, through which we can understand the underlying principles of a social totality. They write:

> In a given social formation, there can be a variety of hegemonic nodal points. Evidently some of them may be highly overdetermined; they may constitute points of condensation of a number of social relations and, thus, become the focal point of a multiplicity of totalizing effects. But insofar as the social is an infinitude not reducible to any underlying unitary principle, the mere idea of a centre of the social has no meaning at all. (Laclau and Mouffe 1985: 139)

Consequently, debates about the relative autonomy of the state are meaningless because they were premised on "the assumption of a sutured society" (139), a premise they reject. As Jessop puts it, Laclau and Mouffe represent an approach to understanding social processes that holds that "the social has an open, unsutured character and that neither its elements nor its totality have a pre-given necessity" (Jessop 1990: 289). As a result the various relations that compose the social result in "societies that are tendentially constituted as an ensemble of totalizing effects in an open relational complex" (290). In their elaboration of this point Laclau and Mouffe use a variety of words and concepts in their attempt to move us away from deterministic thinking. One of their most often used concepts is "articulation." They illustrate the meaning of articulation in the claim that "Since all identity is relational ... the transition from 'elements' to moments can never be complete" (1985: 113). In the description that follows they employ terms such as "floating," "ambiguous," and "overflowing" to characterize the fluidity and non-fixed nature of social existence, social relations, and even their overall notion of the social. One of their more radical conclusions is that "the social *is* articulation insofar as 'society' is impossible" (1995: 114, emphasis in original). Although Jessop is unsure as to whether this argument really means that society is impossible at all, he is clear about what this rejection of totalizing theoretical frameworks means for the study of the state. The state becomes, at most, one part of a larger set of social relations that are constantly contested, produced, and reproduced. Jessop summarizes: "Even if their approach does not require the total deconstruction of the state, it does deny states any positivity and de-privileges them as sites of political struggle" (293).

These comments should not lead us to think that recent theorizing about the state leads only to postulating that the state is an autonomous social actor with interests and activities that have no connection to society, or that it is necessary to give up efforts to develop a systematic theory or understanding of the state because, like other social phenomena, the state is indeterminate, contested, and not subject to systematic analysis or understanding. Some of the most interesting recent thinking about the state has been developed by thinkers associated with an approach commonly referred to as regulation theory. While, as Jessop points out, many complex and sophisticated different ideas and arguments are associated with regulation theory, there are some common assumptions that inform these thinkers. Central among the underlying principles is the assumption that the social and economic structures that typically characterize capitalist society are unstable and incapable of maintaining themselves in the long term without some significant transformations and interventions. These theorists argue that regulatory mechanisms are the basis of the transformations and interventions that make it possible for the capitalist system and its concomitant institutional structures and arrangements to survive. As Jessop points out: "They all focus on the changing social forms and mechanisms in and through which the capital relation is reproduced despite its inherent economic contradictions and emergent conflictual properties" (Jessop 1990: 309). Regulation theorists tend to examine both the economic and extra-economic processes and structural conditions that allow different accumulation regimes to exist and function despite the inherent contradictions and class conflicts that characterize the system. They further assume that there are no abstract necessary or typical systems of regulation that work in all or most capitalist systems. The modes of regulation that characterize a particular society or nation will be the outcome of historically specific institutional arrangements, modes of conduct, and normative rules (309).

Jessop explains that the scholars working within this tradition have shown variations on this theme. Some regulation theorists use concepts such as "regimes of accumulation" or "modes of regulation" to describe historically and nationally specific institutional arrangements and institutions that might characterize the structures and operations of capitalism in specific locales at specific moments in history. For example, while theorists might have used the general descriptor of Keynesian welfare state to describe both Canada and the Unites States at a certain moment, in actual fact the two nations showed significant differences in the forms and structures of their welfare states. In each case different sets of policies and institutional arrangements (regimes of accumulation or modes of regulation) reflected the strength or weakness of labour, various fractions of capital, the role of state agencies, and so on. In Canada, for example, the stronger British Fabian socialist influence in farmers' and workers' movements may have resulted in a mode of regulation that included a significant government role in the provision of medical services. Despite its apparent tendencies to be abstract, regulation theory draws our attention to the need for concrete analysis by denying "that there is a single objective logic of capitalist development that transcends all particularities: the development of capitalism is always mediated through historically specific institutional forms, regulatory institutions, and norms of conduct (Jessop 1990: 309).

The state is able to provide the required modes or systems of regulatory mechanisms because it is "neither an ideal collective capitalist whose functions are determined in the last instance by the imperatives of economic production nor is it a simple parallelogram of pluralist forces" (Jessop 1990: 315). The process of establishing the necessary regulatory system to facilitate continued capital accumulation is deemed to be complex:

> Securing the conditions for capital accumulation or managing an unstable equilibrium of compromise involves not only a complex array of institutions and policies but also a continuing struggle to build consensus and back it with coercion.... The state itself can be seen as a complex ensemble of institutions, networks, procedures, modes of calculation and norms as well as their associated pattern of strategic conduct. (315)

According to Jessop the overall approach that emerges out of the many specific thinkers associated with the regulationist perspective offers a useful antidote to the simplistic or economic reductionism arguments, conventional functionalist positions, and approaches that exaggerate the separateness of the state from the political processes surrounding capital accumulation. Without succumbing to the questionable conclusion about society being impossible that flows out of Laclau and Mouffe, Jessop notes that societies are "relatively structured, sedimented or fixed," bur their maintenance and continued existence require the continued coordination of complex individual and institutional arrangements, which typically involve struggles for hegemony and the use of the ensemble of state institutions. The problem with both

Jessop's and the regulationist school's work is that neither offers much by way of a non-functionalist explanatory framework.

Gregg Olsen and Julia O'Connor have also commented on the issue of functionalist logic permeating non-functional-structuralist analyses of the state. In their edited book, *Power Resource Theory and the Welfare State: A Critical Approach*, Olsen and O'Connor (1998: 5-6) introduce an alternative approach commonly referred to as power resource theory, which "emerged in the late 1970s and early 1980s in an attempt to redress some of the problems with existing mainstream and radical accounts of the welfare state." The approach, which seeks to direct more attention to the potential role of various classes in influencing state policies and actions, emerged out of the work of Gosta Esping-Anderson and Walter Korpi. According to Olsen and O'Connor, the approach rejects the pluralist notions that power is not concentrated, but rather is widely dispersed. The approach also takes unbrage with the tendency among those within the Marxian tradition to see power absolutely concentrated in the hands of the capitalist class. They note that this approach suggests "that the balance of power between labour and capital was fluid, and therefore variable." They add: "While capital would always have the upper hand within a capitalist framework, labour had the potential to access political resources which could increase its power, and thereby allow it to implement social reform and alter distributional inequities to a significant degree" (6).

Walter Korpi (1998: vii) explains that power must be conceptualized as a resource that shifts over time and cannot be readily understood simply in terms of immediately observable behaviours, just as an iceberg cannot be understood by observing the tip that presents itself to us. He goes on to describe an essential feature of the approach: "The power resources approach therefore focuses not only on the direct, but also the indirect consequences of power, indirect consequences mediated through various alternative strategies and actions available to the holders of power resources."

Korpi explains that the exercise and distribution of power occur within specific institutions, with markets, the polity, and the family being the three main institutional sites. As power relations and dynamics change, the precise configuration and operation of institutions will change. Power resource theory has proven to be of use in the actual analysis of the evolution of institutions in which power is exercised and distributed, such as those associated with the welfare state (see Olsen 1999; Bashevkin 2000).

Power resource theory arguments are, then, not all that different from the regulation theory argument that different political, cultural, and historical circumstances tend to generate different regimes of accumulation and modes of regulation. Both positions draw our attention to the need for historical and empirical research that is viewed through a theoretical prism that provides insights into actual mechanisms and modes of exercising power.

The challenges and problems for existing state theories caused by the need to theorize the changing role and functions of the state in the face of global governance and regulatory agencies are but one issue we must face as the twenty-first century unfolds. The next chapter will turn to an even more significant issue: the apparent inability of state theories to recognize, let alone adequately theorize, sex- and gender-based inequalities.

• NINE •

SEX, GENDER, AND FEMINIST THEORY

Most feminists have rejected the usual definition of politics as relating to the polity and the formal political order, arguing for a broader definition that takes in everyday activities, including how we live our gendered lives. The familiar phrase the "political as personal" instructs us to be attentive to the nature of power in our everyday lives. As feminists point out, politics and the political are connected to virtually every human relationship; thus, by urging people to make the political personal, feminism demands, for instance, that we take our commitment to an egalitarian and free world seriously at the level of personal existence; and that we recognize that politics is much more than the formal state structures of the polity. As Catharine MacKinnon affirms: "Gender is a social system that divides power. It is therefore a political system" (1989: 160).

Feminists have thus turned their attention systematically to the analysis of power at both the personal everyday and the state levels, although this work has been only a small part of the whole theoretical project of feminism. These efforts are important because, as we have seen, theorizing the relationships of power that surround sex and gender issues has not been a priority for social and political theory.

The theories and perspectives that we have been considering have all grappled with a common issue: understanding the nature of the polity in capitalist society and the nature of political power in a liberal-democratic state. To be sure, we have encountered major, even radical, differences in how these theories and perspectives understand and explain the structures and processes of political power, but they also share some common features. Indeed, one of the common features of western political thought is an apparent fundamental lacuna. Juliet Mitchell identified the basis of this theoretical and empirical void in the introduction to her groundbreaking essay "Women: The Longest Revolution." That essay became an influential statement, helping to usher in the "Second Wave of Feminism" that had such a significant impact on western society during the second half of the last century. Mitchell (1990: 43) explained:

> The situation of women is different from that of any other social group. This is because they are not one of a number of isolable units but half of a totality: the human species. Women are essential and irreplaceable; they cannot therefore be exploited in the same way that other social groups can. They are fundamental to the human condi-

tion, yet in their economic, social, and political roles they are marginal.

Without digressing into the epistemological issues of the relationship between social reality and social scientific theory, we must note that feminist theory has made women's marginality the focus of its historical, empirical, and theoretical endeavours.

A quick scan of many political theory books provides prima facie evidence that issues relating to sex and gender have been ignored. For example, Patrick Dunleavy and Brendan O'Leary's 1987 book, *Theories of the State: The Politics of Liberal Democracy* includes no index entries under feminist theory and only one under "women's movement." Still, some scholars have argued that the problem is not so much that political theorists have simply ignored women, but rather how women have been theorized. Diana Coole, for example, has argued that women have been included in the projects of western political theory but on the basis of inherently sexist assumptions. She notes that though women are to be found within many western political works, they are located within what the theorists see as a natural hierarchy:

> Within this, women are granted a significant role, perceived as consonant with their nature, which yields them a definitive place in the order of things. It is a place associated with reproduction and domesticity, with the organic, the necessary and the emotional. (Coole 1988: 3)

She also notes that as a result, "Political thought has made a massive and privileged ideological contribution to patriarchy: it has provided arguments and assumptions which have legitimized women's exclusion from public life and their subordination to the private realm" (6).

In a similar vein Carole Pateman (1989: 3) argues that in non-feminist political theory "the public sphere is assumed to be capable of being understood on its own, as if it existed *sui generis*, independently of private sexual relations and domestic life." Pateman further argues: "The power of men over women is excluded from scrutiny and deemed to be irrelevant to political life and democracy by the patriarchal construction of the categories with which political theorists work" (13-14). A review of the historical and empirical evidence regarding the sexual and gender dimensions and implications of state actions serves to convince us that political theory really does need a feminist rectification to highlight the problems of sex, gender, and power.

SEX, GENDER, AND THE STATE: SOME HISTORICAL AND EMPIRICAL STUDIES

In her 1986 article "Gender and Reproduction: Or, Babies and the State," Jane Jenson addresses the issue of the adequacy of Marxian theories to address the question of the oppression of women. She notes, "Everyday observations of the law, welfare programs, educational institutions, and family policy indicate that state actions affect the ways in which feminine and masculine lives are constructed" (Jenson 1986: 201). However, she also notes that observations and descriptions do not constitute an explanation; that is, they do not answer the question of why the state contributes to "gender-based oppression." Jenson's essay has two objectives: to establish that the state in capitalist society is in fact part of the structural oppression of women; and to assist in the development of an adequate theoretical framework to explain why the state would act in that way.

Jenson examines the role of the state in the production and reproduction of what she terms a "healthy and disciplined labour force" in several countries (Jenson 1986: 205). After reviewing historical developments in England and France she concludes that, while there were national differences in policies and practices regarding the roles and participation of women in the labour force, "It is evident that the capitalist state has participated in the reproduction of women's oppression" (213). In her discussion of the findings, Jenson reviews three possible theoretical streams that might offer an explanation. She concludes that, in the final analysis, "It is, therefore, impossible to found a general theoretical statement of the capitalist state's contribution to gender relations on the presumed existence of shared assumptions that the family wage is 'natural,' that the basic family unit is the wage-earning husband and dependent wife and children, or, that the state will act to exclude women from the labour force" (228). She argues for the need to understand and examine historical forces and constructs and that "It is possible to understand the ways in which the state contributes to the oppression of women" (229).

In another important essay, "Masculine Dominance and the State" (1985), Canadian scholar Varda Burstyn critiques the existing concepts commonly used within Marxist analysis to examine class relations and class domination and decides that those concepts, "while illuminating one crucial set of economic class relations have also obscured, much as the use of the word 'Man' to describe humanity has obscured the specific reality of women, another set of class relations–gender–class" (Burstyn 1985: 48). The concept of gender-class is essential to the remainder of Burstyn's argument.

Burstyn suggests a number of distinct concepts and terms to illustrate the nature and significance of male dominance as a transhistorical phenomenon. Indeed, she suggests using the terms male dominance and gender-class to ensure an understanding of the specific form of dominance involved in the historical relations between men and women (Burstyn 1985: 49-50). In setting up the distinctions between economic class, which refers to what Marxists have referred to simply as class, and gender-class, Burstyn first examines the precapitalist emergence of male dominance and the sexual division of labour.

In her subsequent analysis of gender–class relations she emphasizes the features of the sexual division of labour and of women's labour.

Burstyn argues that women's labour must be understood as being both productive and reproductive. Productive labour results in the actual production of things, while reproductive labour results in the production of people. The historical relations between men and women have resulted in male control over the products of both women's productive and reproductive labour. Men not only control women's labour in cultivation, craft production, and capitalist production, but also exhibit control "of children formalized in family patterns and masculine inheritance systems" (Burstyn 1985: 53). In addition, Burstyn stresses that male control over the very sexuality of women adds an important dimension to male control. When combined with male domination of "economic, religious, political, and military systems of power in human societies," this sexual control results in the pervasive form of dominance faced by women:

> Men's freedom from the necessity to care for their own bodies and those of children, the sick and the elderly, through men's appropriation of women's productive labour and men's access to women's bodies and control of their issue—that is, men's appropriation of women's reproductive labour—indicates that we are talking about class relations between men and women. (55)

After establishing the basis and extent of male domination, Burstyn examines the role of the state in masculine dominance. Her overall argument holds that the state has been active in maintaining both the relations of economic-class domination and gender-class domination. The interests of the dominant class in the economic-class system and the interests of males have been served by the state, which "has taken on the crucial role of mediation and regulation to advance capitalism's needs for a given form of labour power and surplus extraction in such a way as to retain masculine privilege and control—masculine domination—in society as a whole" (57).

Burstyn cites numerous examples of how the state serves these dual systems of domination in both capitalist and noncapitalist societies. In addressing the central "why" question she is rather deliberate in isolating the nature of state personnel as an explanation, since state personnel tend to be predominantly men. She states that because she is "of the opinion that the central state systems do represent a massive condensation of real power and do act quite instrumentally—to use a deliberately controversial term—in constant reoccurring ways to enforce class domination, I think it is valid and necessary to understand something about their personnel as well as about their policies and forms of governing" (Burstyn 1985: 72-73). In her subsequent analysis Burstyn examines the systematic exclusion of women from positions within the government, political parties, administrative machinery, and the coercive repressive apparatus. Ultimately her analysis could be deemed to represent an instrumentalist position, because she argues that it is males as a dominant class who occupy the key positions of power and authority in the state apparatus. In her critiques of traditional and contemporary Marxism, Burstyn argues for the inclusion of a new theory of sex-based domination—males over females—within the core of a new critical theory of capitalist society.

If there was any doubt about the extent to which the actions and policies of the Canadian state not only have an immediate impact on relations between the sexes but are also gendered, a collection of essays edited by Janine Brodie (1996b), *Women and Canadian Public Policy*, represents the *coup de grâce*. The book contains numerous articles that examine the extent to which the policies and actions of neo-conservative governments of the 1990s had different impacts on women and men. The conclusion as summarized by Brodie is inescapable: "The new emerging order [is] fraught not only with new dangers for Canadian women, but also with contradictions" (Brodie 1996b: 24). The contradictions, of course, open the door to resistance and struggles for equity and democratization.

In that collection, for instance, Patricia McDermott examines what many people would assume to be necessarily beneficial state policies for women— pay and employment equity legislation. She demonstrates how the Ontario provincial government's decision to treat the wage gap between women and men and the various discriminatory labour practices that segment the labour force as separate problems amenable to different legislative and policy solutions resulted in a failure to satisfactorily address both issues. The end result, after much public debate and political posturing, was a very real danger that the long-sought-after goal of fairness and equity would slip though the cracks (McDermott 1996: 102). In her study of the central issue of new reproductive technologies, Barbara Cameron demonstrates that it is not so much that the Canadian state is developing or intending to develop polices in this area that are detrimental to women, but rather that the new global era is preventing the state from doing anything. Cameron argues that the North American Free Trade Agreement "contains provisions that can be used to limit the capacity of member states of NAFTA to regulate commercial activity within its territory" (123-124). It matters not that such regulations might have an impact on pay or equity or new reproductive technologies; NAFTA very likely forbids them.

Several essays in the collection address the issue of how the neo-conservative and neo-liberal eras of fiscal restraint and deregulation have hurt women. Pat Armstrong ends her discussion of the destruction of the health-care system with a pointed conclusion: "Meanwhile, states are reducing the capacity of women to remain healthy by dismantling social-security programs, by deregulating industries, and by moving away from an equity agenda" (Armstrong 1996: 145).

One section of the book, "Restructuring Private Life," contains a number of powerful essays addressing issues related to questions such as same-sex couples, obscenity law and pornography, and violence against women. In each case the evidence reveals that the various state levels in Canada are powerful forces in the structuring of relations between women and men and in the gendering of society.

These essays, and others in collections such as that edited by M. Patricia Connelly and Pat Armstrong (1992), *Feminism in Action: Studies in Political Economy*, demonstrate definitively that the state is an important player in constructing and regulating sex and gender in advanced capitalist society. The question they tend not to answer is *why* this is so. As important as these historical and empirical studies are, they tend to neglect the larger issue of what sort of theoretical explanations might be most appropriate for explaining these developments and offering answers to the essential why questions.

POWER AND THE POLITY

While the traditional or mainstream literature has tended to ignore the issue of sex, gender, power, and the state, that omission is obviously not the case for feminist theory. Indeed, some long-established traditions seek to explain the gendered nature of the state in capitalist society, and some of the more important streams of feminist thought bear directly on our efforts to understand the role of the state in capitalist society.

Given the complexity, substance, and voluminous nature of late twentieth- and early twenty-first-century feminist thought, many scholars have attempted to classify or categorize feminist theory into distinct schools of thought or approaches. Alison M. Jaggar (1983), Josephine Donovan (1992), Alison M. Jaggar and Paula S. Rothenberg (1984), Patricia Madoo Lengermann and Jill Niebrugge (1996), Zillah R. Eisenstein (1981), Rosemarie Tong (1989), Nancy Mandell (1995), and Roberta Hamilton (1996) all offer somewhat different classificatory schemas. However, there tends to be sufficient agreement to allow us to utilize a broad and somewhat crude division. One useful, though fairly orthodox, approach to the basic contours of feminist theory is to make an analytical distinction between liberal, radical, Marxian, and socialist feminism. While other important streams of feminist thought do exist, including psychoanalytical, existential, lesbian, anarchist, postmodernist, and Third World orientations, here we will concentrate on these more prominent western approaches.

LIBERAL FEMINISM

In their summary of the development of feminist theory, Patricia Madoo Lengermann and Jill Niebrugge-Brantley (1996) note that women have been protesting their social position for centuries, although the development of explicitly feminist social theory is a more recent phenomenon. The issue of

172

women's rights was on the agenda of several early liberal thinkers, including Mary Wollstonecraft, John Stuart Mill, and Harriet Taylor Mill. One could argue that their works mark the beginning of liberal feminism.

One of the first systematic attempts to extend the liberal notions of freedom, individuality, and autonomy to women is found in a 1792 publication, *A Vindication of the Rights of Women* by Mary Wollstonecraft. As we know, the classical liberal thinkers were critical of any action, practice, or social structure that unnecessarily limited individual action, freedom, autonomy, and by inference human development. To be sure, Hobbes had argued that a relatively powerful state or sovereign was necessary, but its fundamental role and purpose were to provide the necessary preconditions for human happiness and fulfilment through exercising people's natural propensities. Locke extended the liberal postulate that human happiness and fulfilment requires a substantial measure of freedom of action, thought, expression, and will, but his thinking was limited by the times in which he lived. Eisenstein (1981: 35) argues that the classical liberal thinkers operated in the context of a certain view of women:

> The seventeenth century inherited the view of women as both intellectually and morally inferior to man. Women's inequality to man was a prevalent precapitalist vision. Her inferiority was rooted in the presumption of her moral weakness as described by the church fathers.

It follows, therefore, that just as Locke and other classical liberal thinkers acknowledged that not all human males were citizens by virtue of their inability to acquire and demonstrate a sufficient capacity for reason, so too women were excluded from full citizenship. Carole Pateman refers to the social contract, a central concept in classical liberal thought, as "The Fraternal Social Contract," and she summarizes the sexual and gender assumption implicit in the classical liberal world view:

> In short, the contract constitutes patriarchal civil society and the modern, ascriptive rule of men over women. Ascription and contract are usually seen as standing at opposite poles, but the social contract is sexually ascriptive in both form (it is made by brothers) and content (the patriarchal right of the fraternity is established). (Pateman 1989: 43)

It was precisely these limitations on the citizenship, freedom, and autonomy of women that Wollstonecraft argued against. As Eisenstein (1981: 91) notes: "Wollstonecraft applies these demands of the bourgeois revolution of reason, personal independence, and individual freedom to women on the same basis that they were extended to men." Given the times and the existing image of women, Wollstonecraft took on some of the most prevalent ideas of the day:

> I still insist that not only the virtue but the *knowledge* of the two sexes should be the same in nature, if not in degree, and that women, considered not only as moral but rational creatures, ought to endeavour to acquire human virtues (or perfections) by the *same* means as men, instead of being educated like a fanciful kind of *half* beings—one of Rousseau's wild chimeras. (Quoted in Coole 1988: 122, emphasis in original)

In an argument that anticipated some of the points that John Stuart Mill was to make later, Wollstonecraft placed considerable emphasis on education as the key to developing women's capacity for reason and thus her full humanness. However, as Coole (1988: 124) points out, Wollstonecraft was also a product of her times. She was also capable, for instance, of arguing that the more fully human were women, the better they would be at their roles of wives and mothers. Coole (1988: 127) summarizes Wollstonecraft's contribution: "Wollstonecraft's agenda for women's emancipation is a typically liberal one: education, civil rights; an opportunity to compete for access to occupations; political rights."

Harriet Taylor and her second husband, John Stuart Mill, undertook collaborative work after their marriage in 1851, further developing the basic logic of Wollstonecraft's analysis of the roles and status of women in English society. Although Mill's famous *On the Subjection of Women* was not written and published until 1869, ten years after Taylor's death, it is clear that many of the ideas it develops resulted from their earlier collaboration (Eisenstein 1986: 114).

As one might expect, Taylor and Mill extended the arguments made by Wollstonecraft. As Eisenstein (1986: 127) notes: "Citizen rights still excluded women and did not recognize women as individuals in the legal-liberal sense of the term. Taylor and Mill, therefore, argue to extend the established freedoms of bourgeois society to women. In Mill's own words:

> That the principle which regulates the existing social relations between the two sexes—the legal subordination of one sex to the other—is wrong in itself, and now one of the chief hindrances to human improvement; and that it ought to be replaced by a principle of perfect equality, admitting no power or privilege on the one side, nor disability on the other. (Quoted in Jaggar and Rothenberg 1984: 105)

Mill provides powerful comparisons, including that of master and slave, to describe the sexual inequalities in his society. However, as several scholars have pointed out, Mill's analysis is limited by his failure to offer concrete solutions to address the situation. Indeed, Eisenstein argues that his acceptance of the existing patriarchal culture along with its familial roles represents a serious contradiction in his analysis. Steven DeLue (1997: 316) agrees: "Even for a thinker such as Mill, who wanted to usher women into the public realm as equals with men, the main problem Mill leaves unattended is the need to reconfigure the private realm in a way that permits women full participation in society."

The ideas and arguments of Wollstonecraft, Taylor, and Mill paved the way for the social and political protests and movements that eventually resulted in the formal incorporation of women into the political structures of western society during the twentieth century. Josephine Donovan (1992: 8) refers to a set of core liberal ideas that informed much feminist thought as the basis tenets of Enlightenment liberal feminism:

> (1) A faith in rationality. With some thinkers, such as Wollstonecraft, Reason and God are nearly synonymous. The individual's reason is the divine spark within; it is one's conscience. With feminists such as Frances Wright and Sarah Grimké the individual conscience is regarded as a more reliable source of truth than any established institution or tradition. (A similar antinomianism had been branded a heresy when expressed by Anne Hutchinson (1591-1643) in colonial Massachusetts.)
>
> (2) A belief that women's and men's souls and rational faculties are the same; in other words, that women and men are ontologically similar.
>
> (3) A belief in education—especially training in critical thinking— as the most effective means to effect social change and transform society.
>
> (4) A view of the individual as an isolated being, who seeks the truth apart from others, who operates as a rational, independent agent, and whose dignity depends on such independence.
>
> (5) Finally, Enlightenment theorists subscribed to the natural rights doctrine, and while the most important theorists did not limit themselves to demanding political rights, the mainstream of the nineteenth-century women's movement settled upon these demands, in particular the demand for the vote.

The demands of early liberal feminists for full citizenship rights and equality, in and before the law, quite naturally resulted in an emphasis on achieving or acquiring what they lacked. Roberta Hamilton (1996: 86-87) explains:

> Suffrage was key to the liberal feminist agenda, for it represented

citizenship. A liberal-democratic state rests upon the right of citizens to choose government. As long as women were excluded from this right, the very notion of equality between the sexes remained moot.

Hamilton describes the struggles, setbacks, and eventual victory for women in this regard. The extension of the franchise to women in Canada occurred in the context of several major worldwide crises, including two world wars and the Great Depression. Then the development of liberal feminist theory arguably entered a period of relative acquiescence during the middle third of the twentieth century. That is not to say that the struggles of women for equity and inclusion in social institutions ended; far from it. It was, however, a time when social science theorizing, especially as applied to the polity, was dominated by thinkers articulating the pluralist and functionalist approaches. Anthony Giddens (1982: 1) uses the phrase "the orthodox consensus" to refer to the views that "dominated sociology, politics and large sectors of the social sciences in general in the postwar period." It was a consensus framed within the context of structural functionalist and pluralist social science. However, this consensus, especially as applied to understanding the roles and positions of women in society, the family, and the state, soon developed into a crisis as more and more women and men realized nirvana had not been reached (Knuttila 1996: 269-70).

Thus began the second wave of feminism. Dorothy Chunn notes that a distinction should be made between early twentieth-century liberal feminists and feminists later in the century. She refers to the earlier women as "maternal feminists" who were as concerned with protecting the role of women as mothers as they were with achieving political equality for women.

> The maternal feminist assumption that nurturing and care giving are "feminine qualities," and providing and protecting are "masculine" traits, reflected an uncritical belief in the normality of the bourgeois family model and acceptance of the idea that the family is one based on a heterosexual marriage relationship in which each member of the nuclear unit has a specific role. The sexual division of labour leaves husband and wife in charge of separate but equal spheres of activity. (Chunn 1995: 180)

This concern was clearly not as central to the liberal feminists of the 1960s or later second wave feminists who conceptualized women and men in terms of sameness (albeit without equality) rather than difference and who challenged the sexual division of labour by arguing for the movement of married women en masse into the public realm (Chunn 1995: 181).

Nancy Mandell (1995: 9) makes a useful distinction between liberal feminism and contemporary liberal feminism, tending to use the latter to refer to developments during the twentieth century. As Jaggar (1983) notes, a new cadre of liberal feminists began to systematically analyze the situation of women in liberal-democratic society, and despite having formally gained full citizenship and despite being protected by charters of rights and constitutional provisions, they were forced to conclude that women still faced serious problems:

> Liberal feminists believe that the treatment of women in contemporary society violates, in one way or another, all of liberalism's political values of equity, liberty, and justice. Their most frequent complaint is that women in contemporary society suffer discrimination on the basis of sex. By this, they mean that this places certain restrictions on women *as a group*, without regard to their individual wishes, interests, abilities, or merits. (Jaggar 1983: 175-76, emphasis in original)

While discrimination against women appeared to be structural, in that women were being denied access to important and powerful roles and positions, for liberal feminists the roots were normative. As Mandell points out, liberal feminists remained concerned about the content of the society's value system and normative orientations. As she states, "They identify socialization and education in shaping individuals as central in constructing gender differences in attitudes, expectations, and behaviours." Liberal feminists hoped that "by reshaping individual beliefs and values, new socialization processes will be created in institutional and non-formal settings." Finally, as a result, "More liberated and egalitarian gender relations will presumably derive from this altered process of social learning" (Mandell 1995: 6). Clearly, although the contemporary liberal-feminist approach has much in common with structural functionalism and pluralism, including an acceptance of the basic structures of western society as appropriate, there are key differences. As Mandell indicates, liberal feminists tend to argue that the key components of any social structure include its value system, normative orientations, and unifying belief systems and moral codes. However, unlike some social and political theorists, liberal feminists argue that the value system has become contaminated with dysfunctional elements in the form of sexist ideas and values that attribute behavioural characteristics or personality attributes purely on the basis of biological sex. When this happens people are more or less automatically streamed into jobs, careers, and roles on the basis of sex and gender rather than ability. Many women face insurmountable barriers in attempting to enter so-called non-traditional occupations and roles. As a result women face various forms of informal, formal, legislated, and everyday discrimination that "diminishes their liberty and autonomy" (Jaggar 1983: 177).

For women, the situation of not having a fair chance to develop all their human abilities and potentials because they are streamed into traditional roles and behaviours is clearly not in accordance with the classical liberal premises of freedom and opportunity for all. For society, a major potential talent pool made up of half of the society is lost. For example, how many potential scientists have been denied an opportunity to contribute to the search for a cure for cancer as a result of women's systematic exclusion from various professions and occupations?

Pat Armstrong and Hugh Armstrong (1990) agree that the liberal-feminist approach places considerable emphasis on socialization, in which values, norms, beliefs, and behaviours are passed on from one generation to another. Because the essence of the problem is located in the society's value and belief system, changes have to be made in that system. Sexist ideas and behaviours have to be confronted and altered. New nonsexist ideas have to be disseminated through the socialization and resocialization processes. In liberal-feminist thought, the general picture is far from hopeless. Because liberal feminists accept the basic soundness of the current social structures, they conclude that all that is really needed is some "fine-tuning." Society's belief system and moral codes have become corrupted with sexist ideas, but the current institutional arrangements are strong enough to ensure that the required reforms and adjustments can be made and that these changes will lead to the eventual development of egalitarian relations between men and women. As Jaggar (1983: 199-200) notes:

> Liberal feminists take their task to be the extension to women of the liberal political values of liberty, equality, autonomy, self-fulfilment and justice, which they believe can be achieved through limited legal reforms. They do not view the oppression of women as a structural feature of the capitalist economic system, so that women's liberation requires the overthrow of that system.

Moreover, the state is seen as a potential ally in the process, providing that women avail themselves of their legitimate opportunities to make an impact on the state through existing means:

> Given these assumptions, liberal feminists take for granted that the state is the proper and indeed the only legitimate authority for enforcing justice in general and women's rights in particular. They see the state as the neutral arbiter of conflicting social interests, whose task is to protect individual rights and so to defend against the tyranny of any individual or group. (Jaggar 1983: 200)

Hamilton points out that for many liberal feminists suffrage became a key item on their political agendas. However, the successful campaign for full citizenship, as defined strictly by the right to vote and participate in elections, proved to be inadequate for addressing the structural and systemic inequalities that women faced: "Many historians argue that the granting of suffrage changed much less than feminists had hoped and their opponents had feared" (Hamilton 1996: 88).

The inadequacies of conventional structural functionalist and pluralist thought were partly responsible for the emergence of various streams of neo-Marxism during the 1960s and 1970s, as we have seen. Similarly, then, the failure of liberal feminism to provide a systematic and coherent analytical and political framework arguably resulted in feminists looking elsewhere for the necessary analytical tools. For some of them, an obvious potential source of analytical assistance would be Marxism.

MARXIAN FEMINISM, AND ENGELS' ORIGIN OF THE FAMILY

Much has been written about the relevance and usefulness of Marx and the concepts he developed for our understanding of sex and gender (Tong, 1989; Donovan, 1992; Sargent, 1986; England, 1993). While opinions on this issue vary, one thing is quite clear: sex and gender relations were not of primary significance in Marx's understanding of the overall structures and dynamics of human society. Marx's work contains systematic accounts of many key sociological issues, including the essential character of human beings, the nature and operation of the capitalist economic order, the nature of human consciousness, the dynamics of political power, and so on, but little explicit treatment of sex and gender. There is, however, one original work dating to the era that Donovan (1992) refers to as "first wave" Marxism.

In 1884, one year after Marx died, Friedrich Engels, the close collaborator and lifelong supporter and friend of Marx, published *The Origin of the Family, Private Property and the State*, in which he attempted to provide the basis of a materialist approach to the development of the family. Drawing heavily on the work of the nineteenth-century anthropologist Lewis H. Morgan, Engels argues that as human society evolves we witness the growth of different forms of familial organization. During the earliest period of human history, referred to as a stage of "savagery," sexual and reproductive relations were organized on the basis of group marriages. The development of pottery, the domestication of animals, and the cultivation of cereal grains marked the second major stage, barbarism. By the end of that period the smelting of iron and the use of an alphabet had come into being. During this second stage, group marriages gave way to paired families.

Engels notes that the rise of paired families and of restrictions concerning who could marry whom was in part due to the biological problems associated with the sexual reproduction of close biological relatives ([1884], 1972: 47). There were, however, other reasons for the definitive emergence of monogamy—reasons that, Engels argues, were social and economic. As human society evolved there was an increasing social surplus; that is, an increasing difference between the total wealth produced in society and the wealth required for subsistence—for keeping the population alive and reproducing. Subsistence living implies a "hand-to-mouth" existence, with no surplus that can be stored and used later. As humans became more productive, a surplus developed and the basis for a class structure emerged, because with a surplus came the possibility of someone or some group controlling the gains and thereby acquiring a measure of economic power. In Europe men tended to appropriate and control the economic surplus, and as a result they came to have more power. Accompanying this process was the growth of a concern, among those men who controlled the society's economic surplus, with the disposition of the surplus. They wanted both to protect their material wealth on a day-to-day basis and to arrange for its intergenerational transfer: the disposition of the wealth after death. Engels argues that men established a system of monogamy and patriarchy in order to control the disposition of their wealth. By controlling women and attempting to ensure that women only had sexual relations with their designated husbands, men could make certain that their wives bore only their own children, and they could be confident that those children would be legitimate heirs to their properties.

According to Engels, the development of a social surplus and the subsequent appropriation of that surplus as private property provided the basis for the emergence of both a system of social class and a system of patriarchy. The root cause of class and patriarchal domination is to be found in the economic structures and processes of the capitalist system. Given that, the elimination of class and male domination could only come through the transformation of class relations. And because men's domination of women is fundamentally rooted in men's desire to provide legitimate and true heirs for their private productive property, Engels argues, the abolition of private productive property would logically mean that there would be no more need for men to oppress women ([1884], 1972: 71).

BEYOND ENGELS: THE VALUE OF DOMESTIC LABOUR

Debates concerning the strengths, weaknesses, and relevance of Engels's arguments have been legion (see Sayers, Evans, and Redclift 1987). The emergence of yet another surge in the continuing struggles of women for equality and the creation of an egalitarian society after the 1960s produced a renewed interest in the potential insights of the work of Marx and Engels. Among the first to plumb the works of Marx for insights into the nature of contemporary sex and gender roles was Margaret Benston. In a 1969 essay, "The Political Economy of Women's Liberation," Benston (1984) argued that a full understanding of the dynamics of sex and gender relations requires a close look at the nature of housework and its relationship to material production in capitalist society.

Benston's analysis of the relationship between housework and the position of women in society draws on the distinction in Marxian economic theory between use value and exchange value. Commodities or items that have a use to somebody are said to embody use value. If you are hungry and I make you a sandwich and give it to you at no charge, the sandwich can be said to have use value only. Commodities or items that are exchanged for money or traded for another commodity are said to embody exchange value. If instead of freely giving away my sandwich I sell it (exchange it for money), the sandwich can be said to have exchange value. Since capitalist market economies are based on production for sale and profit, commodities produced that embody exchange value are more highly prized and are deemed to be more socially important.

The work that women typically do in the home is unpaid and involves the preparation of meals, childcare, housecleaning, and other family service and support work. Benston argues that this work results in the creation of use value for family members, but it results in no exchange value because women do not charge or get paid for what they produce. Housework is, Benston argues, a form of precapitalist work. The problem for women is that their labour in the home is undervalued and not deemed socially important because no exchange value is produced. As a result both women and the work they do are deemed to be less important than the profit-producing work of men. Benston notes that in the perpetuation of the capitalist system the work that women do in the home is essential, because it involves the consumption of various commodities that the capitalist system produces for sale. In addition, by providing a stable and healthy home life women make it possible for men to continue to work and produce surplus value. Women also are available to enter the workforce during times of need, composing a reserve army of labour to be drawn into the labour force during times of labour shortage or crisis.

The key issue that Benston raises—the relationship between women's work in the household and the overall nature of sex and gender relations in the society—became a topic of considerable debate during the 1970s. Peggy Morton (1972) drew our attention to a new issue involved in connecting women and their domestic labour to the larger society when she argued that women produce one of the most important commodities involved in capitalist production: labour power. Morton does not disagree with the claim that women produce use value; she argues that what is important is that in labour power women are producing the essential commodity that capitalists require if they are to appropriate surplus value. As we know, within the Marxian approach labour power is the essential commodity, given that it is the source of surplus value and thus profits. One of the key social roles that the family plays is making it possible for workers to return to work day after day, week after week, month after month, and even year after year by providing them with a place where they get proper nutrition and can rest and relax and get their "batteries recharged." Others, including Mariarosa Dalla Costa (1972) and Wally Seccombe (1974), have supported this position, even emphasizing in stronger terms the role of housework in the production of surplus value in capitalist society. The question of the precise nature of the relationship between domestic labour and the production of surplus value became the topic of what has become known as the domestic labour debate (for an excellent summary of the various positions, see Armstrong and Armstrong 1990: ch. 5).

What is significant about the debate over the precise nature of domestic labour (housework) in capitalist society is that it points out some important weaknesses in Marxian theory in regard to understanding sex and gender relations. Armstrong and Armstrong (1990: 88) note that at a certain point those engaged in developing our understanding of the nature of sex and gender relations "became increasingly disillusioned by a domestic labour debate that seemed to have reached a dead end." The dead end related less to the role of domestic labour than to the lack of attention devoted to the question of why domestic labour has predominantly been the domain of women. The debate also served to raise the issue of the role of the state in organizing and reproducing sex and gender relations in capitalist society. It was an issue that Mary McIntosh addressed in her important essay "The State and the Oppression of Women."

McIntosh (1978: 255) argues that the state is not involved in the direct oppression of women but contributes to the oppression of women "through its support of a specific form of household." She points out the close relationship between the household system and the larger system of capitalist production. It is in the household that the working class and its labour power are reproduced, and it is also in the household that women are maintained as a reserve army of labour. But McIntosh (1978: 259) adds an essential point: the necessity of understanding the role of the family household within the context of a class-based analysis:

> The part played by the state in these institutions is a complex one; and the state, like society, cannot be analyzed simply in terms of "patriarchy." Capitalist society is one in which men as men dominate women; yet it is not this but class domination that is fundamental to the society. It is a society in which the dominant class is composed mainly of men; yet it is not as men but as capitalists that they are dominant.

McIntosh thus argues for the necessity of understanding the structures and functions of both state and family in capitalist society in relation to the interests of capital and the process of reproducing the system. The state functions in the interests of capital through its efforts to ensure that the family continues to be the site of the production and reproduction of labour power.

Patriarchal family structures also facilitate the maintenance of women as a reserve army of labour.

McIntosh discusses a number of state actions geared to maintaining the patriarchal family and the consequent oppression of women: the formalization and legalization of marriage, taxation laws, population policies, social security policies (including income support), welfare and unemployment legislation, and pensions. She argues convincingly that the state has acted to bolster the structures of the patriarchal family. In the end, however, her analysis is weak in its analytical and explanatory capacity—as indeed she herself notes, acknowledging the fundamentally functionalist nature of her argument (260).

A number of fundamental questions emerge out of this discussion, including some vital *why* questions. Why does the state undertake certain actions? How is it that the state knows what actions to take in order to bolster the structures of the patriarchal family? What is the underlying mechanism or dynamic that explains the emergence and continued presence of patriarchy itself? In the final analysis McIntosh, (1978: 284) explains the structures of the family by reference to both state actions and ideology. "The key problem is the relative inflexibility of the family as a social institution structured by ideologies of human nature, tradition, religion and so on, as well as by state policy." But locating ideology as the explanation of family structures does not explain why the state supports these structures, unless the actions of the state are deemed to be determined primarily by ideology.

BEYOND MARXISM: SOCIALIST FEMINISM
The question of whether the oppression of women in capitalist society can be understood as a subset of the overall oppression of the working class became one of the pivotal issues for many feminists.

In her essay "The Unhappy Marriage of Marxism and Feminism: Toward a More Progressive Union," Heidi Hartmann lays out the rationale for the development of a new analytical approach that incorporates insights from and builds on the strengths of both Marxism and feminism. Marxism has provided potentially powerful analytical tools, she says, but it is essentially flawed: "While Marxist analysis provides essential insight into the laws of historical development, and those of capital in particular, the categories of Marxism are sex blind" (Hartmann 1986: 2). Still, "Feminist analysis by itself is inadequate because it has been blind to history and insufficiently materialist." Her proposed solution is a "more progressive union of Marxism and feminism" (3). The analytical fruit of this more progressive union would be a mode of analysis that simultaneously examines the structures and dynamics of both capitalism and patriarchy. Such an analytical approach would allow us to understand the dynamics not only of capitalism's class exploitation but also of patriarchy's sex- and gender-based exploitation and domination. Since feminists and Marxists are not supposed merely to analyze and engage in intellectual debates about inequality, oppression and exploitation, a new theoretical orientation such as this would offer something more practical. Hartmann explains: "As feminist socialists we must organize a practice which addresses both the struggle against patriarchy and the struggle against capitalism" (33).

That essential project is very much the same as the one attempted by Michèle Barrett in *Women's Oppression Today: Problems in Marxist Feminist Analysis*. Barrett offers a more detailed outline of the analytical logic of a socialist-feminist approach and is critical of traditional Marxian, liberal-feminist, and radical-feminist analyses because they fail to provide an adequate way of understanding and explaining the nature of women's oppression in the complex relations that comprise capitalist society. An adequate analytical approach must take into account "the economic organization of households and its accompanying familial ideology, the division of labour and its accompanying relations of production" (Barrett 1980: 40).

Barrett musters a convincing set of arguments against any form of biological determinism, radical-feminist or otherwise. She then engages in an examination of the concept of ideology that is key to her analysis. Barrett is careful not to suggest that the concept can be used in any simplistic manner; yet she maintains that ideology is central to understanding the structuring of notions of sexuality and gender in capitalist society. After examining the role of the educational system in transmitting ideology, she looks at the dynamics of family life. Barrett is critical of the concept of "the family" because it tends to be ahistorical and ideological. As capitalism has developed there have been various forms of family organization, and to postulate the nuclear family as the norm is to impose an unrealistic model or standard on everyone. "The family" is an ideological concept because it includes ideas about what "normal" sex and gender relations are supposed to be. Important to her understanding of family relations is what she terms the "ideology of familialism," which involves, among other things, "ideologies of domesticity and maternity for women, of bread winning and responsibility for men" (Barrett 1980: 206-07). Such powerful ideological formulations of the "normal" family with associated sex and gender roles become a part of the dominant ideology, and they bear an impact on the thinking, character, and lives of people.

Barrett's analysis of the operation and dynamics of families and households makes it clear that the institution and the assumptions about sex and gender behaviours contained therein do not operate in the best interests of women. She explicitly asks the question of who seems to benefit from the nature of patriarchal family relations and the attendant sex and gender relations. Her answer is that it is not most women and not the working class, though perhaps working-class men get some benefits. As for the ruling class, she concludes that they seem to gain the most from the operation of these social structures, though even in this case the benefits are not exactly unambiguous (Barrett 1980: 222-23).

Barrett also examines the role of the state in maintaining and reinforcing the structures and dynamics of the patriarchal family, noting that throughout history there is evidence that the state has participated in creating social conditions and regulations that foster the oppression of women. She writes:

> A model of women's dependence has become entrenched in the relations of production of capitalism, in the division of labour in wage work and between wage labour and domestic labour. As such, an oppression of women that is not in any essentialist sense pre-given by the logic of capitalist development has become necessary for the ongoing reproduction of the mode of production in its present form. (Barrett 1984: 249)

In focusing her analysis on the emergence of the family household system within western capitalist society, Barrett seeks to avoid simple economic-determinist arguments. She attaches considerable importance to ideology and the historical process through which economic, class, and ideological factors combine to create complex social structures. In her theorizing on the state, Barrett tends not to develop an explicit analysis. There is an assumption in her work that the state is tied to and serves the interests of the bourgeoisie, but *how* this actually happens and *why* are not central components of the analysis.

In a similar vein, although in a substantially different manner, Jane Ursel, a sociologist who has studied the historical roles of women in Canada, argues for a revision of Marxian thought in the study of production, reproduction, patriarchy, and the state (Ursel 1986). Ursel examines how the state in Canada has assisted, through legislation, in the maintenance of patriarchy. Her argument is predicated on a revision of the theories of production and reproduction in capitalist society. Because humans must both produce material necessities and reproduce themselves in order to maintain themselves and human society, Ursel (1986: 153) argues that we must recognize at the level of theory the existence not only of modes of production but also of modes of reproduction: the traditional concept of modes of economic production must be integrated with an analytical framework that has as a central element concepts of modes of reproduction. Ursel (1986: 154) suggests that we think of three distinctive modes of reproduction:

> These are (a) *communal patriarchy*, which corresponds with pre-class, kin-based social systems; (b) *family patriarchy*, which corresponds with class-structured social systems characterized by decentralized processes of production; and (c) *social patriarchy*, which corresponds with advanced wage labour systems.

She adds that the object of her analysis is "the transition from familial patriarchy to social patriarchy" and that, "Moreover, it is within these two modes of reproduction that the state emerges as an important mediator between production and reproduction" (154). Ursel sees one common feature in all patriarchal systems: "The essential condition for the subordination of women within any patriarchal system is *control of women's access to the means of their livelihood....* This control is the essence of patriarchy, its universal function and effect" (153). Much of her subsequent argument focuses on the role of the state in the transition from family to social patriarchy.

Ursel's examination of the role of the state as manifest in legislation is predicated on several assumptions concerning the nature and functions of the state in these modes of reproduction.

> Class societies are marked by two fundamental imperatives, the short-term extraction of surplus in the interests of the dominant class, and the long-term reproduction of the labour supply which is in the interest of the system as a whole. An important role of the state in class societies is to ensure a balanced allocation of labour and non-labour resources between the two spheres of production and reproduction so that the system is maintained both in the long and short term. In brief, the state is the guarantor of the rules of class and the rules of patriarchy and must insure that one system does not disrupt the other. (Ursel 1986: 155)

It is clear from this that the state serves both the interests of the dominant class in a class-based mode of production and the dominant interests in the patriarchal mode of production. But Ursel does not specify precisely why the state serves these dominant interests and how the dominant interests make their will known to the state. She is, however, convincing in her presentation of data and arguments. She illustrates that the state indeed takes on new roles and functions that are essential to the maintenance of both the capitalist mode of production and the patriarchal system. She writes:

> The dynamic of the wage labour system to maximize the extraction of surplus requires the unrelenting commodification of labour which ignores the long-term needs of the social system to maintain and reproduce the population. Under capitalism, however, the existence of the population is dependent upon an adequate allocation of resources to the reproductive unit. The state, charged with preserving the system as a whole, is faced with a major challenge in attempting to mediate the now fundamentally contradictory spheres of production and reproduction. It is under these conditions that social patriarchy emerges as a new regulatory role for the state. (157)

Barrett, Hartmann, and Ursel all draw our attention to an important analytical problem in working to understand sex and gender issues. Can sex and gender relations in our society be understood purely within the context of the patriarchal system, with no reference to the existence of the capitalist society? Or are sex and gender relations in our society to be understood primarily as the outcome of the operation and dynamics of the capitalist system, and thus if that system were changed would we tend to see the emergence of more egalitarian sex and gender relations? Or must we, as Barrett and Hartmann suggest, turn our analytical attention to understanding both capitalism and patriarchy and the intersections between the two?

RADICAL FEMINISM

While liberal feminists have focused on changing social institutions and practices by changing sexist values, norms, and ideas, Marxian feminists have debated the precise manner by which women are exploited within the capitalist class structure. Socialist feminists insist that neither approach adequately understands that women in capitalist society are oppressed in a double sense in that they are typically exploited both by the class system and by being female in a patriarchal social system. One other stream of feminist thought, though, argues that none of these approaches is radical enough and that they all miss the most fundamental form of exploitation experienced by all women.

Among the most powerful of the feminist treatises of the last half-century is Shulamith Firestone's *The Dialectic of Sex: The Case for Feminist Revolution* first published in 1970. Firestone maintains that men and women must be understood as being members of separate and distinctive classes. For Firestone, the basis of class is biological and, as in the Marxian analysis, one class has historically been dominant and exploitative. Using the concept of sex-class as the basis of her analysis, Firestone argues that men have dominated and exploited women largely because of women's biological role in species reproduction. The fact that women give birth is at the root of the problem. In her words:

> We have seen how women, biologically distinguished from men, are culturally distinguished from "human." Nature produced the fundamental inequality—half the human race must bear and rear the children of all of them—which was later consolidated, institutionalized, in the interests of men. Reproduction of the species cost women dearly, not only emotionally, psychologically, culturally but even in strict material (physical) terms: before recent methods of contraception, continuous childbirth led to constant "female trouble," early aging, and death. Women were the slave class that maintained the species in order to free the other half for the business of the world—

187

admittedly often its drudge aspects but certainly all its creative aspects as well. (Firestone 1984: 141)

It is therefore as a result of the biological processes of childbirth that women are forced to depend on men for long periods of time, and this dependency has resulted in the emergence of the larger patterns of domination and subordination characteristic of patriarchal society.

Firestone uses analogies drawn from Marxism to compare the struggles of women with those of the exploited proletarian underclass as they seek to overthrow the oppressor. In the case of women as a sex-class the obstacles may be even greater, because one of the root causes is biological. She notes that the first demand of the alternate system must be: "*The freeing of women from the tyranny of their reproductive biology by every means available, and the diffusion of the childbearing and childrearing role to the society as a whole, men as well as women*" (Firestone 1984: 141, emphasis in original). She then discusses some fairly commonly accepted means for diffusing child-rearing responsibilities, including family planning, twenty-four-hour childcare centres, and such. As for the child-bearing function, she writes:

> At the other extreme there are more distant solutions based on the potentials of modern embryology, that is, artificial reproduction, possibilities still so frightening that they are seldom discussed seriously. We have seen that the fear is to some extent justified: in the hands of the current society and under the direction of current scientists (few of whom are female or even feminist), any attempt to use technology to "free" the body is suspect. But we are speculating about post-revolutionary systems, and for the purposes of our discussion we shall assume flexibility and good intentions in those working out the change. (Firestone 1984: 142)

Given, then, that the causes of women's oppression are rooted in biology, the solutions must be radical in the truest sense of the word. Firestone (1984: 136) admits that many people will have difficulty even contemplating what she is suggesting:

> But the reaction of the common man, woman and child—"*That?* Why you can't change *that!* You must be out of your mind!—is closest to the truth. We are talking about something every bit as deep as that. The gut reaction—the assumption that, even when they don't know it, feminists are talking about changing a fundamental biological condition—is an honest one.

The revolution that Firestone is talking about will have an impact on every social institution, including the state; however, like most revolutionary situations it is not possible to prescribe or predict what the new institutions might look like.

An alternative, but also biologically related, explanation for the oppression of women by men is found in the work of Mary O'Brien. In *The Politics of Reproduction* O'Brien locates the roots of patriarchy and male domination in the processes of biological reproduction, but in a manner that is quite different from Firestone's. O'Brien (1981: 11) agrees that Marxian-style "class analysis cannot wholly comprehend the genesis and actuality of male dominance." She acknowledges the fundamental fact that biological reproduction is an essential species activity: "The unifying thread in all this is human history, but human history perceived as a social process which has as an absolutely and inescapably necessary substructure the process of human reproduction" (13). Elsewhere she states the matter even more clearly: "Yet it is the reproduction process, I submit, that is the material base of the social relations of reproduction, and is also the material base of generic community (O'Brien 1988: 102). The explicit reference to a Marxian concept, substructure, is quite deliberate because O'Brien goes on to utilize other concepts borrowed from Marx. Of particular importance are the concepts of productive labour and alienation.

O'Brien examines the differential biological roles played by women and men in the process of reproduction. As a result of the physical act of copulation the man becomes alienated from his seed. The woman, on the other hand, plays the central role, literally engaged in productive and reproductive labour for the entire gestation period as she biologically nurtures a new human life. Following Marx, O'Brien postulates that men and women develop different forms of consciousness and understandings. As for women, there is no doubt about the role and importance that they play in biological reproduction. Nor is there any doubt about the role that their labour, or their maternal status, plays. The situation is different for men. They have been alienated from the reproductive process since ejaculation and play no significant productive role after copulation, and their parental status may even be questioned. As a result men seek to appropriate and control what they had been alienated from—the child and mother under the rubric of their family (O'Brien 1981: Ch. 1). In so doing men are able to simultaneously secure several benefits: "Thus the appropriation of the child is at the same time the appropriation of the mother's alienated labour. It is in this sense that paternal right is the right of the appropriator. Paternity may well have been man's first experience of the joys of getting something for nothing" (O'Brien 1988: 105). What has emerged in history, then, is complex institutional and social practices that serve to legitimate, perpetrate, and ensure male domination.

Yet another, more recent, discussion in feminist thought has centred on the question of "diversity and commonality" (see, for instance, Code 1993; see also Bannerji 2000 who has begun this task by integrating gender and race—

and class—into an understanding of nation-building). While feminists of various streams have "rallied around a common cause in their opposition to patriarchy," celebrating the sisterhood of all women, the idea of "difference" has also become prominent as new theories of race have been added to the older theories of gender. It has been argued that women have "failed to take into account the effects of institutionalized racism" and that factors of ethnic, racial, and sexual diversity have to be more adequately incorporated into feminist analysis. As theorist Lorraine Code puts it, "The historical goal of achieving equality for women has to be refined and redefined if it is to retain any legitimacy as a feminist project" (Burt, Code, and Dorney 1993: 48).

A final word on how radical feminism views the polity. Alison Jaggar (1983: 100) explains the implications of the radical-feminist critique for political theory: "Radical feminism is far more than an attempt to make existing political theory consistent or to plug its gaps. Instead, it constitutes an entirely new way of perceiving or even identifying political phenomena." Elsewhere she explains that radical feminism is not like traditional political theory:

> Radical feminism ... has different political values; it asks and seeks to answer different questions; it focuses on different areas; and it has developed a very different mode of expression. The first radical feminist writings most closely resembled those of traditional political theory: although lively and polemical, their authors seemed to be trying to produce political analyses of women's situation that were formally identical with traditional analyses. As the radical feminist movement mushroomed, however, its forms of expression became increasingly imaginative and "non-linear." Radical feminists created new music, new poetry, new drama, and new science fiction. Even the prose writing of radical feminism became more impassioned, meta-phorical and epigrammatic. Every available linguistic resource was employed to jolt the audience out of its accustomed ways of perceiving the world and to reveal "a counter-reality, a mutually guaranteed support of female experience undistorted by male interpretation." (Jaggar 1983: 287)

Most often feminist theories, then, have not yet articulated systematic theories of the state that explain how and why the state seems to be able to produce and reproduce patriarchal social practices and structures. There have been exceptions, as in the work of law professor Catharine MacKinnon, whose work *Toward a Feminist Theory of the State* explicitly addresses the issue of the sex- and gender-based actions and logic of the liberal state in capitalist society. In her preface MacKinnon (1989: xi) explains her objective:

As the work progressed, publication of earlier versions of parts of this book ... gave me the benefit of the misunderstandings, distortions, and misreadings of a wide readership. This experience suggests that it must be said that this book does not try to explain everything. It attempts an analysis of gender which can explain the pervasive and crucial place sex occupies as a dimension that is socially pervasive and, in its own sense, structural. It seeks to understand gender as a form of power and power in its gendered forms. To look for the place of gender in everything is not to reduce everything to gender.

Before turning her attention to the issue of the state, MacKinnon (1989: 80) discusses the relationship of feminist analysis to Marxism and the difficulties of achieving a synthesis, because "Taking women's conditions seriously revises existing definitions of social exploitation"—often an impossible task for Marxists because they tend to slip into tautologies about the capitalist system. Her conclusion is therefore "that it is necessary to recast the vision of the totality to be explained."

She herself recasts that vision by arguing that the state, through its actions, policies, and legislation relating to issues such as rape and sexual coercion, abortion, pornography, and sexual equality, is very much a patriarchal state. In her final chapter, "Toward Feminist Jurisprudence," she calls for an alternative standpoint to replace the existing male-dominated worldview:

> In male supremacist societies, the male standpoint dominates civil society in the form of the objective standard—that standpoint which, because it dominates in the world, does not appear to function as a standpoint at all. Under its aegis, men dominate women and children, three-quarters of the world. Family and kinship rules and sexual mores guarantee reproductive ownership and sexual access and control to men as a group. Hierarchies among men are ordered on the basis of race and class, stratifying women as well. The state incorporates these facts of social power in and as law. Two things happen: law becomes legitimate, and social dominance becomes invisible. Liberal legalism is thus a medium for making male dominance both invisible and legitimate by adopting the male point of view in law at the same time as it enforces that view on society. (MacKinnon 1989: 237)

In western society, MacKinnon (1989: 169) maintains: "The state, through law, institutionalizes male power over women through institutionalizing the male point of view in law. Its first state act is to see women from the standpoint of male dominance; its next act is to treat them that way. She summarizes with a powerful statement: "However autonomous of class the liberal state may appear, it is not autonomous of sex. Male power is systemic. Coercive, legitimized, and epistemic, it *is* the regime" (170). To the extent that her alternative feminist or female-oriented jurisprudence might seem radical, one-sided, and utopian, MacKinnon ends her book with an important note:

> Equality will require change, not reflection—a new jurisprudence, a new relation between life and law. Law that does not dominate life is as difficult to envision as a society in which men do not dominate women, and for the same reasons. To the extent feminist law embodies women's point of view, it will be said that its law is not neutral. But existing law is not neutral. It will be said that it undermines the legitimacy of the legal system. But the legitimacy of existing law is based on force at women's expense. Women have never consented to its rule—suggesting that the system's legitimacy needs repair that women are in a position to provide. It will be said that feminist law is special pleading for a particular group and one cannot start that or where will it end. But existing law is already special pleading for a particular group, where it has ended. The question is not where it will stop, but whether it will start for any group but the dominant one. It will be said that feminist law cannot win and will not work. But this is premature. Its possibilities cannot be assessed in the abstract but must engage the world. A feminist theory of the state has barely been imagined; systematically, it has never been tried. (249)

One further vital issue that, unfortunately, we will only touch on briefly here is the question of the state in its relation to gay and lesbian politics. Brenda Crossman's (1996) analysis of the struggle in Ontario over the Equity Rights Statute Amendment Law, which would have removed formal discrimination against gays and lesbians, is instructive in that it demonstrates two points: first, that the state is vitally involved in sexual politics; and second, that its tendencies are towards maintaining patriarchy. R.W. Connell (1990: 519) reached this conclusion on the basis of other evidence: "This adds up to a convincing picture of the state as an active player in gender politics. Nobody acquainted with the facts revealed in this research can any longer accept the silence about gender in the traditional state theory, whether liberal, socialist, or conservative." In his study *Masculinities*, Connell points out:

> The state, for instance, is a masculine institution. To say this is not to imply that the personalities of the top male office-holders somehow seep through and stain the institution. It is to say something much stronger: that the state organizational practices are structures in relation to the reproductive arena. The overwhelming majority of top office-holders are men because there is a gender configuring of

recruitment and promotion, a gender configuring of the internal division of labour and systems of control, a gender configuring of policymaking, practical routines, and ways of mobilizing pleasure and consent. (Connell 1995: 73)

There can be no doubt, then, that the state in capitalist society is vitally important to the construction, production, and reproduction of sex and gender relations. While the ideas outlined in this chapter are disparate in their premises, articulation, and conclusions, they all draw our attention to the importance of power as a dimension of sex and gender relations. What they do not all do, however, is extend their analysis of power to the arena of the polity. What we need are analytical frameworks and approaches that will allow us to better analyze, understand, and explain *how* and *why* the state seems to act so as to produce, maintain, and reproduce the structures and daily inequalities that are the hallmarks of patriarchal society.

• TEN •

CONCLUSION:
CRITIQUING STATE THEORIES

The study and analysis of the state remain mired in controversy and disagreement. Despite hundreds of years of debate and thousands of books and articles, social scientists have not developed a single approach that enjoys widespread support and acceptance, nor are they ever likely to do so. As a result, students of human society interested in understanding the polity and political power are required to comprehend and evaluate the heuristic value of a myriad of different positions. But how can we begin to determine the adequacy of these different approaches?

The central problem to address in attempting to evaluative alternate theoretical positions is the matter of establishing a basis for evaluation. Several potential approaches can be used for this, including the standard positivist approach of empirical verifiability. Evaluating theories on the basis of empirical data assumes an acceptance of objective external data that are theory-neutral. That is, it is possible to assume that regardless of one's theoretical position or orientation empirical data do exist, and this material can be collected and used as a basis of comparative analysis. George Ritzer (1975: 110) and Thomas Kuhn (1962: Ch. III), among others, argue that this position is open to question. If what is accepted as "data" or "evidence" is in part determined by one's theory, an alternative basis of comparison may be required. Many social scientists still maintain that empirical support is the "court of last appeal." This aspect of theory evaluation has several dimensions, one being the capacity of a theory to generate verifiable hypotheses. Can we use a theory or perspective to generate a hypothesis that we can subsequently test with empirical data?

In addition to this empirical if not positivist criterion, theories might also be evaluated on the basis of their capacity to offer explanations for a particular database or empirical/historical phenomenon or event. Critical evaluation might thus involve, first, determining if support for the theory can be garnered and, second, determining the capacity of the theory to explain a range of empirical data that might be encountered in social investigation.

A second approach might be to follow the lead of John Wilson (1983), Alvin Gouldner (1970), and others who have argued that theories are complicated sets of concepts, propositions, and arguments that tend to be predicated on basic assumptions that are often unstated and implicit. These background assumptions—to borrow Gouldner's term—are often the implicit and unstated basis of more particular theoretical statements. It follows that a theory might be evaluated on the basis of its overall coherence and logic, along with a consideration of the extent and manner by which the background and domain assumptions of a theory represent an integrated argument. Theories in the social sciences are most often complex entities containing a variety of postulations, correlations, and assumptions. The degree of internal consistency between and among these various aspects of a theoretical approach is an important basis for evaluating a theory's capacity to explain. An elementary requirement for a theory to be deemed acceptable is that it be internally self-consistent. We can use this third approach as a basis of evaluation when considering alternative approaches.

We can evaluate theories, then, by examining the basic assumptions on which they are predicated—assumptions that often provide the overall logic for their explanations. We can also compare theories by looking at their internal logical and argumentative consistency. Finally, we can evaluate theories by looking at their capacity to explain given databases and by considering the extent to which data can be garnered to support a theory's central postulations.

The following discussion is intended to raise questions that address core issues for some of the various approaches or theories of the state in capitalist society. Some of these questions address fundamental assumptions and amount to a demand that we re-examine the basic premises of the theories, while others are more empirical in nature. Ultimately an adequate theory should generate that research, if only because such a theory must attempt to actually explain the world we live in.

CRITICAL ISSUES FOR CLASSICAL LIBERALISM

A key element of the classical liberal position from Hobbes and Locke through the utilitarian thinkers is their advocacy of the existence of some form of human nature. Hobbes and Locke both maintain that there was a presocial fixed and eternal human nature that required rational, self-interested, possessive individuals to contemplate and subsequently consummate a social contract, giving rise to a market-based society with an appropriate form of the state. The assumption was that market relations were natural to humans and that the basic possessive individualism of market-oriented humans could only be "socialized" by the presence of a state. The notion that humans are self-seeking utilitarians continued in the work of Mill and Bentham.

The basis of these assumptions should certainly be questioned, especially in the light of the works of cultural anthropologists over the last two centuries. Given the data collected in cross-cultural studies, anthropology, sociology, and social psychology, are we able to support the concept of a fixed and static, possessive, individualistic human nature?

The classical liberal notion of self-seeking individuals as human nature, and market society as fixed and natural, contains definite implications for the study of a broad range of issues including sex, gender, and economic inequality. In Locke's work human rationality ultimately becomes equated with the possession of property; however, he himself recognized the limitations that nature imposes on appropriation for every member of the species. At some point the possibility of every human mixing their labour with nature so as to appropriate it as private property ceases to exist. The result is the emergence of humans without property and without the possibility of acquiring property. If we extend this argument to its logical conclusion, we can argue that market society produces inequalities, and if we push the argument further it produces classes.

If fundamental inequalities among humans are a necessary outcome of market relations, what are the implications for an understanding of the state? What are the legitimate functions of the state in a market society? Is the state's sole legitimate function the provision of a basis for market transactions and the enforcement of contracts? If so, what measure of control do participants have over the state's actions? How do we prevent the functioning of the market from producing massive inequalities? How do we ensure democracy in the face of massive inequalities? In wrestling with this question classical liberalism tended to limit democratic participation to those, for example, with property, or those deemed mentally competent. What limitations on full democratic participation are we willing to accept? How are we to attempt to legitimize participation?

CRITICAL ISSUES FOR SOCIOLOGICAL FUNCTIONALISM

Compared to the classical liberals, thinkers included under the rubric of sociological conceptions of the state use a substantially different set of fundamental assumptions. Like their classical liberal predecessors, Comte and Durkheim were concerned with the problem of social order. For the early sociologists however, the basis of disorder is not human nature, but, rather, either the lack of a moral or normative code in society or the existence of weak, ineffective moral codes. Comte and Durkheim understood social order as based on a shared normative value system that all members of a society understand and accept and that therefore provides the basis of social interaction.

The establishment of a shared normative orientation is only one of the key problems faced by human social systems. Sociological functionalism, especially as systematically developed by Parsons, tends to assume that social institutions perform basic *functions* for society as a whole. According to this thinking, the analysis of any institution begins with an understanding of the particular function that institutions perform for society as a whole.

In relation to these assumptions, we must question the argument that normative orientations or moral codes can provide the basis of social order. In addition, we must concern ourselves with the origins and formulation of moral codes. What are the implications of the tendency of sociological theorists, with the exception of Weber, to ignore or downplay inequality, change, contradiction, and even conflict?

If we combine these concerns, a series of questions emerges. Can we ignore the inequalities of income characteristic of market society? Can we understand the process by which a society's norms and values are formulated without reference to inequalities and relations of power? Can we assume that a given set of norms and values is somehow "society's as a whole"? Can we assume that relations of power and domination are not a fundamental aspect of human relations? Can we assume that stability, order, and consensus are the normal conditions of human society?

CRITICAL ISSUES FOR ELITE AND PLURALIST THEORY

By definition, elite theorists accept the inevitability of social, economic, and political inequalities. Because, at least in the classical positions, this condition was partly attributed to biological factors, this assumption stands open to challenge. No matter what complex of environmental and genetic factors produces human behaviours, all simple determinist arguments must be challenged. Evidence must be provided to support such contentions and alternative explanations of human conduct and characteristics must be addressed and refuted.

As illustrated by our review of Michels (1962), with its emphasis on the development and role of social organizations, elite theory need not rely on arguments based on biological factors. Michels accepts the inevitability of a certain organizational imperative as leading to oligarchy. While the problems that Michels identifies are very real, is the process indeed inevitable? Are there means by which organizations can structurally seek to diminish the processes leading towards leadership control? Are genuine mass-based democratic organizations, parties, and institutions possible? Does the fact that such institutions and organizations have not been the norm in the past mean that we disregard their possible development in the future? Is it not possible for humans to learn from the past and seek to counter the problems facing democracy in the future? Is there an alternative to merely accepting inequalities as a necessary aspect of the human condition?

Some elite theorists argue that the basis of elite membership is rooted in the special characteristics of those key organizational and institutional positions. This position fails to explain, however, why some individuals come to occupy those positions and others do not. If the answer is education, or the development through training of some special attribute, it then becomes necessary to explain the existence of educational differences. Does the element of class position, perhaps, provide a more adequate explanation of the basis of these sorts of individual differences?

In modern pluralist theory the mode of theorizing about the state tends not to be based on any identifiable concept of human nature, although Bentley

(1935) and Merriam (1964) tend to view conflict as inevitable. They suggest that an element of human nature is involved. Contemporary pluralists such as Dahl also view conflict as inevitable, but see the basis of conflict in the plurality of groups that emerge in modern industrial society. In suggesting that the state or government is the key centre of decision-making and the location of legitimate conflict and competition between differing groups, modern pluralists make a major assumption: that the various groups, parties, or associations compete on more or less equal terms. This is the key tenet of pluralism, and it raises fundamental questions.

Are the various interest groups, associations, and parties that attempt to influence the state decision-making process in any sense fundamentally, more or less, equal? Do all citizens have more or less equal opportunity to organize, lobby, and influence the electoral process, thereby influencing the state? Is it not possible that economic inequalities, which pluralists recognize as existing, might be the basis of a class system? If so, how can we be sure there is no class that is able to translate economic power into political power effectively? If all groups are not more or less equal, or if there are economic inequalities that render certain groups more politically powerful, a fundamental tenet of pluralism is surely undermined.

Like functionalist theory, pluralism assumes the existence of some broadly conceived social or national interest that the state or government serves. Such a notion must imply a lack of substantial divisions, class or otherwise, in the society. Is it possible in an advanced industrial society to assume that the manifold differences within the population can be subsumed under the rubric of some "national interest"? If this is indeed possible, how can we be sure that it is not a form of normative or ideological domination? Is it possible that a powerful group or class is able to influence a society's norms and values, thereby "setting the agenda" and thus influencing the content and direction of political debate?

A final question flowing out of these points relates to another fundamental point of the pluralist approach: Does history confirm that in the long run the political process produces no consistent winners or losers? Is there "give and take" or "wins and losses" for all those attempting to influence state policy? It goes without saying that the answers to these questions are crucial to the pluralist thesis.

CRITICAL ISSUES FOR MARXISTS: TRADITIONAL AND NEO

Much of Marx's analysis and critique of capitalist society is predicated on a concept of species being. The basis of the materialist approach is an assumed primacy of economic activity in human existence, a point that Marx argues is empirically demonstrable. Was this a simple overconcentration on one dimension of human existence?

In Marx's work on the state, which of the two apparent alternate approaches represents his position? Is the state an autonomous institution that functions to maintain the capitalist system? What is the relationship of the state to the other institutions, especially the economic? Phrased somewhat differently: Is the state a part of the superstructure whose structures, actions, and policies simply reflect the "requirements" of the economically dominant class? Is the state an autonomous arena of human practice, linked to but not simply determined by economic structures and relations? Marx's failure to complete his analytical theoretical exposition on the state left a legacy of uncertainty that still haunts neo-Marxist theory.

In articulating their view of the state in essentially functionalist terms, some neo-Marxists make it difficult to differentiate themselves from more orthodox functionalists. In discussing institutions in essentially functionalist terms, do some neo-Marxists merely substitute the "dominant class" for "society" and develop a new functionalism? What is the real difference between analysis that views the state in functional terms, as an institution that functions to maintain a system in the interests of the society, and analysis that postulates that the state functions to maintain the system in the interests of a specific class? Are both approaches not somewhat tautological and circular, especially at the level of empirical analysis? Theda Skocpol (1980) and Colin Crouch (1979) have criticized some neo-Marxists for their functionalist tendencies. Crouch (1979: 3) in particular argues that by slipping into this functionalist mode of analysis Marxists have provided "no acceptable answer to the fundamental question: Why must the state in capitalist society serve the interest of capitalism?"

The central task of neo-Marxist theory thus becomes a matter of answering this question in non-functionalist terms. Although one might argue that Szymanski's approach, for instance, offers a capacity to deal with this issue, he also provides an inadequate analysis of the relationship of the state to the large social structures. The problems with the theory of base-superstructure once again emerge.

TOWARDS AN ALTERNATIVE FRAMEWORK
Human beings are a unique species in that we are cultural and social and not instinctual animals. Our many unique physiological traits, including our huge and complex brain organ, have allowed us to develop social solutions and ways of dealing with our various individual and species needs, drives, and problems. Human social structures, including various institutional orders, must be understood as having developed as a result of humans acting socially and deliberately in response to these individuals and species needs, drives, and problems. The emergence and development of social arrangements, structures, and institutions are part of an important process for human development, because once these structures develop and emerge they in turn become a central determinant of subsequent behaviour.

As a species humans face a number of problems, are influenced by a number of drives, and must deal with a number of needs; however, not all of these factors are of equal importance for our individual and species survival. Two sets of needs or problems are paramount. First, if we are to survive, we must provide ourselves with the necessary material basis for our physical existence—we must have food, clothing, and shelter, for instance. In addition, if we are to survive as a species we must engage in biological reproduction to ensure that the current generation will not be the last. Without these activities there can be no individuals or no continuing society. Clearly, these activities represent an essential core of activities around which all other human social practices emerge and revolve. Before there can be a formal political order, an organized educational system, or even systematic religious practices, we must satisfy our material needs and ensure biological reproduction.

The relationship between those human practices and activities associated with material production and species reproduction and the larger social structure, such as the state or the polity, is complex. The social structure consists of various social arrangements and social practices, which we call institutions. These institutions are what social scientists call the economy, the family, the polity, religion, and the educational order; and they are part of a larger whole or totality connected through a complicated reciprocal set of relationships. Because we are an intelligent and communicative species, the development and operation of these various institutions have been accompanied by the emergence of sets of ideas, stocks of knowledge, and ideologies related to how things are done or should be done and in general to how the world works. Each of these sets of organized institutionalized practices has its own internal structures and patterns of organization as well as its own complex relationships with the other institutional orders that make up the social totality.

The social structure of a modern capitalist society can be analytically dissected into several broad areas of human practice. The economy (practices relating to material production) and the household system (practices relating to species reproduction) are central and fundamental to the existence of individual humans and society as a whole. Other institutional orders or clusters are the polity (the political order, or state) and the wide range of other social interactions, practices, and activities that comprise our social existence, all of which are part of what we will term "civil society." As John Urry (1981) points out, the concept of civil society includes a large number of practices and structures that are essential to the existence of humans. Its broad rubric includes practices and arrangements commonly associated with education, religion, recreation, and the media. In essence, civil society can be taken to include most areas of human action and practice not associated with reproduction, production, or the polity.

Using a series of concentric circles to depict these complex relationships, we would place the household and economic orders at the core since they represent the fundamental institutionalized social practices that underpin the continued survival of individual human beings and the species as a whole. The next circle represents the ideas, ideologies, and stocks of knowledge that humans produce and generate as they go about the social activities of biological reproduction and material production. The bold lines radiating outward, which indicate a primary influence, and the dotted lines pointing inward towards the core, which indicate reciprocal, but less significant, influences and causality. The multiple practices and institutions that make up civil society are structured, moulded, and shaped by our reproductive and productive activities and are mediated through an attendant and associated polity and the stocks of knowledge that we generate as we go about producing satisfaction for our material needs and biologically reproducing ourselves.

The task of social analysis is to fill in the details concerning the structure and organization of the various practices that make up the economy, the household, civil society, and the state. Such a task requires the development of a theoretically informed mode of social analysis capable of operating at several levels of abstraction. We must, for instance, be able to make analytical

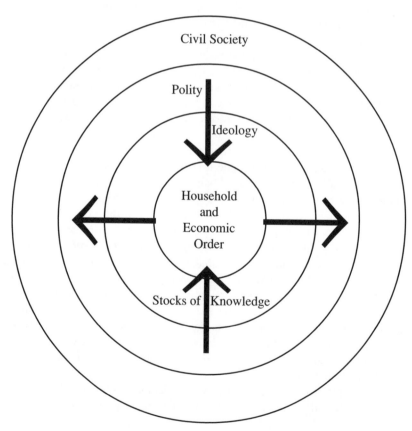

statements about how the capitalist system operates in the abstract as well as about how the system operates at the level of a particular society at a specific moment in time. Social analysis continually moves from one level of abstraction to another, engaging in analysis of a concrete society at one moment and then making generalizations about the nature of social phenomena in similar types of societies the next. Understanding the nature and operation of the state in a liberal-democratic society means gaining a grasp on the nature of the society's economic and household orders both at the general or abstract level and at the particular, empirical, and concrete level. In addition it is necessary to understand the nature and structure of civil society and, of course, of the structure and organization of the polity.

Within this social structure, a number of factors establish the unique role and structure of the liberal-democratic state:

- The state is more formally organized and structured than any other institutional order. The organized nature of the state is often apparent in the existence of a formal constitutional structure.
- The state's existence is usually associated with the existence of a specific territory and a claim for the legitimate right to use violence to protect its territory and structures.
- The actions and policies of the state have a major impact on other institutional orders. Decisions, actions, and policies taken within the structures of the polity can have an impact on virtually every member of society in every other realm of practice.
- The importance of the state for other institutional practices is evident in the fact that control over the state is often the central concern of those seeking to implement radical programs of social change.

THE ECONOMY

In a capitalist society economic activity is organized on the basis of private ownership of the society's productive resources, with the production, distribution, and consumption of wealth governed by social relations centred on the dynamics of the market. A fundamental characteristic of all market economies is the presence of a class structure. Class position, based on the insights of Marx and Weber, is fundamentally determined by a person's structural relationship to society's productive resources and by the resources a person brings to the marketplace. For instance, people who bring capital to the marketplace and who, as a result, are in ownership positions are in a different class from those entering the market with only their labour power to sell. The class structure of an advanced capitalist nation contains several groupings, including: 1) the corporate ruling class; 2) the petite bourgeoisie; 3) a new middle class; 4) the working class; and 5) the poor (Clegg, Boreham, and Dow 1986; Bilton et al. 1987).

The corporate ruling class is made up of people who own the major economic enterprises in society. The petite bourgeoisie includes people who own some productive property from which they receive income but who employ either no workers or only a small number of workers (Clegg, Boreham, and Dow 1986, suggest fewer than ten). The new middle class is composed of a heterogeneous group of individuals whose major role in the economy is, first, to help the owners of the major productive enterprises realize profits and, second, to assist in the general operation of the various state systems that work for the maintenance and reproduction of the larger social system. This grouping would include various legal and financial professionals. The working class is made up of people whose primary source of income is the sale of their labour power, mainly to those in the corporate ruling class. The poor are people who are either chronically unemployed or employed on a seasonal basis; as a result they have no stable long-term connections with the larger patterns of economic activity.

Because the class structures of capitalist society are extremely complex, there are internal divisions within the corporate ruling class, both among various sectors of the corporate ruling class and among the representatives of industrial, resource, financial, banking, and merchandising capital. Similarly, among the members of the petite bourgeoisie there are fractions representing different sectors of the economy, different regions, or other different interests. The new middle class and the working class can also be subdivided into fractions representing different sectors of the economy, occupations, and types and levels of skills. Ultimately, whatever the grouping or class, a person's position in the economic order is determined by market position, which is the central determinant of that person's share of the social surplus.

THE HOUSEHOLD SYSTEM

Given that the survival of the human species is dependent on continued biological reproduction—a process involving the development of complex social arrangements and relationships between the sexes and including the development of arrangements for the care and raising of extremely dependent human infants—such reproductive activity must be analyzed as a central dimension of human social existence.

In the past social scientists tended to ignore the systematic study of reproductive relations, gender relations, and patterns of interaction between the sexes. As a result it is only quite recently that we have begun to see the emergence of a set of basic concepts and terms to assist understanding of human social relations within the household system. For example, the term *patriarchy* is now used to direct our attention to key characteristics of the household system that have emerged in the west. In most if not all of the capitalist world we exist within the confines of a patriarchal household system. While there are many continuing debates about the precise meaning of the term, for our purposes it is enough to define a patriarchal system as one in which men dominate women.

The domination of women by men can take several forms. For instance, a sex-based division of labour in which women do the major portion of domestic labour, including childcare, typically characterizes the patriarchal household. A patriarchal system also usually involves a devaluation of women's tasks in and out of the household—and much of this work consists of performing services for men. What is significant about the patriarchal system we live in today is the extent to which male domination has become a central aspect of virtually all aspects of society. In the various institutions—particularly in the economy, most aspects of civil society, and the state—the key positions of power and control are almost always occupied by men; and many of the institutional orders seem to operate primarily to perpetuate male dominance.

Given the centrality of patriarchal relations in our society, to understand the role of the state we clearly require an approach that allows us to understand the basis of and dynamics of patriarchy. Many thinkers and theorists, including Mary O'Brien (1981), have convincingly argued that the very existence of patriarchy makes the concept difficult to understand and use, because social science thinking itself is male-dominated. O'Brien's reference to male-stream thought is meant to indicate that our very modes of understanding social experiences and processes have themselves become part of the patterns of domination inherent in a patriarchal system (O'Brien 1981: 6).

But the existence of long-standing traditions of male-stream thinking in the western social sciences has now been successfully and dramatically challenged by the emergence of varied streams of feminist thinking and theory, which have begun to redress the fundamental flaws in the established approaches and theories. This feminist thinking clearly represents the most vibrant and exciting direction in modern scholarship, and it is clear that this literature must form the core of our analysis of these processes, whether that analysis utilizes some form of dual systems approach or not (See England 1993).

MECHANISMS OF POWER: CONNECTING THE POLITY

If social analysis directed at the polity is to avoid the simplicity and teleological thinking that characterize various kinds of functionalist thought, theorists must develop an approach that provides for the possibility of empirical research into state actions and decisions. It is not enough to explain an action of policy in terms of its functional importance or contribution to society, capital accumulation, or even patriarchy. Unfortunately, most of the existing approaches have significant weaknesses in their basic premises and, in many cases, functionalist proclivities, and it is important to develop an approach that breaks out of this pattern—that is, to develop a non-functionalist approach that is capable of facilitating empirical research.

In looking at the operation of the state in liberal-democratic society we can note some basic premises. To begin with, liberal-democratic states are highly structured, complex, bureaucratic, and formal institutions. In most liberal democracies the structures and operation of the state are formally established and recognized within codified written constitutions. The state structures are composed of the government, various bureaucracies and agencies, and the military and judiciary. While the operation of all branches of the polity can have an impact on society, in liberal-democratic systems the core of the decision-making and policy formation process resides within the government, that is, within the legislative and executive branches. Although there are instances in which state bureaucracies and agencies have altered the intended impact of government policies and actions, the legislature is the ultimate decision-making body.

A central question here is: How can we come to understand the political practices and processes that are central to the operation of the liberal-democratic state? More specifically we might ask: How do individuals, classes, and groups in capitalist society influence the processes, operation, decision-making, and activities of the liberal-democratic state?

To answer such questions, Szymanski's ideas about linkages to the state or what he calls mechanisms of power seem like a useful point of departure (see Chapter Six). The essence of the approach resides in the argument that the dominant class in liberal-democratic society influences the state through a system of direct and indirect linkages. Extending this mode of analysis, we could argue that these modes of control or linkages to the state are available not only to classes whose bases are in the economy but also to groups and social forces whose bases are best understood within the context of the domestic system or civil society. For example, sexist ideologies, which necessarily emerge from a patriarchal organization of reproduction, can make an impact on the operation of the state; or male-dominated organizations can attempt to use mechanisms of power to compel the state to take particular actions. What we need to clarify is the nature of these linkages or mechanisms of power through which individuals, groups, and classes can have an effect.

The electoral process is one obvious direct mechanism of power. It involves a variety of processes, from the funding of the electoral process and political parties to the actual presentation and election of candidates. These activities work to influence the actual selection of those individuals involved in state decision-making. The precise options open will vary depending on the nature of the system; for instance, depending on whether it is parliamentary or republican; or depending on the voting procedures—whether they are preferential or "first past the post." The nature of political party structures also varies from social formation to social formation, with different options and possibilities available in different locations at different conjunctures.

A second direct mechanism of power quite unrelated to personnel selection is the lobbying process. Again depending on the precise nature of the system, lobbying and pressure group tactics of various sorts can be directed at the president, the cabinet, backbenchers, or even the agencies and bureaucracies. This sort of activity provides a potential mechanism of power for those interested in influencing the state, and it is most often an activity open to empirical investigation, in that it is possible to determine precisely if, when, and how the mechanism is used.

A third direct mechanism of power available to those attempting to influence the state is the policy-formation process. Most industrial liberal democracies have witnessed the emergence of a variety of policy-formation "think-tank organizations" in recent years. Though not of the calibre or importance of organizations such as the Trilateral Commission, organizations in Britain such as the Adam Smith Institute and the Institute of Economic Affairs and in Canada such as the Fraser Institute and the C.D. Howe Institute are active in advising governments and in publishing papers and reports, all purporting to offer sound and even scientific advice to governments. The coverage that such reports and events receive in the mass media makes it difficult for governments and state personnel to ignore them. In addition governments often solicit the "scientific" advice of such organizations when planning policy decisions.

In addition to these direct means of influencing state policy there are more structural or indirect mechanisms related to the larger social and economic environment. These are economic and ideological mechanisms. One such indirect means is the use of the "ideological mechanism of power." The use of ideological power represents an important but often subtle means through which the actions and policies of the state can be influenced, and the mechanism must be understood in terms of the capacity to influence the ideology or belief and value system of society as a whole. This often means, for example, attempting to equate one's own interests with the "national interest" or the "general will." When a group, individual, or class is able to establish these equations it becomes more difficult for the state to manoeuvre because certain actions can be perceived as being against the "national interest," "freedom," or the "public good."

This ideological mechanism has at least two dimensions. Firstly, it may be possible to influence key institutions such as the mass media or schools to adopt a certain ideology or value system presented in terms of the "national interest" or the "public good." Included in such a process might be the general notion that government intervention is always negative while individual entrepreneurial efforts must be good. Secondly, it is also possible for this mechanism to be used in a more explicit and specific sense: for instance, in attempts to argue that a specific polity or action that is of direct benefit to a particular class or group is actually in the "national interest" or against the "national interest." Those with a material and economic interest in free trade might, for example, seek to convince everyone in Canada that this particular policy is one that will benefit every member of society.

This mechanism of power does not necessarily imply the intentional creation or manipulation of "public opinion," though that, of course, does sometimes occur. Much of what makes up a society's value and ideological system emerges and is articulated in an unintentional and unintended—even haphazard—manner as the various institutional practices take place. Sexism, racism, and even classism represent systems of belief that, once they become established as part of the value system of a society, emerge as powerful factors in the determination of state policy and actions. State policy-makers and decision-makers may very well act within the bounds of the accepted "logic" of "how things are" as determined by the general belief and value system. Works such as those by John Thompson (1984), Robert Connell (1983), and Jorge Larrain (1979) discuss these issues, as does Michèle Barrett (1980). Connell and Barrett stand out because they explicitly discuss both classism and the role of familial ideology.

Another indirect but very important mechanism of power relates to the relationship between the economy and the state. A number of writers operating from different problematics have argued that capital and business possess a massive advantage over other classes, especially when it comes to relations with the state (Miliband 1973; Lindblom 1982; Block 1977). While the argument is sometimes posed in terms of the capacity of the capitalist class to influence the direct mechanism of power, it is important to understand that economic power—control over what Giddens calls allocative resources—constitutes a mechanism of power in its own right.

Colin Crouch (1979), Fred Block (1977), and Albert Szymanski (1978) all argue that activities and conditions within the economy fundamentally influence the operations of the state. According to Crouch, social stability in the broadest sense is dependent on a "healthy" economy, that is, on continuing investment, stable and increasing employment, and general economic prosperity. The class that determines the pattern of investment and economic development therefore has substantial power to influence the larger environment within which the state operates. Block makes the same point, noting that a critical element in economic activity in capitalist society is "business confidence" and that those classes controlling the society's allocative resources have the capacity to influence the operations of the state through their control of "economic planning." The extent to which a class or group is capable of influencing the larger economic processes in a capitalist society will be a central determinant of its capacity to use this mechanism of power. Given that social stability tends to depend on economic stability, at least in capitalist societies, control over economic resources can thus be translated into political power.

RE-EVALUATING STATE THEORIES

Many of the theories we have been considering offer broad structuralist approaches to the state. As a result they become entrapped within the circularity of functionalist thought. The state is seen as functioning for society, or for the dominant class or males, but these approaches often do not explain how society, the ruling class, or males influence the state to ensure that it functions in their interest. One of the strengths of the alternative approach, looking at "mechanisms of power," is that it brings the human actor clearly into social analysis while recognizing that human actors operate within the context of social structure. States or state structures do not make decisions or take actions; human beings do, but they do so within the confines and dynamics of existing structures. The mechanisms of power are in theory available to all citizens in a liberal-democratic society; however, it is clear that the ability to engage or utilize most of these mechanisms of power is based on access to economic and other resources.

To be politically successful—whether in running for office, organizing a lobby, establishing a policy-analysis organization, or effectively organizing ideological and public relations campaigns—requires economic resources. In turn the use of economic resources as a mechanism of power usually depends upon membership in a class that provides access to those economic resources. In a class-structured society in which there is an unequal distribution of economic power and resources, there will be significant differences in the capacities of individuals and classes to use these mechanisms of power.

Although class is an important determinant of the capacity to influence the state, groups and individuals from civil society, or the domestic system can also have an impact on the operation of the state. In an important essay Connell (1990) summarizes the growing literature on the patriarchal nature of the state and presents a definitive argument about the central role of the state in sex and gender relations. He points to the need for a more adequate theoretical understanding of how and why such state interventions have occurred. As well, the notion of mechanism of power can help further the analysis of the operation of the state, because when it is understood in the context of capitalist and patriarchal social relations it helps us move beyond reductionist class-based explanations. Indeed, this approach offers the possibility of understanding the state as a site of conflict and competition, albeit most often between grossly unequal forces. Nevertheless, history demonstrates occasions when workers, farmers, women's groups, and others have effectively used these mechanisms of power in order to wrestle concessions from the state. For example, social movements, such as environmentalists or peace activists, whose base of support cannot be solely understood in terms of class structures, can adopt the mechanisms of power. It is also possible to establish connections between, on the one hand, various social and economic processes within patriarchal society and, on the other, state actions and policies. Such a task involves analyzing not only the concrete and empirical influences of individuals and groups on the mechanisms of power but also the structural process, such as how sexist ideologies influence the social environment within which the state acts; or the personalities of those involved in policy formulation and implementation.

A new approach to the study of the structures and operation of the state in liberal-democratic society is clearly required. As more and more aspects of our lives unfold within the context of large, complex, and centralized bureaucratic organizations, the modern world seems to be more and more out of our control. Every dimension of our existence is seen to fall under the jurisdiction of some mammoth organization exercising centralized power, whether it is the corporations that control the production and distribution of our material necessities, the trade unions that are supposed to protect us from these giant companies, the government that claims to represent us as it wages war and kills innocent civilians, or even our churches with their orthodoxies to guard. To many people it seems as if the human individuals who make up society have less and less capacity to influence these structures. Thus it may well be time to re-examine the very nature of the role and distribution of power in all our social organizations and relations, with an eye to working towards the true democratization of these relations.

This book introduces readers to the dominant ideas that have emerged as Western social science has sought to understand the polity in capitalist society. But it is also imperative that readers engage in a critical evaluation of the capacity of these ideas to explain one of the central issues in our society: the distribution of power.

Clearly, the existing approaches fall short in both theorizing and empirically explaining the nature of power in capitalist patriarchal society. An adequate approach must be capable of answering a series of key questions, such as: Does the approach explain concrete and specific state policies and actions in a non-functionalist, non-reductionist, and non-teleological manner? Do the approaches offer an adequate theoretical basis for social analysis and in particular an analysis of the polity? Do the approaches involve empirical and historical research? Can the approaches explain the multiple dimensions of sexual, economic, and other social inequalities?

If we can develop an approach to state theory that comes to grips with these questions, we will be on our way to addressing the central issue of power. And the act of addressing the issue of power is surely the first step towards creating a truly humane and democratic society.

REFERENCES

Albrow, Martin. 1977. *The Global Age*. Stanford: Stanford University Press.

Althusser, Louis and Etiénne Balibar. 1970. *Reading Capital*. London: NLB.

Andreski, Stanislav (ed.). 1974. *The Essential Comte* New York: Barnes and Noble.

Armstrong, Pat and Hugh Armstrong. 1983. "Classless Sex: Towards Feminist Marxism." *Studies in Political Economy*, No. 10, Winter.

_____. 1984. *The Double Ghetto: Canadian Women and Their Segregated Work*. (Revised ed.) Toronto: McClelland and Stewart.

_____. 1990. *Theorizing Women's Work*. Toronto: Garamond Press, 1990.

Armstrong, Patricia. 1996. "Unravelling the Safety Net: Transformations in Health Care and Their Impact on Women." In Janine Brodie, (ed.), *Women and Canadian Public Policy*. Toronto: Harcourt Brace.

Avineri, Shlomo. 1968. *The Social and Political Thought of Karl Marx* London: Cambridge University Press.

_____. 1972. *Hegel's Theory of the Modern State*. London: Cambridge University Press.

Bakunin, Mikhail. 1960. As quoted in Paul Eltzbacher, *Anarchism*. London: Freedom.

_____.1966. "Marx, the Bismark of Socialism." In L.I. Kimermann, (ed.), *Patterns of Anarchy*. New York: Anchor Books.

_____. 1971. "God and the State" and "Statism and Anarchy." In Marshall Shatz. (ed.), *The Essential Works of Anarchism*. New York: Bentham Books.

_____. 1977. "Church and State," "The Illusion of Universal Franchise," "Perils of the Marxist State," "What is Authority." In George Woodcock, (ed.), *The Anarchist Reader*. Sussex: Harvester Press.

Bannerji, Himani. 2000. *The Dark Side of the Nation: Essays on Multiculturalism, Nationalism and Gender*. Toronto: Canadian Scholars'.

Baran, Paul A. and Paul M. Sweezy. 1966. *Monopoly Capital*. New York: Monthly Review.

Barrett, Michèle. 1980. *Women's Oppression Today: Problems in Marxist Feminist Analysis*. London: Verso.

_____. 1984. "Women's Oppression: A Reply." *New Left Review,* 146, July/August.

Bashevkin, Sylvia. 2000. "Rethinking Retrenchment: North American Social Policy During the Early Clinton and Chretien Years." *Canadian Journal of Political Science*, March, XXXIII:1.

Benston, Margaret. 1984. "The Political Economy of Women's Liberation." In Alison M. Jaggar and Paula S. Rothenberg, (eds.), *Feminist Frameworks*. New York: McGraw-Hill.

Bentham, Jeremy. 1960. *A Fragment on Government*. Oxford: Basil Blackwell.

Bentley, Arthur F. 1935. *The Process of Government*. Evanstown: Principia Press.

Bilton, Tony, Kevin Bonnett, Philip Jones, Michelle Stanworth, Ken Sheard and Andrew Wesbter. 1987. *Introductory Sociology*. London: Macmillan.

Block, Fred. 1977. "The Ruling Class Does Not Rule." *Socialist Register,* May-June.

Bourricaud, Francois. 1981. *The Sociology of Talcott Parsons*. Chicago: University of Chicago Press.

Boyer, Robert. 1996. "State and Market: A New Engagement for the Twenty-First

Century." In Robert Boyer and Daniel Drache, (eds.), *States Against Markets: The Limits of Globalization*. London: Routledge.

Boyer, Robert and Daniel Drache (eds.). 1996. *States Against Markets: The Limits of Globalization*. London: Routledge.

Bragdon, H.W. and S.P. McCutchen. 1954. *History of a Free People*. New York: Macmillan.

Brenner, Johanna and Maria Ramis. 1984. "Rethinking Women's Oppression." *New Left Review*, 144, March/April.

Brodie, Janine (ed.). 1996a. "New State Forms, New Political Spaces." In Robert Boyer and Daniel Drache, (eds.), *States Against Markets*. London: Routledge.

_____. 1996b. *Women and Canadian Public Policy*. Toronto: Harcourt Brace.

Brown, Laura Kimberley. 1996. "Canada, Globalization and Free Trade: The Past is New." In Raymond-M Hebert, (ed.), *Re(Defining) Canada: A Prospective Look at our Country in the 21st Century*. Winnipeg: Presses Universitaires Se Saint-Boniface.

Burstyn, Varda. 1985. "Masculine Domination and the State." In *Women, Class, Family and the State*. Toronto: Garamond.

Burt, Sandra, Lorraine Code and Lindsay Dorney. 1993. *Changing Patterns of Women in Canada*. Toronto: McClelland & Stewart.

Cameron, Barbara. 1996. "Brave New Worlds for Women: NAFTA and New Reproductive Technologies." In Janine Brodie, (ed.), *Women and Canadian Public Policy*. Toronto: Harcourt Brace.

Carmichael, D.J.C. 1983. "C.B. Macpherson's 'Hobbes': A Critique." *Canadian Journal of Political Science*, XVI: 1, March.

Carnoy, Martin. 1984. *The State and Political Theory*. Princeton: Princeton University Press.

Carter, April. 1971. *The Political Theory of Anarchism*. London: Routledge and Kegan Paul.

Chomsky, Noam. 1998. "Power in the Global Arena." *New Left Review*, 230, July/Aug.

Clegg, Stewart, Paul Boreham and Geoff Dow. 1986. *Class Politics and the Economy*. London: Routledge and Kegan Paul.

Clough, S.B. and C.W. Cole. 1967. *Economic History of Europe*. Boston: D.C. Heath.

Code, Lorraine. 1993. "Feminist Theory." In Sandra Burt, Lorraine Code and Lindsay Dorney, (eds.), *Changing Patterns: Women in Canada*. (2nd edition) Toronto: McClelland & Stewart.

Comte, August. 1875. *The System of Positive Polity*. (4 vols.) New York: Burt Franklin.

_____. 1953. *The Positive Philosophy*. (2 vols.) New York: D. Appleton.

Connell, R.W. 1983. *Which Way is Up?* North Sydney: George, Allen and Unwin.

_____. 1987. *Gender and Power*. Sydney: Allen and Unwin.

_____. 1990. "The State, Gender and Sexual Politics." *Theory and Society*, 19.

_____. 1995. *Masculinities*. Berkeley: University of California Press.

Connelly, Patricia. 1983. "On Marxism and Feminism." *Studies in Political Economy*, 13, Fall.

Connelly, M. Patricia and Pat Armstrong (eds.). 1992. *Feminism in Action: Studies in Political Economy*. Toronto: Canadian Scholars.

Coole, Diana. 1988. *Women in Political Theory*. Boulder: Harvester Wheatsheaf.

Coser, Lewis. 1977. *Masters of the Sociological Thought*. New York: Harcourt Brace Jovanovich.

REFERENCES

Courchene, Thomas J. 1996. "Globalization, Free Trade and the Canadian Political Economy." In Raymond-M Hebert (ed.), *Re(Defining) Canada: A Prospective Look at our Country in the 21st Century.* Winnipeg: Presses Universitaires Se Saint-Boniface.

Crossman, Brenda. 1996. "Same-Sex Couples and the Politics of Family Status." In Janine Brodie, (ed.), *Women and Canadian Public Policy.* Toronto: Harcourt Brace.

Crouch, Colin. 1979. "The State, Capital and Liberal Democracy." In Colin Crouch, (ed.), *State Economy and Contemporary Capitalism.* New York: St. Martin's Press.

Dahl, Robert. 1965. *Modern Political Analysis.* Englewood Cliffs: Prentice-Hall.

_____. 1967. *Pluralist Democracy in the United States.* Chicago: Rand McNally.

_____. 1972. *Democracy in the United States: Promise and Performance.* Chicago: Rand McNally.

_____. 1990. *After the Revolution? Authority in a Good Society.* New Haven: Yale University Press.

Dalla Costa, Mariarosa. 1972. "Women and the Subservience of Community." In Mariarosa Dalla Costa and James Selma, (eds.), *The Power of Women and Subservience of Community.* Bristol: Falling Wall.

DeLue, Steven. 1997. *Political Thinking, Political Theory, and Civil Society.* Boston: Allyn and Bacon.

Dobb, M. 1946. *Studies in the Development of Capitalism.* London: Routledge and Kegan Paul.

_____. 1963. *Studies in the Development of Capitalism.* London: Routledge and Kegan Paul.

Donovan, Josephine. 1992. *Feminist Theory: The Intellectual Traditions of American Feminism.* New York: Continuum.

Dunleavy, Patrick and Brendan O'Leary. 1987. *Theories of the State: The Politics of Liberal Democracy.* London: Macmillan.

Durkheim, Emile. 1933. *The Rules of Sociological Method.* New York: Free Press.

_____. 1964. *The Division of Labour in Society.* New York: Free Press.

Eisenberg, Avigail. 1995. *Reconstructing Political Pluralism.* New York: State University Press of New York.

Eisenstein, Zillah R. 1981. *The Radical Future of Liberal Feminism.* Boston: Northeastern University Press.

Eldridge, John 1983. *C. Wright Mills.* Sussex: Ellis Horwood.

Engels, Frederick. [1884] 1972. *The Origin of the Family, Private Property and the State.* Moscow: Progress.

_____. 1935. *Socialism: Utopian and Scientific.* New York: International.

England, Paula (ed.). 1993. *Theory on Gender/Feminism on Theory.* New York: Aldine De Gruyter.

Evans, B.Mitchell, Stephen McBride and John Shields. 1998. "National Governance Versus Globalization: Canadian Democracy in Question." *Socialist Studies Bulletin,* 54, October-December.

Field, G. Lowell and John Higley. 1972. *Elitism.* London: Routledge and Kegan Paul.

Firestone, Shulamith. 1984. "The Dialectic of Sex." In Alison M. Jaggar and Paula S. Rothenberg, (eds.), *Feminist Frameworks.* New York: McGraw-Hill.

Fletcher, Ronald. 1971. *The Making of Sociology.* (2 vols.) London: Nelson.

Frank, Andre Gunder and Barry K. Gills (eds.). 1993. *The World System: Five Hundred Years or Five Thousand?* London: Routledge.

Fudge, Judy and Harry Glasbeek. 1997. "A Challenge to the Inevitability of Globalization: The Logic of Repositioning the State as the Terrain of Contest." In Jay Drydyk and Peter Penz, (eds.), *Global Justice, Global Democracy.* Winnipeg/Halifax: Society for Socialist Studies/Fernwood.

Gamble, Andrew. 1981. *An Introduction to Modern Social and Political Thought.* London: Macmillan.

Giddens, Anthony. 1971. *Capitalism and the Rise of Modern Social Theory.* Cambridge: Cambridge University Press.

_____. 1972. *Emile Durkheim: Selected Writings.* Cambridge: Cambridge University Press.

_____. 1972. *Politics and Sociology in the Thought of Max Weber.* London: Macmillan.

_____. 1978. *Emile Durkheim.* Glasgow: Collins.

_____. 1979. *Central Problems in Social Theory.* Berkeley: University of California Press.

_____. 1981. *A Contemporary Critique of Historical Materialism.* Berkeley: University of California Press.

_____. 1982. *Sociology.* New York: Harcourt Brace Jovanovich.

_____. 1982. *Profiles and Critiques in Social Theory.* Berkeley: University of California Press.

_____. 1984. *The Constitution of Society.* Cambridge: Polity.

Globe and Mail. 1995. "Don't Mess With Moody's." February 27.

_____. 1995. "Dollar Shows What World Thinks of Budget." March 3.

_____. 1995. "Is Moody's the Newest Superpower?" March 6.

Gold, David A., Lo, Y.H. Clarence and Eric Olin Wright. 1975. "Recent Developments in Marxist Theories of the State." *Monthly Review*, 27(5) October; and 27(6) November.

Goldman, Emma. 1970. "Anarchism: What it Really Stands For." In Robert Hoffman, (ed.), *Anarchism,* New York: Atherton.

Gouldner, Alvin W. 1970. *The Coming Crisis of Western Sociology.* New York: Avon.

Gramsci, Antonio. 1975. *Selections from the Prison Notebooks.* New York: International.

_____. 1977. *Selections from Political Writings 1910-1920.* New York: International.

Grant, George. 1965. *Lament for a Nation.* Ottawa: Carleton University Press.

Green, Joyce. 1996. "Resistance Is Possible." *Canadian Woman Studies,* 16(3).

Hamilton, Alexander, James Madison and John Jay. 1961. *The Federalist Papers.* New York: Mentor.

Hamilton, Peter. 1983. *Talcott Parsons.* Chichester: Ellis Horwood.

Hamilton, Roberta. 1996. *Gendering the Vertical Mosaic: Feminist Perspectives on Canadian Society.* Toronto: Copp Clark.

Hammond, J.L. and B. Hammond. 1966. *The Rise of Modern Industry.* London: Methuen.

Hansen, Karen V. and Ilene J. Philipson (eds.). 1990. *Women, Class and the Feminist Imagination: A Socialist-Feminist Reader.* Philadelphia: Temple University Press.

Harrison, Frank. 1983. *The Modern State.* Montreal: Black Rose.

_____. 1986. "Culture and Correction." In Dimitrios Roussopoulos, (ed.), *The Anarchist Papers.* Montreal: Black Rose.

REFERENCES

_____. 1987. "Book Review, *Anarchism: A Theoretical Analysis* by Alan Ritter." *Our Generation,* 18(2).

Hartmann, Heidi. 1986. "The Unhappy Marriage of Marxism and Feminism: Towards a More Progressive Union." In Lynda Sargent, (ed.), *The Unhappy Marriage of Marxism and Feminism: A Debate on Class and Patriarchy.* London: Pluto.

Hegel, G.W.F. 1967. *The Phenomenology of Mind.* New York: Harper and Row.

Heilbroner, Robert. 1968. *The Making of Economic Society.* Englewood Cliffs: Prentice Hall.

_____. 1992. *Twenty First Century Capitalism.* Concord, ON: Anansi.

Held, David. 1980. *Introduction of Critical Theory.* Berkeley: University of California Press.

_____ (ed.). 1983. *States and Societies.* Oxford: Martin Robertson.

_____ (ed.). 1991. *Political Theory Today.* Stanford: Stanford University Press.

_____. 1995. *Democracy and the Global Order: From the Modern State to Cosmopolitan Governance.* Cambridge: Polity.

Hewett, Marsha. 1986. "Emma Goldman: The Case for Anarcho-Feminism." In Dimitrios Roussopoulos, (ed.), *The Anarchist Papers,* Montreal: Black Rose.

Hobbes, Thomas. 1968. *Leviathan.* Harmondsworth: Penguin.

Hobsbaum, E.J. 1975. *The Age of Capital: 1848-1875.* London: Abacus.

Hocking, William Ernest. 1970. "The Philosophical Anarchist." In Robert Hoffman, (ed.), *Anarchism.* New York: Atherton.

Hoffman, Robert. 1970. "Introduction." In Robert Hoffman, (ed.), *Anarchism,* New York: Atherton.

Holloway, John and S. Picciotto (eds.). 1979. *State and Capital.* London: Edward Arnold.

Howard, M.C. and J.E. King. 1975. *The Political Economy of Marx.* Essex: Longman.

Hunt, Elgin F. and David W. Colander. 1984. *Social Science: An Introduction to the Study of Society.* New York: Macmillan.

Hunt, E.K. 1990. *Property and Prophets: The Evolution of Economic Institutions and Ideologies.* London: Harper and Row.

Jacoby, Russell. 1971. "Towards a Critique of Automatic Marxism: The Politics of Philosophy From Lukacs to the Frankfurt School." *Telos,* 10, Winter.

Jaggar, Alison M. 1983. *Feminist Politics and Human Nature.* Lanham, Maryland: Rowman & Littlefield.

Jenson, Jane. 1986. "Gender and Reproduction: Or, Babies and the State." *Studies in Political Economy,* 20, Summer.

Jessop, Bob. 1982. *The Capitalist State.* Oxford: Martin Robertson.

_____. 1990. *State Theories: Putting the Capitalist States in Their Places.* University Park, Penn: Pennsylvania State University Press.

Kapstein, Ethan B. *Governing the Global Economy: International Finance and the State.* Cambridge: Harvard University Press.

Kariel, Henry S. 1968. "Pluralism." In David L. Sills, (ed.), *International Encyclopedia of the Social Sciences.* New York: Macmillan and Free.

Knuttila, Murray. 1996. *Introducing Sociology: A Critical Perspective.* Toronto: Oxford University Press.

Korpi, Walter. 1998. "The Iceberg of Power Below the Surface: A Preface to Power Resource Theory." In Julia O'Connor and Greg Olsen, (eds.), *Power Resource Theory and the Welfare State: A Critical Approach.* Toronto: University of Toronto Press.

Korten, David C. 1995. *When Corporations Rule the World*. West Hartford and San Francisco: Kumarian and Berrett-Koehler Publishers.

Kropotkin, Peter. 1960. As quoted in Paul Eltzbacher, *Anarchism*. London: Freedom.

_____. 1966. "A Scientific Approach to Communist Anarchism." In L.I. Kimermann, (ed.), *Patterns of Anarchy*. New York: Anchor.

_____. 1971. "The Conquest of Bread" and "The Repentant Nobleman." In Marshall Shatz, (ed.), *The Essential Works of Anarchism*. New York: Bentham.

_____. 1977. "The Uselessness of Laws," "Prison and its Effects," "Anarchism and Violence," "The Paris Commune 1871," "Crime in a Free World," "On the Wage System." In George Woodcock, (ed.), *The Anarchist Reader*. Sussex: Harvester.

_____. 1989. "Anarchism." *Our Generation*, Spring.

Kuhn, Annette and AnnMarie Wolpe (eds.). 1978. *Feminism and Materialism: Women and Modes of Production*. London: Routledge and Kegan Paul.

Kuhn, Thomas S. 1962. *The Structure of Scientific Revolutions*. Chicago: University of Chicago Press.

Laclau, Ernesto. 1975. "The Specificity of the Political: The Poulantzas-Miliband Debate." *Economy and Society*, 4.

Laclau, Ernesto and Chantal Mouffe. 1985. *Hegemony and Socialist Strategy*. London: Verso.

_____. 1990. "Post-Marxism Without Apologies." In Ernesto Laclau, *New Reflections on the Revolution of Our Time*. London: Verso.

Larrain, Jorge. 1979. *The Concept of Ideology*. London: Hutchinson.

Lenin, V.I. 1965. *The State and Revolution*. Peking: Foreign Languages.

Lewis, Jane. 1985. "The Debate on Sex and Class." *New Left Review*, 149, January/February.

Lindblom, Charles E. 1982. "Another State of Mind." *American Political Science Review*, 76.

Lipset, Seymore Martin. 1968. "Political Sociology." In Talcott Parsons, (ed.), *American Sociology*. New York: Basic.

Locke, John. 1952. *The Second Treatise of Government*. Indianapolis: Bobbs Merrill.

Lukes, Steven. 1973. *Emile Durkheim*. Middlesex: Penguin.

Mackie, Marlene. 1983. "Gender Relations." In Robert Hagedorn, (ed.), *Sociology*. Toronto: Holt Rinehart and Winston.

MacKinnon, Catharine A. 1989. *Toward a Feminist Theory of the State*. Cambridge: Harvard University Press.

Macpherson, C.B. 1962. *The Political Theory of Possessive Individualism*. London: Oxford University Press.

_____. 1975. *Democratic Theory*. Oxford: Clarendon.

_____. 1983. "Leviathan Restored: A Reply to Carmichael." *Canadian Journal of Political Science*, XVI: 4, December.

Madison, James. 1961. "No. 10." *The Federalist Papers*. New York: Mentor.

Madoo Lengermann, Patricia and Jill Niebrugge. 1988. "Contemporary Feminist Theory." In George Ritzer, *Modern Sociological Theory*. New York: McGraw-Hill.

Mandell, Nancy (ed.). 1995. *Feminist Issues: Race, Class and Sexuality*. Scarborough, ON: Prentice Hall.

Mandell, Nancy and Ann Duffy (eds.), 1995. *Canadian Families: Diversity, Conflict and Change*. Toronto: Harcourt Brace.

Marcham, F.G. 1950. *A History of England*. New York: Macmillan.

Marcuse, Herbert. 1960. *Reason and Revolution*. Boston: Beacon.

Maroney, Heather Jon and Meg Luxton (eds.). 1987. *Feminism and Political Economy: Women's Work, Women's Struggles*. Toronto: Methuen.

Martindale, Don. 1975. *Prominent Sociologists Since World War II*. Columbus: Charles Merrill.

Martinussen, John. 1997. *State, Society and Market: A Guide to Competing Theories of Development*. London and Halifax: Zed and Fernwood.

Marx, Karl. 1964. *The Economic and Philosophical Manuscripts*. New York: International.

_____. 1970a.*Critique of Hegel's Philosophy of Right*. Cambridge University Press.

_____. 1972a. *The Class Struggles in France*. Moscow: International.

_____. 1972b. *The Eighteenth Brumaire of Louis Bonaparte*. In Robert Tucker, (ed.), *The Marx Engels Reader*. New York: W.W. Norton.

_____. 1973. *Grundrisse*. Middlesex: Penguin.

_____. 1977. *Contribution to the Critique of Political Economy*. Moscow: Progress.

Marx, Karl and Frederick Engels. 1952. *Manifesto of the Communist Party*. Moscow: Progress.

_____. 1970b. *The German Ideology*. New York: International .

_____. 1973. *Selected Works*. Moscow: Progress.

McBride, Stephen and John Shields. 1993. *Dismantling a Nation: Canada and the New World Order*. Halifax: Fernwood.

McDermott, Patricia. 1996. "Pay and Employment Equity: Why Separate Policies?" In Janine Brodie, (ed.), *Women and Canadian Public Policy*. Toronto: Harcourt Brace.

McIntosh, Mary. 1978. "The State and the Oppression of Women." In Annette Kuhn and Ann Marie Wolpe, (eds.), *Feminism and Materialism: Women and Modes of Production*. London: Routledge and Kegan Paul.

McLaren, Arlene Tigar (ed.). 1988. *Gender and Society: Creating a Canadian Women's Sociology*. Toronto: Copp Clark Pitman.

McLellan, David. 1970. *Marx Before Marxism*. Middlesex: Penguin.

_____. 1971. *The Thought of Karl Marx*. London: Macmillan.

_____ (ed.). 1977. *Karl Marx: Selected Writings*. Oxford: Oxford University Press.

Merriam, Charles E. 1964. *Political Power*. New York: Collier Macmillan.

Merrington, John. 1977. "Theory and Practice in Gramsci's Marxism." *Western Marxism: A Critical Reader* (edited by New Left Review). London: New Left Review.

Michels, Robert. 1962. *Political Parties*. New York: Free Press.

Miliband, Ralph. 1965. "Marx and the State." *Socialist Register*.

_____. 1972. "Reply to Nicos Poulantzas." In Robin Blackburn, (ed.), *Ideology in Social Science,* Glasgow: Fontana/Collins.

_____. 1973. *The State in Capitalist Society*. London: Quartet.

_____. 1973. "Poulantzas and the Capitalist State." *New Left Review*, 82, November-December.

_____. 1977. *Marxism and Politics*. Oxford: Oxford University Press.

Mill, John Stuart. 1947. *On Liberty*. New York: Appleton-Century Crofts.

_____. 1958. *Considerations on Representative Government*. New York: Library of Liberal Arts.

_____. [1896] 1984. "The Subjection of Women." In Alison M. Jaggar and Paula S.

Rothenberg, (eds.), *Feminist Frameworks*. New York: McGraw-Hill.

Mills, C.W. and Hans Gerth (eds.). 1958. *From Max Weber*. New York: Oxford University Press.

_____. 1959. *The Power Elite*. New York: Oxford University Press.

Mitchell, Broadus. 1967. *Postscripts to Economic History*. Ottawa: Littlefield, Adams.

_____. 1967. *Postscripts to Economic History*. Totowa: New Jersey.

Morton, Peggy. 1972. "Women's Work is Never Done." In *Women Unite*. Toronto: Women's Press.

Mosca, Gaetano. 1939. *The Ruling Class*. New York: McGraw-Hill.

Mouffe, Chantal. 1993. *The Return of the Political*. London: Verso.

Nelson, Brian R. 1982. *Western Political Thought*. Englewood Cliffs: Prentice-Hall.

Nicholson, Linda J. (ed.). 1990. *Feminism/Postmodernism*. New York: Routledge.

Norlinger, Eric A. 1981. *On the Autonomy of the Democratic State*. Cambridge: Harvard University Press.

O'Brien, Mary. 1981. *The Politics of Reproduction*. London: Routledge and Kegan Paul.

_____. 1988. "The Dialectics of Reproduction." In Arlene Tigar McLaren, (ed.), *Gender and Society: Creating a Canadian Women's Sociology,* Toronto: Copp Clark Pitman.

O'Connor, James. 1973. *The Fiscal Crisis of the State*. New York: St. Martin's.

O'Connor, Julia and Gregg Olsen. 1998. "Understanding the Welfare State: Power Resource Theory and Its Critics." In Julia O'Connor and Gregg Olsen, (eds.), *Power Resource Theory and the Welfare State: A Critical Approach*. Toronto: University of Toronto Press.

Offe, Claus. 1984. *The Contradictions of the Welfare State*. Cambridge MIT Press.

_____. 1996. *Modernity and the State: East, West*. Cambridge: MIT Press.

Olsen, Gregg. 1999. "Half Empty or Half Full? The Swedish Welfare State in Transition." *Canadian Review of Sociology and Anthropology*, 26:2.

O'Malley, Joseph. 1970. "Introduction and Notes." In Karl Marx, *Critique of Hegel's Philosophy of Right*. Cambridge: Cambridge University Press.

Palmer, R.R. 1957. *A History of the Modern World*. New York: Alfred Knopf.

Panitch, Leo. 1977. "The Role and Nature of the Canadian State." In Leo Panitch, (ed.), *The Canadian State: Political Economy and Political Power*. Toronto: University of Toronto Press.

Pareto, Vilfredo. 1976. *Sociological Writings*. Oxford: Basil Blackwell.

Parsons, Talcott. 1951. *Essays in Sociological Theory*. New York: Free Press.

_____. 1964.*The Social System*. New York: Free Press.

_____. 1969. *Politics and Social Structure*. New York: Free Press.

_____. 1971. *The System of Modern Societies*. Englewood Cliffs: Prentice-Hall.

_____. 1978. "The Concept of Society: The Components and Their Interrelations." In Alan Wells, (ed.), *Contemporary Sociological Theory*. Santa Monica: Goodyear.

Pateman, Carole. 1989. *The Disorder of Women: Democracy, Feminism and Political Theory*. Stanford: University of Stanford Press.

Paul, Jeffrey. 1981. *Reading Nozick*. Totowa, NJ: Rowman and Littlefield.

Piven, Fox Frances and Richard Cloward. 1998. "Eras of Power." *Monthly Review*, January.

Pocklington, T.C. 1985. *Liberal Democracy in Canada and the United States*. Toronto: Holt Rinehart and Winston.

REFERENCES

Polyani, Karl. 1971. *The Great Transformation*. Boston: Beacon.

Porter, John. 1965. *The Vertical Mosaic*. Toronto: University of Toronto Press.

Poulantzas, Nicos. 1972. "The Problem of the Capitalist State." In Robin Blackburn, (ed.), *Ideology in Social Science*. Glasgow: Fontana Collins.

_____. 1973. *Political Power and Social Classes*. London: NLB and Sheed Ward.

_____. 1975. *Classes in Contemporary Capitalism*. London: New Left.

_____. 1976. "The Capitalist State: A Reply to Miliband and Laclau." *New Left Review*, 95, January-February.

Proudhon, Pierre-Joseph. 1960. As quoted in Paul Eltzbacher, *Anarchism*. London: Freedom.

_____. 1971. "General Idea of the Revolution in the Nineteenth Century." In Marshall Shatz, (ed.), *The Essential Works of Anarchism*. New York: Bentham.

_____. 1977. "The Birth of Anarchy: the Death of Property," "Parliamentary Isolation," "To Karl Marx," "The Principle of the Revolution," "The Old Society and the New," "The Revolution and the Nation." In George Woodcock, (ed.), *The Anarchist Reader*. Sussex: Harvester.

Redekop, John H. 1978. *Approaches to Canadian Politics*. Scarborough: Prentice-Hall.

Ritzer, George. 1975. *Sociology: A Multiple Paradigm Science*. Boston: Allyn and Bacon.

_____. 1983. *Sociological Theory*. New York: Alfred A. Knopf.

Rocher, Guy. 1974. *Talcott Parsons and American Sociology*. London: Thomas Nelson.

Ross, Robert J.S. and Kent Trachte. 1980. *Global Capitalism: The New Leviathan*. Albany: State University of New York Press.

Rossides, Daniel W. 1968. *Society as a Functional Process: An Introduction to Sociology*. Toronto: McGraw-Hill.

_____. 1978. *The History and Nature of Sociological Theory*. Boston: Houghton Mifflin.

Rostow, W.W. 1965. *The Stages of Economic Growth*. Cambridge: Cambridge University Press.

Roussopoulos, Dimitrios (ed.). 1986. *The Anarchist Papers*. Montreal: Black Rose.

Sabine, George H. 1961. *A History of Political Theory*. New York: Holt, Rinehart and Winston.

Sargent, Lynda (ed.). 1986. *The Unhappy Marriage of Marxism and Feminism: A Debate on Class and Patriarchy*. London, Pluto.

Sassoon, Anne Showstack. 1983. "Hegemony." In Tom Bottomore, (ed.), *A Dictionary of Marxist Thought*. Cambridge, MA: Harvard University Press.

Sayers, Janet, Mary Evans and Nanneke Redclift (eds.). 1987. *Engels Revisited*. London: Tavistock.

Seccombe, Wally. 1974. "The Housewife and Hew Labour Under Capitalism." *New Left Review*, 83, Jan./Feb.

Shatz, Marshall (ed.). 1971. *The Essential Works of Anarchism*. New York: Bantam.

Skocpol, Theda. 1980. "Political Response to Capitalist Crisis: Neo-Marxist Theories of the State and the New Deal." *Politics and Society*, 10(2).

_____. 1985. "Bringing the State Back In: Strategies of Analysis in Current Research." In Peter Evans, Dietrich Rueschemeyer and Theda Skocpol, (eds.), *Bringing the State Back In*. Cambridge: Cambridge University Press.

Smith, Adam. [1776] 1969. *An Inquiry into the Nature and Causes of the Wealth of Nations*. Port Washington, NY: Kennikat.

Sweezy, Paul M. 1942. *The Theory of Capitalist Development*. New York: Modern Reader.

Sweezy, Paul and Paul Baran. 1966. *Monopoly Capital*. New York: Monthly Review.

Sydie, R. A. 1987. *Natural Women—Cultured Men: A Feminist Perspective on Sociological Theory*. Toronto: Methuen.

Szymanski, Albert. 1978. *The Capitalist State and the Politics of Class*. Cambridge: Winthrop.

Tabb, William. 1997. "Globalization Is *An* Issue, The Power of Capital is *The* Issue." *Monthly Review*, June.

Teeple, Gary. 1995. *Globalization and the Decline of Social Reform*. Toronto and New Jersey: Garamond and Humanities.

_____. 2000. *Globalization and the Decline of Social Reform into the Twenty-first Century*. Toronto: Garamond.

Theodorson, G.A. and A.G. Theodorson. 1969. *Modern Dictionary of Sociology*. New York: Crowell.

Therborne, Goran. 1978. *What Does the Ruling Class Do When it Rules?* London: NLB.

Thomas, H. and W. Hamm. 1947. *Modern Europe*. Toronto: Clarke, Irwin.

Thompson, Dennis F. 1976. *John Stuart Mill and Representative Government*. Princeton: Princeton University Press.

Thompson, E.P. 1968.*The Making of the English Working Class*. Middlesex: Penguin.

_____. 1978. *The Poverty of Theory and Other Essays*. New York: Monthly Review.

Thompson, John B. 1984. *Studies in the Theory of Ideology*. Berkeley: University of California Press.

Thompson, Kenneth. 1976. *August Comte: The Foundations of Sociology*. London: Thomas Nelson.

_____. 1982. *Emile Durkheim*. New York: Travistock.

Tong, Rosemarie. 1989. *Feminist Thought: A Comprehensive Introduction*. Boulder, Col: Westview.

Tumin, Melvin M. 1967. *Social Stratification: The Forms and Functions of Inequality*. Englewood Cliffs: Prentice Hall.

Urry, David and Julia Urry. 1995. *Collins Dictionary of Sociology*. Glasgow: Harper Collins.

Urry, John. 1981. *The Anatomy of Capitalist Society*. London: Macmillan.

Ursel, Jane. 1986. "The State and the Maintenance of Patriarchy: A Case Study of Family, Labour and Welfare Legislation in Canada." In James Dickinson and Bob Russell, (eds.), *Family, Economy and State*. Toronto: Garamond.

Wallerstein, Immanuel. 1974. *The Modern World System*. New York: Academic.

Weber, Max. 1949. *The Methodology of the Social Sciences*. New York: Free Press.

_____. 1949. *The Protestant Ethic and the Spirit of Capitalism*. New York: Free Press.

_____. 1978. *Economy and Society*. Berkeley: University of California Press.

Weiss, Linda. 1997. "Globalization and the Myth of the Powerless State." *New Left Review*, 225, Sept./Oct.

Wilson, John. 1983. *Social Theory*. Englewood Cliffs: Prentice-Hall.

Wolf, Eric. 1982. *Europe and the People Without History*. Berkeley: University of California Press.

REFERENCES

Wood, Ellen Meiksins. 1996. *Democracy Against Capitalism: Renewing Historical Materialism*. Cambridge: Cambridge University Press.

_____. 1998. "Class Compacts, The Welfare State, and Epochal Shifts." *Monthly Review*, January.

Woodcock, George. 1977. *The Anarchist Reader*. Sussex: Harvester.

Wright, Eric Olin. 1979. *Class, Crisis and the State*. London: NLB.

Zeitlin, Irving M. 1981. *Ideology and the Development of Sociological Theory*. Englewood Cliffs: Prentice-Hall.